DALLAS
COWBOYS

The Complete Illustrated History

Jaime Aron

Foreword by Roger Staubach

MVP
BOOKS

First published in 2010 by MVP Books, an imprint of MBI Publishing Company, 400 First Avenue North, Suite 300, Minneapolis, MN 55401 USA

Text copyright © 2010 by Jaime Aron

MVP Books titles are also available at discounts in bulk quantity for industrial or sales-promotional use. For details write to Special Sales Manager at MBI Publishing Company, 400 First Avenue North, Suite 300, Minneapolis, MN 55401 USA.

To find out more about our books, visit us online at www.mvpbooks.com.

Library of Congress Cataloging-in-Publication Data

Aron, Jaime.
    Dallas Cowboys : the complete illustrated history / Jaime Aron ; foreword by Roger Staubach.
        p. cm.
    Includes bibliographical references and index.
    ISBN 978-0-7603-3520-8 (hb w/ jkt)
    1. Dallas Cowboys (Football team)—History. I. Title.
    GV956.D3A76 2010
    796.332'6407642812—dc22
                        2009050061

Edited by Josh Leventhal
Designed by Mandy Kimlinger
Layout by Greg Nettles

Printed in China

On the frontispiece: Tom Landry statue at Cowboys Stadium, 2009 (Al Messerschmidt/Getty Images).

On the title page: Troy Aikman, 1990 (George Gojkovich/Getty Images).

On the back cover: Bob Lilly, circa 1970 (Focus on Sport/Getty Images); Tom Landry, January, 1979 (Heinz Kluetmeier/*Sports Illustrated*/Getty Images); Emmitt Smith, 1995 (Focus on Sport/Getty Images); Tony Dorsett, circa 1980 (Focus on Sport/Getty Images); Cowboys Stadium, 2009 (Ronald Martinez/ Getty Images); Harvey Martin, Larry Cole, and Jethro Pugh, January 1976 (Focus on Sport/Getty Images); Eddie LeBaron, circa 1960 (Walter Iooss Jr./ *Sports Illustrated*/Getty Images); Troy Aikman, 2000 (Craig Jones/Allsport / Getty Images); Tony Romo, 2009 (Ronald Martinez/Getty Images).

In memory of

Coach. You are

missed every day.

CONTENTS

FOREWORD

BY ROGER STAUBACH

Roger Staubach in action, 1970s. *Focus on Sport/ Getty Images*

For 50 years, the Dallas Cowboys have had two constants: A blue star on a shiny silver helmet and a tradition of great quarterbacks.

Don Meredith laid the foundation, and Craig Morton kept it going. Craig and I competed for a few years, then I became keeper of the flame. Danny White took over for me and—eventually—Troy Aikman revived the legacy. Now, it is Tony Romo's turn. There have been others, of course, but fans tend to consider each of us as being symbolic of a certain era in Cowboys history.

It's a pretty exclusive fraternity, and I'm proud to be part of it.

Don Meredith was one of the toughest, most determined players I ever saw. Maybe it takes another quarterback to fully appreciate the punishment his body endured over the years it took to get the Cowboys from expansion team to championship contender. Had the Cowboys beaten the Green Bay Packers in the 1966 or 1967 NFL Championship games, he'd probably be in the Hall of Fame. As it was, Dandy

Don and the Cowboys gave those Packers clubs a tougher fight than they faced in the Super Bowls that followed; that's how good those Dallas teams were.

Instead, I had the privilege of being the quarterback when the Cowboys became world champions for the first time. Coach Landry had us unbelievably well prepared for that Super Bowl, and it showed. I will always remember the huge smile he had after we won that game. It made me smile, too, because I knew how fortunate I was to play for Coach Landry.

I also was fortunate to have a foot in two generations of championship teams—when we won our second Super Bowl, practically our entire roster had turned over. While I wish we could've gotten past the Steelers for another title or two, the fact that we played in five Super Bowls during the 1970s is quite an accomplishment. It's a big reason we became known as "America's Team."

When I retired, I believed Danny White would keep it going. Like Meredith, he came ever so close to getting it done. Danny broke many of my passing records but had some heartbreaking losses in NFC Championship games. I wish more people recognized what a great quarterback he was.

After some rough years, the Cowboys landed the guy I call my favorite quarterback of all time: Troy Aikman. He had everything you want in a quarterback—a strong arm, an analytical mind, and an ego that understood he was part of a team. Most of all, he was a tremendous leader. Troy could've thrown for more yards, but he never worried about statistics. He just wanted to win. And win he did; three Super Bowls and more victories in the 1990s than any quarterback in any decade. I'm especially glad one of those Super Bowl wins came against the Steelers.

Tony Romo is the newest link in our chain. Like me, he had to wait for his big chance. Like Danny, he's put up big numbers. Like Don, he's endured his share of agonizing losses. We're all looking forward to Tony taking the Cowboys back to the Super Bowl. He's already won over my grandkids. They prefer wearing his jersey to mine.

Staubach poses with his Heisman Trophy and his Pro Football Hall of Fame bust. *NFL/Getty Images*

While quarterbacks get a lot of attention, it takes a lot more parts to have a winning organization. Luckily, the Cowboys have had great owners, coaches, scouts, and—most of all—rosters filled with talented players. The Ring of Honor isn't big enough to hold all those who deserve to be remembered, but the pages of this book certainly will give them their due.

Enjoy looking back at the first 50 years of Dallas Cowboys history. Here's hoping the next 50 are even better.

INTRODUCTION

Don Meredith helped to lead the Dallas Cowboys from expansion team to championship contender during the 1960s. *Diamond Images/Getty Images*

Over their first 50 seasons, the Dallas Cowboys became the most talked about, most written about, most envied, most loved, and most hated team in the NFL, maybe among all teams in all sports.

The star on their helmets is a global icon. Fans everywhere knew about the stadium with the hole in the roof and the smart-alecky reason for it: "So God can watch His team." And now the team has upgraded to a $1.2 billion arena that just might be the grandest sports venue since the Colosseum opened in Rome back in the first century.

The "Hail Mary" is one of the most famous plays in NFL history. The "Ice Bowl" is one of the most famous games. The NFL Films shot of Tom Landry's silhouette has become one of the sport's most classic images.

Emmitt Smith is the league's career rushing leader. Nobody will ever run for a longer touchdown than Tony Dorsett's 99-yarder.

They were once jeered as "Next Year's Champions" because they had trouble winning the big one. Now they are "America's Team," with five Super Bowl trophies and a record eight appearances in the big game.

Bob Lilly was the first player the team ever drafted, and he became the first member of the team's Ring of Honor, then the club's first inductee into the Pro Football Hall of Fame. No wonder he's known as "Mr. Cowboy."

Don Meredith was the first player under contract, signing a "personal services" deal before the NFL gave Clint Murchison Jr. the franchise. This move was another tone-setter because quarterback became the team's signature position.

Roger Staubach won the team's first Super Bowl, and the second, and was the top-rated quarterback in NFL history when he retired. Yet Staubach himself considers Troy Aikman better than he was; Troy did win three Super Bowls. All told, "quarterback of the Dallas Cowboys" has become the ultimate position in all of pro sports, much like center field for the New York Yankees once was. The rub is that you have to succeed. If you do, the world will be at your command. For proof, look no further than the rise of Tony Romo, who judged the Miss Universe pageant, played in celebrity golf events, and dated singers and movie stars before he even won a playoff game.

Jerry Jones likes to say the Cowboys are the top property in television entertainment, and it's hard to argue against his point. The NFL draws the highest ratings, and the Cowboys consistently draw the highest ratings of any team. That's why they always get the best time slots—the Monday night appearances, when that was the jewel, and now Sunday nights, plus the mid-afternoon game that's beamed to most of the country. Whatever game or NFL studio show you are watching, there's a good chance a former Cowboys player or coach will be part of the broadcast. Ask anyone 50 or younger if they remember a Thanksgiving without the Cowboys on television.

The team was sold for the highest price ever paid for a sports club. Twice.

There are season-ticket owners in all 50 states. The team sells more merchandise than several other clubs combined. Heck, the Cowboys Cheerleaders outsell some teams. (Can you believe it took that long to mention the cheerleaders?)

That's the thing about this franchise: there is so much of everything.

One of the more remarkable aspects of the first 50 seasons is that the Cowboys have always been

Roger Staubach transformed the Cowboys from "Next Year's Champions" to "America's Team" with two Super Bowl victories in the 1970s. *NFL/Getty Images*

interesting. Maybe there were some eras when it wasn't much fun being a fan, but in looking back, it is easy to connect the dots, to follow the narrative arc.

In the early 1960s, Landry was putting together a complex scheme that he knew would one day outsmart everyone. He just didn't have talented enough players to make it work. Tex Schramm took care of that part, upgrading the roster through some shrewd deals and with the aid of his revolutionary computerized scouting system, which spit out the right names based on information plugged in by Gil Brandt and his legion of sources.

A 5-foot-7 Korean War hero-turned-lawyer named Eddie LeBaron was the first quarterback in club history, holding the job down until Meredith was ready to take over. Dandy Don brought the Cowboys oh-so-close to championships in 1966 and 1967, luring fans into believing in the club, only to break their hearts with early playoff losses in 1968

Troy Aikman was under center for three Super Bowl titles in the span of four years. He is also the franchise leader in passing yards, completions, and touchdowns *George Rose/ Getty Images*

and 1969. He retired after that, only 31 years old but having endured enough pain and agony—physically, for sure, but also mentally because he was always the fans' whipping boy and often Landry's too.

Craig Morton got the Cowboys to the Super Bowl in 1970, but it wasn't until Staubach took over a year later that they finally became Super Bowl champions. He led them back to the big game three more times (1975, 1977, and 1978), wrapping a pair of four-point losses around a second championship. The losing quarterback in Dallas' second Super Bowl win? Morton, then playing for the Denver Broncos.

Staubach retired in part because he thought Danny White was ready to take over. White's years were another tease. He put up huge numbers and got the Cowboys within one win of the Super Bowl in his first three seasons, but he never took that final step.

By the mid-1980s, the rest of the league had caught up with Dallas' scouting system and Landry's innovations. The Cowboys were falling apart, and nobody could stop it.

As much as folks wanted Landry to be replaced and a new era to begin, no one wanted to see him go out the way he did—fired by new owner Jerry Jones the minute he took over and put himself in charge of "socks and jocks." Who was this guy? And what the hell were he and Jimmy Johnson doing to this team?

They had the No. 1 overall pick and wisely spent it on Troy Aikman. But, soon after, they gave up the next year's No. 1 on another quarterback to compete with Aikman. Then they lost their first five games and traded their only Pro Bowl player, Herschel Walker.

They went 1–15 in 1989, the worst since Landry's 0–11–1 debut. Yet they really did have a plan.

Parlaying the picks they got for Walker into all sorts of players and picks, the Cowboys turned things around quickly. Johnson was voted coach of the year in 1990 and then guided the team into the playoffs in 1991.

With Aikman handing off to Emmitt Smith or passing to Michael Irvin, the Cowboys became Super Bowl champions in 1992, 1993, and 1995. It was the greatest four-year run by any team, especially considering they were one game shy of the title game in their "down" year.

A messy spat between Johnson and Jones led to a coaching change after the second title. Barry Switzer held the fort down while the great players were still in their prime, but the fun faded quickly.

Landry's office, which remained his and only his for 29 years, might as well have had a turnstile after that.

Switzer gave way to Chan Gailey, who gave way to Dave Campo. Gailey became the first coach to never win a Super Bowl or even a playoff game. Campo became the first to never make the playoffs or have a winning season.

The problem wasn't the coaches as much as the roster. Irvin retired, then Aikman did, but only after Jones ruined his salary cap by trying to load up for one last title run behind No. 8.

The post-Aikman era began with four starting quarterbacks in one season. The franchise was a mess. The only highlight was Smith's march toward Walter Payton's rushing record. The day he got it, Dallas lost. It would be Smith's last year with the Cowboys.

Then Jones swallowed some of his ego and hired a real "football guy," Bill Parcells. He got the club back into the playoffs in his first season and over four years put the franchise back on solid footing. He never won a Super Bowl, or even a playoff game, but Parcells definitely left the Cowboys better than he found them—especially with Romo at quarterback.

An undrafted rookie, Romo arrived the same year as Parcells. There probably wouldn't have been room to keep him the next year, but then incumbent starter Quincy Carter cleared a path by earning his release.

Romo didn't get on the field until his third season, and it was only as the holder. Finally, in his fourth season, he replaced Drew Bledsoe and became an instant sensation. He set numerous passing records while leading the Cowboys to a record-tying 13 wins in his first full season, which also was the first season for coach Wade Phillips. Another playoff flop followed, but Dallas had another quarterback it could count on, and that's always been the most important first step to success.

Dallas' next championship quarterback? Having captured his first postseason win in January 2010, Tony Romo hopes to lead the Cowboys back to the top.
Ronald Martinez/Getty Images

LeBaron, Meredith, Staubach, White, Aikman, and Romo—each quarterback clearly represents an era in team history.

So that's how this book is organized: by quarterback.

Through pictures and words, the following 10 chapters will take you through the first 50 years of Dallas Cowboys history—the highs and lows, on the field and off. You will read about the big games and the big controversies, the star players and the scandals.

Sprinkled throughout are segments like "Polishing the Star," detailing history and traditions; "Rivalry in Review," which spotlights rivals from the division and beyond; and "You Make the Call," which offers up topics for fans to ponder and debate.

For those of you who lived through these seasons, enjoy the memories. For those of you learning as you go, you will understand how and why the Cowboys became "America's Team."

And, yes, the cheerleaders are in here too.

THE EDDIE LeBARON ERA

THE EARLY DAYS: 1960–1962

BIRTH OF A FRANCHISE

Pro football first arrived in Dallas in 1952, when the New York Yanks of the National Football League were sold to the league office, and commissioner Bert Bell awarded the franchise to a group of local businessmen.

Team owner Clint Murchison Jr. and his first quarterback, Eddie LeBaron, had a tough road ahead in their first season. The team steadily improved over the next few years before LeBaron handed the QB reins to up-and-comer Don Meredith. *Ralph Crane/ Time Life Pictures/ Getty Images*

They called their new club the Dallas Texans and made the Cotton Bowl their home stadium. It seemed like a perfect plan. After all, the only thing more popular than high school football on Friday nights was college football on Saturdays. Now, folks could round out their weekends with a pro football game on Sundays.

The first Texans game was a big enough deal that Gov. Allen Shivers showed up. At a pre-game ceremony, he declared it his pleasure to welcome "this new era in sports in Texas."

Well, that era lasted just seven games. Only four were in Dallas. All were losses, and few people even noticed, much less showed up.

The owners were losing so much money that they told Bell to take his team back. So the Texans became nomads, playing their remaining games on the road. They actually won one to finish 1–11. They left their mark on NFL history by being the last franchise to fold.

Among those who turned out to Texans games was a short, stocky guy with a buzz cut and glasses named Clint Murchison Jr. An heir to one of the great oil fortunes, he had wanted to buy the Texans. Disappointed, he spent the next several years trying to buy other teams.

Murchison's big chance came in 1959. The NFL was talking about adding two teams in 1961, then the league sped up its plans when a group of wannabe owners got together and announced their intention to launch the American Football League in 1960.

Two teams in this maverick league were going to be located in Texas, including one led by the league's driving force, Lamar Hunt, another Dallas-area oil heir. NFL leaders knew they needed a presence in the Lone Star State too; their southernmost team at the time was in Washington, D.C.

Murchison went to Chicago and got the support of legendary Bears boss George Halas. He was so confident about getting a team that he went out to hire a general manager. At Halas' urging, Murchison convinced CBS Sports executive Texas E. "Tex" Schramm to come aboard.

A graduate of the University of Texas, Schramm had been a sportswriter in Austin before going to work for the Los Angeles Rams, starting as their public relations man and working his way up to general manager before leaving for CBS. He had been in television for several years, having turned down job offers from pro football and pro basketball teams. Schramm accepted Murchison's offer because he liked the challenge of building a team from scratch—and because Murchison promised to stay out of his way.

Schramm was living in New York at the time, so naturally he followed the Giants. That season, 1959, the Giants posted a league-best record of 10–2 and gave up the fewest points, drawing a lot of praise for defensive assistant Tom Landry.

"He is an innovator who will make a big name for himself in the coaching ranks before he's through," Giants head coach Jim Lee Howell said.

The Houston Oilers of the AFL were also trying to hire Landry, but Schramm had a few things going for him. Landry already knew the NFL, and he spent his offseasons selling insurance in Dallas. He had also already had one bad experience with a rival league, having signed out of college with the New York Yankees of the All-America Football Conference. The AAFC folded after his rookie season of 1949.

On December 28, 1959, the day after the Giants lost the NFL title game to the Baltimore Colts, Schramm introduced Landry as head coach of the Dallas Rangers.

Yes, Rangers.

Receiver Gene Felkins, of the original Dallas Texans, drops a pass against the Green Bay Packers in November 1952. It was one of many mishaps for the short-lived franchise. *Vernon Biever/NFL/Getty Images*

General manager Tex Schramm (left) and the newly named head coach, Tom Landry, December 28, 1959. *AP Images*

COWBOY LEGENDS
CLINT MURCHISON JR.

Days before the Cowboys played in their first Super Bowl, Tom Landry received a note from his boss.

I have taught you all I can. From now on, you're on your own.
Sincerely,
CLINT

Murchison was kidding, of course. It was typical of his fun-loving, large-living persona, which included owning a Caribbean island, a posh California hotel, an eatery in New York he called the Dallas Cowboy Restaurant (until the league made him change it), and a chunk of a $1.25 billion family fortune in an era when it was rare to have $1.25 million.

In 1966, *Life* magazine described Murchison (pronounced MURK-i-son) as a "smart, unorthodox, funny man with an M.I.T. master's in mathematics [and] a passion for football. . . . Murchison is the sort of fellow who expects—and gets—75 cents change each time he hands one of his four children a dollar for a hot dog. He throws fiscal caution to the winds, however, when it comes to building a football team or executing a practical joke."

In November 1960, on the Cowboys' first trip to Chicago, Murchison rented a live bear and had the animal's trainer dress up in a cowboy outfit, then he put them on display in the lobby of the Sheraton Hotel the day before the game. He invited photographers to watch this demonstration of the Cowboys beating the Bears—the pretend cowboy shooting his pistol and the bear falling over, right on cue. Murchison then brought the bear and the trainer to his private party and got them both drunk. Yes, both man and animal. Once the bear started rampaging, he was somehow corralled onto an elevator and released into the lobby.

Another vintage move came at the end of the 1961 season, before a game in Washington.

Murchison knew the halftime show featured Santa Claus drawn by Alaskan huskies. So the night before the game he had

Lynn Pelham/Time Life Pictures/
Getty Images

the field seeded with chicken feed and had 200 chickens flown in from Texas and stashed in the bowels of the stadium. The plan was to release the birds during "Jingle Bells." The chickens would go after the feed, the dogs would go after the chickens, and madness would ensue. The plan was foiled by some stadium workers, but the prank continued. For weeks, Redskins owner George Preston Marshall received calls in which all he heard were clucking sounds. He changed his phone numbers several times, yet the calls kept coming. (Perhaps Murchison's friend J. Edgar Hoover, the head of the FBI, helped provide the new numbers?) Marshall was so irate he complained to NFL commissioner Pete Rozelle. The calls ceased, but a year later, what became known as the Cowboy Chicken Club managed to sneak a man wearing a chicken suit onto the field before a game in Washington. He released a chicken, then turned a cartwheel and fled into the stands as the teams came out.

Friends said Murchison was too smart for his own good. For years, he wriggled out of mistakes or forgot about them through gambling, womanizing, drinking, and taking drugs. He became religious late in life—after marrying Gil Brandt's ex-wife—but couldn't escape the financial traps he'd set for himself.

As inflation grew and interest rates soared, Murchison kept borrowing money. Even selling the Cowboys for $80 million didn't help. He was hundreds of millions of dollars in debt when he died in March 1987 at age 63.

Murchison is not in the Ring of Honor, and it's a shame. The team's founder belongs there to perpetuate the memory of the guy who made everything possible. Consider these words from Landry, spoken at Murchison's memorial service:

"A lot of people were wondering why we were successful. I got my praise, Tex got his praise, Gil got his . . . but it was Clint Murchison that brought us together. It was his roots. Stability is the only way that you can have a long-running successful organization in pro football, and he gave us the stability that we wanted."

ORIGIN OF THE NICKNAME AND LOGO

At first, this club was called the Dallas Steers.

Tex Schramm put a stop to that: "You don't want your whole football team being castrated." So they switched the name to Dallas Rangers.

"It came to me right away, like a bolt from the blue: THE DALLAS RANGERS," team founder Clint Murchison Jr. said. "Now there, I declared, was a name for a football team if there was one. Its connotations were historical, proud, tough. My grandfather, who was one, would have loved it."

It was such a good nickname that it was already taken.

A minor league baseball team in the American Association was already using it. Yet as the NFL team was starting up, the baseball team was going out of business, so the baseball owner told the football folks they could have it.

Then they decided to keep the baseball team—and the nickname.

Murchison wanted to keep it too. Dallas, he insisted, "was surely big enough to hold two Rangers," pointing out that New York had two Giants and St. Louis had two Cardinals.

Schramm talked him into changing.

Murchison was jealous of Lamar Hunt for beating him to the name Texans. ("If you don't think I got even for that, drive out to Irving and check the name of the stadium," Murchison later wrote.)

He also declared that "all the animals, at least all the good ones [Tigers, Bears, Lions] were used up."

From a list of 12 candidates, 3 finalists were chosen. Murchison didn't like any and put off a decision. He was about to board a plane when Schramm called and told him to pick one already.

"OK," Murchison said. "Let's go with Cowboys."

So on March 20, 1960, a headline in *The Dallas Morning News* read, "One Ranger Skips Town," referring to the fact that the football team was going with a new name.

"We just decided it would be in the best interests of everyone if we changed our name," Schramm said in the accompanying article. "So from now on we are the Cowboys."

Murchison considered it a temporary thing, figuring he could switch back to Rangers, or something else, in a few years.

He was serious. In March 1965, he told the newspapers to put it up for discussion among fans.

As he wrote in a note to a Dallas sportswriter, the tally came in as follows:

- Keep the name Cowboys, 1,138.
- Change the name to Rangers, 2.
- Murchison is stupid, 8.

Once they started with the Cowboys name, "the rest was easy," Murchison wrote years later.

"The team color was a cinch. Lamar had red, so we took blue. It took me eight years to finish the decal design, but you will eventually become used to it, even as I have to the name."

Yeah, that star logo seems to have caught on quite nicely.

WASHINGTON REDSKINS

The bad blood between the Dallas Cowboys and Washington Redskins began before the teams ever met on the field.

Redskins owner George Preston Marshall did his best to keep Dallas from getting a franchise. Among the reasons, Marshall once told George Halas, was that he considered prospective owner Clint Murchison Jr. "personally obnoxious."

"If he thinks I'm obnoxious now," Murchison wrote, "how will he feel when he meets me?"

Murchison needed Marshall's support because the expansion vote had to be unanimous. In search of a way to persuade Marshall, Murchison lucked into the rights to the song, "Hail to the Redskins."

The importance of this song was summed up best by a *Washington Post* writer who said that taking that song from Marshall would be like taking "Dixie" from the South, "Anchors Aweigh" from the Navy, or "Blue Suede Shoes" from Elvis Presley.

The tune was penned by bandleader Barnee Breeskin and Marshall's then-wife, Corinne Griffith. Breeskin owned the rights and had his own spat with Marshall. When Breeskin caught wind of Murchison's battle with Marshall, he offered the song to Murchison to use as leverage. Adding a degree of separation, the deal ran through Murchison associate Tom Webb.

On the morning of the expansion vote, Murchison went to Marshall's hotel suite and introduced himself. Marshall brought up the song, of course, and Murchison vowed to take care of it with one call.

Then, as planned, Murchison called Webb.

Murchison pulled off a phony conversation requesting the rights. Murchison pretended Webb was holding firm, telling Marshall, "He thinks you're a no-good bastard, apparently, and he's just not going to let you have the song." Marshall pleaded

with Murchison to try again, offering his support of Dallas' expansion bid in exchange for the song rights. Finally, Webb gave in.

In 1973, long after this story had become part of the lore of both teams, another layer of intrigue emerged—in *Playboy* magazine, of all places.

Bobby Baker, a former aide to President Lyndon Johnson, told of a $25,000 bribe one of Murchison's associates gave Senator Estes Kefauver, the chair of an anti-monopoly committee that was deciding whether to declare the Redskins Network a monopoly. From that influential perch, and flush with Murchison's money, Kefauver could have recommended that Marshall support Dallas' bid.

Whichever version you choose to believe, the fact is that the Dallas and Washington teams have been fighting like cowboys and Indians ever since.

The history of the two teams is filled with memorable matchups and off-field shenanigans—like George Allen's spying accusations in 1967 or Harvey Martin's wreath-throwing in 1979—supporting the various surveys that rank this rivalry among the best in the NFL, even in all of sports. (See Murchison's profile for more on his personal tweaking of Marshall.)

The longstanding Dallas-Washington enmity further entered the popular consciousness when it served as the backdrop for two memorable commercials featuring legendary coach Tom Landry.

In one American Express ad, the stone-faced Landry, dressed as a cowboy and standing in a dusty saloon, proclaims, "You never know when you'll be surrounded by Redskins." In another ad, for a hotel chain, Landry pops out of a suitcase wearing his trademark fedora and grabs a guitar and croons, "Mamas, don't let your babies grow up to be . . . Redskins."

After briefly calling his team the Steers, Murchison took a shine to the name Rangers and used it for months. A minor-league baseball team already was using it, but the club was supposed to be going out of business. When it didn't, Schramm convinced Murchison to pick something else. He reluctantly agreed to make a change and just as reluctantly accepted "Cowboys."

Landry received a five-year contract at $34,500 per season. Just as Murchison vowed to stay out of Schramm's business, the GM promised his coach total control of on-field decisions.

The only thing left for Murchison to do was actually get the franchise.

NFL owners met at a Miami Beach hotel in January 1960. Before talking about expansion, they had to hire a commissioner to replace Bell, who had died the previous October. After days of debate, the owners chose Pete Rozelle, who had gotten his start in pro football working for Schramm in the Rams' PR department.

Once they got around to talking about adding teams, Redskins owner George Preston Marshall starting causing problems—again.

When NFL owners originally voted to counter the AFL by expanding their league, the tally was 11–1, with Marshall the lone dissenter. The Redskins were proud of being the southernmost team in the NFL—"the team of Dixie," they bragged—and Marshall wanted it to stay that way. He also wasn't very fond of Murchison, who years before had tried to buy the Redskins from him. In the end, Marshall turned out to be no match for ol' Clint.

The prank-loving multimillionaire oilman had purchased the rights to Marshall's beloved "Hail to the Redskins" fight song, and he wouldn't give them up unless Marshall let Dallas in. The Redskins owner relented, and on January 28, 1960, Murchison—along with his brother John, his secret, silent co-partner, and minority owner Bedford Wynne—owned an NFL franchise.

The cost was only $50,000, but another $550,000 fee was required to compensate the other teams for the players Dallas would take in an expansion draft to stock its roster.

The college draft had been held in November as a pre-emptive move against the upstart AFL. As a result, Dallas could only pick from other teams' has-beens and never-weres. The 12 existing teams each offered nine players, and the Cowboys could take three from each club. Schramm got the list in March and had 24 hours to choose.

Schramm actually had some other players already locked up, having signed them before Dallas even got the franchise. They were good ones too: quarterback Don Meredith and running back Don Perkins.

Meredith was already a star in Dallas at Southern Methodist University, making him an important target for both of the city's new pro teams. Hunt was a big SMU supporter, so he especially wanted Meredith for his AFL team, which by now had revived the name Dallas Texans. Schramm lured Meredith with a $150,000, five-year "personal services" contract, which guaranteed that he would be paid even if the NFL team didn't make it. The Cowboys pulled this off thanks, in part, to Halas, who had drafted Meredith; the Bears then handed over his rights for a third-round pick in 1962.

SMU quarterback Don Meredith was highly sought after by both of Dallas' pro football teams. *Southern Methodist/Collegiate Images/Getty Images*

Perkins also signed a personal services contract. The thanks there go to Sen. Clinton Anderson of New Mexico, who was pals with Murchison. Perkins went to school at New Mexico, and Anderson basically told him it would be in his best interests to sign with Dallas. The Cowboys gave the Colts a mere ninth-round pick in 1962 for Perkins' rights.

Things were going so well that Schramm tried to sign LSU star Billy Cannon too. Schramm backed off after Rozelle, when he was still GM of the Rams, warned Schramm that he might soon have a great roster, but he also might alienate so many people that Dallas wouldn't get awarded a franchise.

Schramm also had another sleuth gathering players: Gil Brandt, a former baby photographer whose hobby was scouring the land for pro football talent, long before that became popular.

While in college at Wisconsin, Brandt wrote to college sports departments posing as a high school coach looking for game film of star players. He began compiling lists of the best prospects and eventually developed a nationwide network of connections. They were essentially informants, passing along things Brandt needed to know, including tips on athletes in other sports who weren't playing football but could. In later years, Brandt would send information to college seniors noting how many undrafted players the Cowboys signed, thus encouraging them to try out for the Cowboys. Considering how many of those undrafted players turned into vital players, it was a brilliant move. Another innovation Brandt would bring—not just to the Cowboys, but to all of scouting—was relying on the 40-yard dash instead of the 100-yard dash to gauge foot speed.

"The first time I called him, I gave him the names of three or four free-agent players we were interested in," Schramm said of Brandt. "In two days, he had all of them signed. He was amazing. It was obvious he was a person who put no limit on the time or energy necessary to get the job done."

In 1960, Brandt's job was to scrounge up guys who were unhappy or who'd walked away from their teams. That's how the Cowboys gathered Eddie LeBaron, Jerry Tubbs, Gene Babb, and a year later, Chuck Howley.

Over those first six months, the team had been renamed, the roster was coming together, and the rest of the organization was being set up for what proved to be the long haul. For instance, Schramm "borrowed" Kay Lang from the Rams' ticket office to set up the same department in Dallas. She stuck around for 25 years. Her sister, Marge Lang Kelley, would become Landry's secretary for 18 years.

Nobody knew it, but the Cowboys were in great shape. They had an incredibly innovative coach, a wily general manager, and a keen talent scout. They also had an owner who was thrilled to be nothing more than their biggest fan, and a few players who would prove to be among the greatest in franchise history.

All they needed was time.

YOU'VE GOT TO START SOMEWHERE

Tom Landry's first training-camp roster was about as big as the phone book in some small Texas towns. There were 193 candidates, including a 5-foot-4 receiver, a rodeo cowboy, and a fullback who was much better at playing piano.

The easiest way to start weeding out folks was the Landry Mile. Backs and receivers had to finish in six minutes, linemen got an extra 30 seconds. This would have been a lot tougher in the Dallas heat, but the Cowboys held their first camp at Pacific College in Forest Grove, Oregon, about 20 miles west of Portland, with the snow-capped Mount Hood visible in the distance.

One guy needed more than nine minutes; he didn't make the cut. Receiver Frank Clarke finished first; he would last eight seasons, among the longest tenures of the inaugural group.

The Cowboys took quarterback Don Heinrich from the Giants in the expansion draft and were considering him to help groom Don Meredith. Then they persuaded Eddie LeBaron to come aboard.

LeBaron had recently passed the Texas bar exam and was planning to retire from football after seven seasons with the Redskins. To get his rights from Washington, the Cowboys gave up a first-round pick in 1961 (their first-ever pick, remember, because they missed the 1960 draft) and a sixth-rounder.

Although LeBaron's college coach had been the venerable Amos Alonzo Stagg, LeBaron wasn't *that* old, only 30. The bigger limitation should've been his size: generously listed at 5-foot-9. But LeBaron

TEX SCHRAMM

Tex Schramm didn't come up with the name "America's Team." But he knew marketing gold when he heard it and made darn sure the tag stuck.

Schramm had a knack for knowing what people would like, even before they knew it.

Go back to his days in TV, when he convinced CBS to give the Olympics wall-to-wall coverage, steered by an anchor, just like a political convention. It's been done that way ever since.

In Dallas, he hired Tom Landry and Gil Brandt and created the computerized scouting system. His theory on scouting was that if you look where everyone else looks, you won't be any better than they are. So he took out-of-the-box gambles and came up with Roger Staubach, Bob Hayes, and Herschel Walker; Chad Hennings was another such pick who paid off years after Schramm left the club. There also were what-the-heck picks who didn't pan out, like Pat Riley and Carl Lewis.

Schramm turned the team newsletter into a global propaganda campaign, such as sending freebies to college trainers so prospective players could keep up with the Cowboys while getting their ankles taped. He built an international radio network every team envied. The Ring of Honor was his idea, and he served as both judge and jury.

The cheerleaders were his doing, as was the Thanksgiving game. He made the Cowboys the first team to wear white at home, realizing the benefit of making opponents wear dark colors in the Texas heat.

"Tex was the architect of the Cowboys," Landry said.

He was just as instrumental in building the NFL.

Schramm negotiated the AFL - NFL merger, helped design the wild-card playoff system, pushed through instant replay, and is to thank or blame for wind strips atop goalposts, wider sideline borders, spiking the ball to stop the clock, and referees announcing penalties to the crowd. The full list of his innovations is much longer, but you get the point.

"He had a unique combination of the big picture and the details," said NFL senior vice president of public relations Greg Aiello, who spent 10 years working for Schramm in the team's PR department before joining the league office.

A native of Los Angeles, Schramm had family roots in San Antonio and went to college in Austin. He had a showman's love of the spotlight and was never shy on opinions. He made sure

players understood the media's role; if a player didn't return a reporter's phone call fast enough, he'd make them do it.

His vision was clear. He wanted to make the Cowboys as big as the New York Yankees, the colossal force on the pro sports scene when the NFL was beginning to hit its stride.

"I want to look and say I was a part of greatness," he once said.

There's a bust at the Pro Football Hall of Fame, and a spot in the Ring of Honor, as proof that he succeeded.

Schramm died in July 2003 at age 83, but his legacy endures in Dallas and throughout pro football.

proved during his years with the Redskins that he knew what he was doing.

Don Perkins was supposed to have been the team's main ball carrier, but he broke a foot at the college all-star game and would miss the season. That opened up playing time for Gene Babb, who had quit the 49ers after being demoted and was working as a coach and an art teacher at Ranger Junior College when the Cowboys tracked him down. Jerry Tubbs had been Babb's teammate in San Francisco, and he, too, had a new career lined up, working for Coca-Cola. But those plans fell through. Dallas took him in the expansion draft, and needing the money, Tubbs showed up at training camp. Just before the season started, the Cowboys lucked out again when Cleveland cut former All-Pro receiver Billy Howton, and they were able to add him.

Of the 36 players picked in the expansion draft, only three would last at least five seasons with the team: Tubbs, Clarke, and offensive lineman Bob Fry. But in 1960, the Cowboys kept 22 of those picks.

The team's first offices were housed in a section of an auto club. "People would crowd in there to map routes for trips, and I'd be over in a corner discussing player contracts on the phone," Schramm recalled. The Cowboys practiced at Burnett Field, a broken-down baseball park infested with everything from rats that chewed on shoulder pads to scorpions that hid in cleats. The offense met in the clubhouse behind first base, the defense behind third base. When it rained, the field and the showers would get flooded, attracting even more critters.

In the years between the 1952 Dallas Texans and the arrival of the Cowboys in 1960, pro football still visited Dallas every year for the annual Salesmanship Club game at the Cotton Bowl, a fundraiser benefiting a camp for underprivileged children. The Cowboys

COWBOY LEGENDS
EDDIE LeBARON

Eddie LeBaron was the perfect guy to take the first snaps for the Dallas Cowboys—even if he was only 5-foot-7 and 160 pounds.

"We needed a cagey veteran like LeBaron, who could help teach Meredith the tricks of his trade and give us some starting experience until Don and the rest of the team matured," Tom Landry wrote in his autobiography.

Known as "The Little General," LeBaron was the NFL's rookie of the year in 1952 and the passing leader in 1958. He was about to retire and start a law career when the Cowboys asked him to help groom Don Meredith. He promised to stay for three years but lasted four. It was the kind of loyalty you'd expect from a Marine who received a Bronze Star for bravery and several Purple Hearts while on the frontlines in Korea.

Although Dallas only won 4 of the 26 games LeBaron started, he should be remembered more for starting the club's incredible lineage at the most important position. And, of course, he did throw the first touchdown pass and led the fourth-quarter rally that produced the first victory.

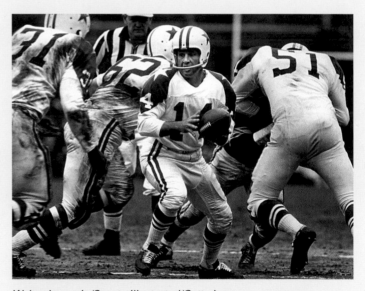

Walter Iooss Jr./Sports Illustrated/Getty Images

"LeBaron is a man I thoroughly respect," Meredith said. "He got the most from his ability, and very few ever do that in any field."

LeBaron finally became a full-time lawyer after the 1963 season. He kept a hand in football too, working with the league and the players' association, then joining the Falcons, first as general manager, then chief operating officer.

continued the tradition, and the team's first-ever home game, albeit an exhibition, drew 40,000 fans on a hot Saturday night in August.

Most fans were there to see the reigning NFL champions from Baltimore, featuring Johnny Unitas, Alan Ameche, Eugene "Big Daddy" Lipscomb, and SMU's own Raymond Berry. (The Colts, by the way, started in 1953 from the remnants of the 1952 Texans. Art Donovan and Gino Marchetti were the lone Texans still playing for the Colts in 1960.)

Dallas led 10–7 until Unitas threw a 62-yard touchdown pass on a fourth-and-10, giving Baltimore a 14–10 victory. Still, it was a relatively promising showing for the new club.

The real debut game—against Bobby Layne and the Pittsburgh Steelers—drew commissioner Pete Rozelle and Hollywood stars Roy Rogers and Dale Evans atop Trigger and Buttercup. The locals didn't take kindly to the show-biz version of cowboys and let them know it. Schramm later called the fans' abuse of his guests one of his biggest embarrassments.

Only eight years before, Dallas hadn't been interested enough in pro football to support one team, but now two clubs were vying for affection—and business. The going theory was that whichever team won first would win everyone over; the Cowboys were hoping the established stars and teams of their league would be a bigger drawing card. Alas, despite mailing out 200,000 letters to prospective buyers, only 2,165 season tickets were sold.

The best seats in the house went for $4.60. It was only two bucks to sit in the end zone, and adults could bring up to five kids for free. Still, only 30,000 people showed up for the opener, and only about 13,000 of them paid to get in. It also rained that day, leaving the field sloppy. Plus, the game was on

COWBOY LEGENDS
DON PERKINS

Don't let the glittering fame of Cowboys quarterbacks obscure an important point: This club has an incredible tradition at running back too.

And it all started with Don Perkins.

Perkins missed the expansion season because of an injury, then played eight seasons. He turned 1,500 carries into 6,217 yards and 42 touchdowns. Tony Dorsett and Emmitt Smith are the only players in team history with more. In just his second NFL game, Perkins rushed for 108 yards against the Vikings, notching the first 100-yard rushing game in franchise history.

At 5-foot 10, 204 pounds, Perkins wasn't the biggest guy. He wasn't the fastest, either. But he always got the job done, finishing among the top 10 rushers in the NFL every season. He made six Pro Bowls and was All-Pro once. When he retired, only four NFL players had ever run for more yards.

In his final season, the team's media guide referred to Perkins as "the pro's pro."

Perkins arrived and left the same time as Meredith, and he was enshrined into the Ring of Honor with him in 1976.

NFL/Getty Images

The Cleveland Browns needed only 25 yards from Jim Brown while handing the Cowboys their worst loss of their debut season, 48–7, in front of a sparse Cotton Bowl crowd on October 16, 1960.
AP Images

a Saturday night; the Texans had the stadium on Sunday. That meant the Cowboys were competing with the most popular night of television, up against favorites like *Gunsmoke, Have Gun Will Travel, Perry Mason,* and *Bonanza.*

On the first offensive series in franchise history, LeBaron threw a short pass to tight end Jim Doran, who took off for a 75-yard touchdown. Then, a long pass to Clarke set up a 7-yard touchdown pass to Fred Dugan. Just like that, Dallas was up 14–0.

It was the biggest lead the Cowboys would have all season.

Layne tied the game with a 49-yard touchdown pass in the third quarter, then threw a 65-yarder in the final minutes to beat Dallas 35–28. The Cowboys came close again the next week, losing 27–25 to Philadelphia, but the game drew only 18,500 fans.

The encouraging sign of two narrow losses was wiped out when the Cowboys went to Washington. LeBaron was playing against his old mates, and owner Clint Murchison Jr. was looking to jostle his new rival, Redskins owner George Preston Marshall. Not only did Washington win 26–14, it was the Redskins' only victory that season.

The rest of the Cowboys' season was typical for an expansion team. Jim Brown and the Browns trounced them 48–7 in Week 4, then they lost to St. Louis a week later on a short field goal in the final minute. After the Colts stomped them 45–7, Meredith got his first start and went 9-of-28 for 75 yards and three interceptions in a 25-point loss to the Rams. Heinrich started the next game, and Dallas lost 41–7 to Green Bay.

The home finale was on November 20 against San Francisco. A crowd of supposedly 10,000 saw the Cowboys fall to 0–9. After losing in Chicago, the Cowboys went to New York for Landry's debut in the city where he played and coached throughout the 1950s.

Playing in front of 55,033 fans, their largest crowd of the year, the Cowboys trailed by two touchdowns early but hung tough. They were down only 31–24 in the fourth quarter when LeBaron threw an 11-yard touchdown pass to Howton. The game finished tied at 31. Finally, they didn't lose! The players even had fans awaiting their arrival at Love Field to congratulate them.

OK, it was only two people holding a sign that read, "Well Done, Cowboys." Still, it was something.

The season ended with a loss at Detroit. Their 0–11–1 record was the worst in the NFL since 1944, when two teams went winless while their best players were fighting World War II. Even the 1952 Texans had won a game.

L. G. "Long Gone" DuPre led the 1960 Cowboys in rushing with a pathetic 362 yards. All three quarterbacks completed less than half of their passes—unless you give LeBaron credit for the 25 caught by opponents. Perhaps the club's biggest accomplishment was sending someone to the Pro Bowl; Doran made it for having 31 receptions and 554 yards.

The reality was, these players couldn't grasp what Landry wanted them to do. The older players were too set in their ways, and the younger players were in over their heads. The few in between resented being forced to be part of this club; more than one whined, moaned, and insulted Landry in hopes of getting released.

LeBaron told Landry that if he dumbed things down a little, they might be able to win a few games.

"That's probably right," Landry replied. "But I'm putting in a system to compete with the New York Giants and the Cleveland Browns."

FIRST WIN, FIRST TEASE

It's a good thing Bob Lilly liked Texas so much.

A college superstar at TCU, Lilly was drafted by the AFL's Dallas Texans and was considering signing with them. He warned NFL teams that the only one in the league he'd consider was the Cowboys.

Dallas was supposed to have the second overall pick, behind the newcomer Minnesota Vikings, but

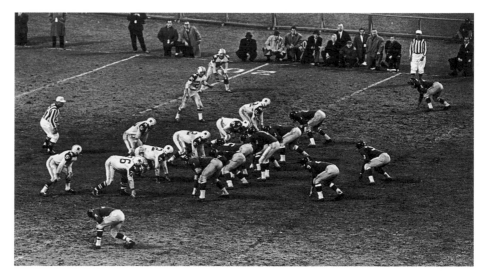

The Cowboys got their only non-loss of the 1960 season in a tie with the New York Giants on December 4. *Robert Riger/Getty Images*

that pick had already been sent to the Redskins for Eddie LeBaron. So Schramm traded offensive lineman Paul Dickson and a first-round pick in 1962 for the thirteenth and final pick of the first round. Schramm used that pick to draft the man who would become known as "Mr. Cowboy."

The Cowboys' front-office savvy was on full display that offseason. Brandt signed Oregon State sprinter Amos Marsh, and Schramm brought Chuck Howley back to the NFL after an 18-month layoff.

A first-round pick by the Bears in 1958, Howley quit after his second season because of a knee injury. He went home to West Virginia and bought a gas station. Realizing he was feeling better, he told former teammate Don Healy, who had been an expansion pick of the Cowboys, that he was thinking about a comeback. Healy passed word along to Schramm. The Bears gave up Howley's rights for two 1963 draft picks.

Minnesota's arrival caused a reshuffling of the NFL. The Cowboys moved from the Western Conference to the Eastern, joining the Giants, Eagles, Browns, Cardinals, Steelers, and Redskins. In addition, the regular season was expanded from 12 games to 14.

Cowboys training camp was held at St. Olaf College in Northfield, Minnesota. With Perkins fully recovered and Marsh also joining the backfield,

COWBOY LEGENDS
BOB LILLY

Bob Lilly was the first player ever drafted by the Cowboys, and he was quite the prototype: Big, strong, tough.

And, of course, talented.

Lilly played all 14 games in all 14 of his seasons and was so good that he made the NFL's All-Decade Team for the 1960s *and* 1970s.

When the Cowboys lost their first Super Bowl, he was the guy who hurled his helmet in disgust. When they won it all the next year, he made the game's biggest play. And when the NFL Man of the Year award started, he was among the team's first-year winners.

Known as "Mr. Cowboy," he was the first inductee into the Ring of Honor and the first tried-and-true Cowboys player to make the Hall of Fame. Since 1985, the team has given out the Bob Lilly Award. It's voted on by fans to honor a player for sportsmanship, dedication, leadership, and achievement.

When he went into the Ring, he was introduced as "the greatest Cowboy of them all," and there weren't any dissenters. Tom Landry, never one big on praise, made an exception for "the greatest player I've ever coached."

The Cowboys don't retire any numbers. The closest they've come is with his No. 74.

Focus on Sport/Getty Images

No one else has ever worn it in a regular-season game and probably no one ever will. So the next time you see someone wearing it during the preseason, here's a hint: that guy ain't making the team; if he does, it won't be as No. 74.

Landry moved Babb to linebacker. He also put Lilly at left defensive end, thinking his speed would be of best use there. It wasn't, and it would take Landry two years to figure it out.

Although the Cowboys had yet to win a game, Murchison liked what he saw. Or maybe he just wanted to boost ticket sales. Whatever the reason, he predicted that Dallas would win 8 to 10 games and that the December 3 home finale against Cleveland would determine the winner of the Eastern Conference.

A month into the season, Murchison's prediction was looking pretty good.

The Cowboys opened at home against Pittsburgh again, this time with Meredith at quarterback. He threw a 44-yard touchdown pass to Clarke for an early lead, then LeBaron came in and threw a 45-yard touchdown pass to Howton on a flea-flicker. The quarterbacks shuffled in and out all game, a move Landry would use many times through the years.

After Meredith threw a late interception that the Steelers returned for a go-ahead touchdown, Landry went back to LeBaron. He tied the game with a TD pass to Dick Bielski with 56 seconds left. Then Jerry Tubbs intercepted Layne at the Dallas 38 with 10 seconds to go. LeBaron threw a 40-yard pass to Howton, setting up rookie Allen Green for the potential game-winning kick.

Green already had missed two field goals and had a punt blocked. But he knew how to make a kick under pressure, having booted Ole Miss past Arkansas and LSU the season before. He did it again, nailing a 27-yarder that gave Dallas a 27–24 victory—the first in franchise history.

The second win came the very next week, in Minnesota, where Meredith outdueled Fran Tarkenton and Perkins posted the club's first 100-yard rushing game. Although a loss at Cleveland followed, the Cowboys played the Vikings again and notched another first: a shutout.

At 3–1, the Cowboys were tied for first place in the conference. It was all downhill from there.

Dallas went 1–8–1 the rest of the way, beating the New York club the team had tied the year before and tying a Washington team that won only one game all season.

Six of Dallas' seven home games drew 25,000 fans or less. The one exception provided a glimmer of hope: When the Cowboys were 3–1, attendance was 41,500.

There were other silver linings too. LeBaron and Meredith both completed more than 50 percent of their passes, Clarke led the league at 22.4 yards per reception, and the rookie Perkins earned a trip to the Pro Bowl.

All things considered, it was a pretty successful second season.

POINTS APLENTY—ON BOTH SIDES OF THE BALL

These days, play calls are sent directly to quarterbacks through speakers in their helmets. But in the Cowboys' third season, Landry wanted to look his guys in the eye and tell them what to do. So he came up with the "quarterback messenger system."

LeBaron and Meredith alternated every snap. Whoever was out on a given play stood next to Landry on the sideline so they could discuss what they were seeing and thinking. LeBaron actually liked it.

In November, Tex Maule wrote an article in *Sports Illustrated* titled, "A Shuttle Shakes Up the Pros." Maule—who'd worked under Tex Schramm in the public-relations department of the Los Angeles Rams back in the 1950s—praised Landry and his system for transforming "the had-nothing Dallas Cowboys into an NFL contender."

Chuck Howley's return to the NFL in 1961 was eagerly appreciated by the Cowboys. *NFL/Getty Images*

And at that point they were contenders, with a 4–3–1 record and the league's highest-scoring offense.

After losing all five preseason games, the Cowboys scored a club-record 35 points in the regular-season opener, with Clarke catching 10 passes for 241 yards and 3 touchdowns. However, the defense gave up just as many points that day and Dallas had to settle for a tie.

A week later, the offense put up 28 points against the Steelers—and the defense gave up 30. The difference proved to be a 99-yard LeBaron-to-Clarke touchdown pass that was wiped out because lineman Andy Cvercko was caught holding in the end zone. Instead of Dallas getting at least six points for a touchdown, Pittsburgh was given two points for a safety.

More big plays came in a 41–19 victory over Philadelphia in Week 5, including a spectacular

NFL first: a pair of 100-yard returns for touchdowns. That had never been done in one game, much less by one team—and the Cowboys did it in a single quarter. First, Marsh returned a kickoff 101 yards, then rookie Mike Gaechter took an interception 100 yards for another score. Earlier, Meredith threw a 57-yard touchdown pass to Clarke.

Dallas stomped Pittsburgh 42–27 a week later, with LeBaron throwing five touchdown passes—a club record that's been tied but never broken.

After a winless debut campaign, Coach Tom Landry (kneeling) and his assistants had nowhere to go but up heading into the 1961 season. *AP Images*

The Cowboys were six games into the season and already had broken their single-game scoring record three times.

They were coming off a 38–10 victory over Washington when the *Sports Illustrated* article came out. They won only once in the remaining six games—and broke the points record again in that one win, scoring 45 against Cleveland.

At 5–8–1, the Cowboys were still headed in the right direction, especially on offense. Their 398 points matched the New York Giants, who were the league's runners-up. Only the champion Green Bay Packers scored more.

The messenger system left Meredith and LeBaron sharing the credit. Dandy Don threw for more yards (1,679 to 1,436), had one less interception, and took one less sack. The Little General threw for one more touchdown, had a slightly higher completion percentage, and, because he threw fewer passes, had a higher rating. Meredith started nine games to LeBaron's five, but it was LeBaron who was invited to the Pro Bowl, the first such honor for a Dallas quarterback.

Clarke led the NFL with 14 touchdown receptions and 22.2 yards per catch. Perkins ran for 945 yards and became the team's first All-Pro. He was so reliable, and Dallas' play-calling so predictable, that a first-down handoff to No. 43 drew chants of "Hey diddle diddle, Perkins up the middle."

The defense was the problem, of course. They allowed 402 points, which would stand as the most in club history until 2004, and by then the season was two games longer.

Landry knew from the start that things were going to be bad. Even though he brought in his former New York Giants protégé, Dick Nolan, to coach the defensive backs, Landry asked Nolan to suit up too. Nolan played all season, then became a valuable member of the coaching staff through 1967. He returned again in 1982 and would remain through Jimmy Johnson's first two seasons.

Nolan's first crop of pupils in Dallas included two quite raw rookies: Gaechter, who had been a record-setting sprinter at Oregon before joining the football team his senior year; and Cornell Green, a basketball star at Utah State who had never played

"The Little General," Eddie LeBaron retreats from the onrushing Eugene "Big Daddy" Lipscomb of the Pittsburgh Steelers. *Robert Riger/Getty Images*

Don Meredith gets the call from Coach Landry and heads into the huddle during a game against the St. Louis Cardinals, October 1962. *Marvin E. Newman/ Sports Illustrated/ Getty Images*

THE COMPUTER

While Tex Schramm was running CBS' coverage of the 1960 Winter Olympics, IBM was handling the scorekeeping for all the sports at all the venues. Their offices were in the same building, and Schramm wandered over to learn about IBM's powerful new machines.

Already hired by the Cowboys, Schramm was trying to determine how computers might help a football team. He knew the biggest crapshoot was the draft, so he talked to programmers about whether it would be possible to enter all the information into a machine to calculate—using only facts, stripping aside personal biases—which players had the greatest potential for success.

In 1962, Salam Qureishi of the IBM subsidiary Service Bureau Corporation came to Dallas to develop such a program. A native of India, Qureishi was a soccer fan who knew nothing about American football, but he was willing to learn.

Qureishi spent several months coming up with a set of questions that would form the basis of the evaluation system. He spent several more years refining it. After all, it's not easy turning intangibles like desire and competitiveness into algorithms.

Tom Landry and Tex Schramm review potential draft picks the old-fashioned way— before computers entered the picture. *AP Images*

The Cowboys gave it a test run in 1964. The machine spit out the top 100 players in the draft pool and, sure enough, 87 of them became pros; 11 of the computer's top 15 became NFL starters.

Schramm was such a believer that he persuaded Clint Murchison Jr. to start his own computer company, Optimum Systems Inc., and let Qureishi run it. It was a pre-emptive move to keep other teams from hiring him. The Cowboys also paid IBM to hand over every copy of the software, lest it turn up in enemy hands.

In 1968, the Cowboys expanded their use of the computer to analyze teams' tendencies—how often they ran on third-and-short, threw on first-and-10, etc.

While the Cowboys used these programs for many more years, Qureishi lasted only until 1970. Murchison fired him because he wanted a better businessman in charge. (A regrettable move, considering that Murchison's company tanked, while Qureishi launched his own firm, Sysorex, and became a very, very rich man.)

Qureishi's innovations served the team very well for a very long time. Even just the perception that the Cowboys had the computer on their side went a long way toward enhancing their image. It became another reason for football fans to love them or hate them.

football. Green knew so little about the sport that he wore his hip pads backward during the first three preseason games.

Green would eventually make five Pro Bowls in a 13-year NFL career. So would defensive end George Andrie, another rookie in 1962. Gaechter remained a solid player throughout the decade. Another newcomer was tight end Pettis Norman, who was discovered at Johnson C. Smith University in Charlotte, North Carolina, and given a signing bonus of 500 one-dollar bills.

The roster was coming together, and the offense was clicking. One more important thing took place following the team's third season: The Cowboys won the battle for the city of Dallas.

In May 1963, Lamar Hunt announced he was moving his team to Kansas City and renaming them the Chiefs.

The notion that whichever team became the bigger winner faster would capture the fan base didn't pan out.

The Texans were AFL champions in 1962 but still couldn't make enough money to keep up the fight—even though the Cowboys had yet to break .500 and were still drawing as little as 12,692 fans. Realizing that Murchison wasn't going anywhere, Hunt decided to stop butting heads with the Cowboys.

Having won their city, the Cowboys could now target the rest of the NFL.

POLISHING THE STAR
THE BATTLE FOR DALLAS

When the Cowboys and Texans began fighting for the hearts and wallets of Dallas citizens, Curtis Sanford—founder of the Cotton Bowl game—proposed that the teams square off and decide matters on the field. Winner stays.

Once both teams started losing money, the stakes changed. The Cowboys and Texans would play, and the loser had to stay, or so the joke went.

The Cowboys got a leg up on the Texans by partnering with the Salesmanship Club for their preseason game, already a big local event. In 1960 and 1962 through 1964, that meaningless August exhibition drew more fans than any regular-season Cowboys games.

The Texans drew more fans than the Cowboys, but they spent a lot of money on promotions. They tied ticket sales to purchases of cigarettes, chips, gasoline, pretty much anything they could. At their first game, they had a parade, an army of clowns and floats, and free balloons for kids.

There were battles for players too. In 1961, both teams drafted Bob Lilly and E. J. Holub. The Cowboys got one, and the Texans got the other.

Sometimes, mailmen mixed up the last names of Cowboys GM Tex Schramm and Texans coach Hank Stram and delivered

envelopes and packages to the wrong place. They held onto anything of value and tossed out complaints or anything else that might need to be addressed.

The owners had their own incidents of mistaken identity.

As bespectacled scions of oil barons, and just a few years apart in age, Clint Murchison Jr. and Lamar Hunt made fun of being confused for each other, and they developed a friendly rivalry.

In 1960, Murchison showed up at a luncheon wearing a red Texans blazer, wishing everyone a Merry Christmas. A week later, Murchison was having a party when a friend showed up with a giant, gift-wrapped box. When Murchison pulled the ribbon, out popped Hunt.

For Hunt's 50th birthday, a video tribute was put together featuring segments with all sorts of celebrities. It ends with the camera closing in on a large, gift-wrapped box, the contents of which can be heard asking, "Ready? Now?" Out pops Murchison, again wearing a Texans blazer.

"Hey, Lamar," he asked, "when are y'all movin' out to Texas Stadium?"

2

THE DON MEREDITH ERA

NEXT YEAR'S CHAMPIONS: 1963–1968

With the Texans out of the way, the Cowboys had Dallas all to themselves heading into 1963. But the spotlight wasn't necessarily a good thing.

The team was still in its formative years, stuck with players who were too old or simply not very good. However, the balance between those types and quality players was starting to even out.

THE PREDICTION AND THE PRESIDENT

On the cover of the September 9, 1963, issue of *Sports Illustrated*, linebacker Chuck Howley is seen breaking through an offensive line, poised to pulverize a quarterback, running back, or both.

The headline above him reads, "Dallas Defense Can Win In The East."

"Dandy Don" Meredith took the Cowboys to new heights by the mid-1960s—but the local hero and three-time Pro Bowler could only get them oh-so-close to glory before he retired in 1969 at the age of 31. *NFL/Getty Images*

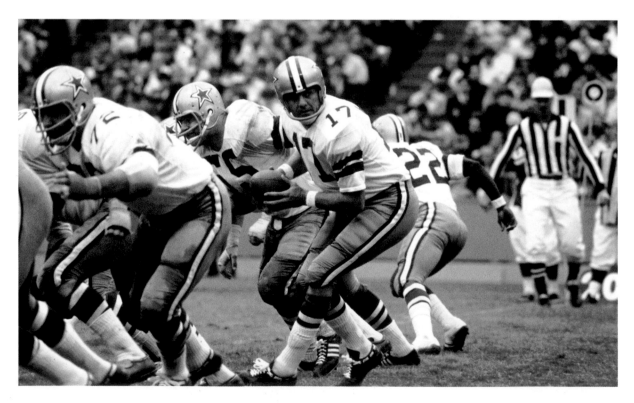

COWBOY LEGENDS
LEE ROY JORDAN

For 14 years, Lee Roy Jordan led the "Doomsday Defense" with his words and actions.

Jordan embodied everything Tom Landry wanted in a middle linebacker, the most important position in his defense: He was smart enough to know his job and everyone else's, plus strong enough and fast enough to make tackles all over the field.

Jordan arrived in 1963 and left after 1976, having started 154 consecutive games and made 1,236 tackles, at that time the most in franchise history. He played in three Super Bowls, winning one. He was picked for the Pro Bowl five times and named All-Pro twice.

As his college coach, Bear Bryant, said, "If they stay inbounds, Lee Roy will get them."

Jordan didn't make it to the Ring of Honor until 1989, but there's a story behind that.

Tex Schramm held a grudge against Jordan over a contract dispute and kept him out. Once Jerry Jones took over, Jordan was his first selection. "You've got a hell of a long memory," Jordan said of Jones during the ceremony.

Surrounded by his six predecessors in the Ring, Jordan said, "Many of the guys felt like I did. They were team players. That was the most important thing for me."

Tony Tomsic/NFL/
Getty Images

Was this a joke?

Everyone knew the Cowboys had an outstanding offense. Howley and Bob Lilly were good, but the overall defense wasn't, even after adding rookie linebacker Lee Roy Jordan.

But the Cowboys were coming off their first winning preseason, and *SI*'s Tex Maule decided to praise this up-and-coming team.

"That was a mean thing to do," receiver Frank Clarke said years later.

After winning five games the previous year, the Cowboys could be expected to improve a little—not all the way to league champions, though.

Especially not after what happened in Dallas on November 22, 1963.

The Cowboys lost their first four games and were 3–7 the day President John F. Kennedy rode in an open convertible through downtown Dallas.

His assassination was a turning point for the country and its citizens, especially those in Dallas. It also affected the guys on Dallas' NFL club, the city's only major pro sports team at the time. When the Cowboys went on the road—as they did two days later, in Cleveland, in a game that kicked off a few hours after Jack Ruby shot JFK's alleged assassin—they were viciously booed.

"They called us everything—murderers," Lilly recalled years later. "Like we had something to do with it. . . . We didn't get over it for weeks. . . . It affected us, no question about it."

(NFL commissioner Pete Rozelle would later regret his decision for the league to hold games that weekend, something successor Paul Tagliabue took to heart when he suspended the season for one week following the September 11, 2001, terrorist bombings.)

The 1963 season began at a fourth different training site in as many years.

Former Army star running back Glenn Davis had invited the Cowboys to be the Rams' annual opponent in a preseason charity game, and Schramm asked for a nearby spot to train. Davis steered them to Thousand Oaks, California, and the campus of California Lutheran College. They would stay for 26 years, watching the community grow from a population of around 10,000 to more than 100,000.

This was the year coach Tom Landry finally accepted that Lilly didn't have the flat-out speed to be an end rushing from the outside. Lilly's speed was in explosive bursts, so Landry moved him to tackle, in the middle of the line. Perfect.

When the Cowboys started 1–6, Landry made a tougher decision. He told Eddie LeBaron thanks for all he'd done to get the franchise going, but with this season pretty much lost, he had to prepare for the

future. Don Meredith would be the starting quarterback the rest of the way.

Meredith started out bumpy: Lose, win, lose, win. But he flashed his talent by throwing for 460 yards—the sixth-highest total in league history—against San Francisco, albeit in a 31–24 loss. Then Kennedy was killed and the season was ruined.

Dallas finished 4–10, one less victory than the previous season and nowhere near Maule's prediction.

At season's end, LeBaron retired and so did Billy Howton, who'd become the NFL's career leader in receptions and yards receiving. Losing a quarterback and receiver at the same time would be tough for a lot of teams, and even tougher for a team in need of a boost as badly as Dallas was.

THE EXTENSION AND A DRAFT TO REMEMBER

Fans were starting to grumble.

Tom Landry had been in charge for four years, and there hadn't been much progress. Wasn't he supposed to be some kind of genius?

When team owner Clint Murchison Jr. gathered reporters and photographers on February 5, 1964, people showed up expecting to be told Landry had been fired. It turned out to be quite the opposite. The coach was getting a 10-year contract extension.

"This is in line with my philosophy that if you get a good man, you have to keep him," Murchison said.

Then Schramm pulled off one of the greatest drafts in NFL history, securing the services of three future Hall of Famers: Mel Renfro in the second round, Bob Hayes in the seventh, and Roger Staubach in the tenth.

Hayes and Staubach were "futures" picks, which meant they still had a year of college eligibility left and couldn't be signed until then. In previous drafts, the Cowboys had been so desperate for live bodies that they couldn't spend them like that. They still needed help right away, to be sure, but these guys eventually would be worth the wait.

"Bullet Bob" was headed to the Tokyo Olympics, where he'd win the 100 meters in a world-record-tying 10.0 seconds, then run a miraculous anchor leg in the 400-meter relay to bring home another gold medal. Staubach was coming off a Heisman

Bob Lilly tackles Jim Brown during a 27–17 loss to Cleveland on November 24, 1963, two days after the assassination of President John F. Kennedy.
Tony Tomsic/Sports Illustrated/Getty Images

COWBOY LEGENDS
DON MEREDITH

Don Meredith is the tragic hero in Cowboys history.

Fans struggled to love him. When they did, it never was for very long. Tom Landry often didn't know what to make of him, either. Dandy Don snapped his fingers in the huddle and sang country-western songs between plays. Landry considered Meredith not serious enough to be a leader, although teammates thought otherwise. They appreciated his grit and courage, and were drawn in by his charisma and passion.

"If Meredith had led us over a cliff, I would have been the first one to follow. He was that great of a leader," offensive lineman Jim Boeke said. "All the guys liked him and wanted to play for him. . . . He just had an incredible way of motivating people."

Added lineman Ralph Neely, "People get a kick out of being around him."

His toughness was legendary.

The Army tried taking him in 1964, but he couldn't pass his physical. And that was before the most grueling season of his career, when he forever won over teammates by persevering on his spindly, aching legs.

"People kept saying, 'How can the kid do it?'" Meredith said. "I'll admit I liked getting that sympathy. But it wasn't really a matter of courage as much as determination. Nobody is going to beat me. I knew if I didn't get up they would have beaten me. I couldn't stand the thought of that."

So maybe courage was his tragic flaw. Fans would've said it was choking in big games.

During a winning streak in 1965, the Cowboys drew 76,251 spectators to the Cotton Bowl, their first-ever sellout, to see how Dallas stacked up against the Cleveland Browns. Meredith threw interceptions from the Cleveland 1 and the 32, both in the final two minutes, and the Cowboys lost 24–17. In *The Dallas Morning News* the next day, Gary Cartwright opened his story with these lines:

Outlined against a grey November sky, the Four Horsemen rode again Sunday.
You know them: Pestilence, death, famine and Meredith.

Meredith threw the interception that ended the 1966 title game, wasn't very good in the Ice Bowl, and was benched in the 1968 playoff game that turned out to be the last game of his career.

He was only 31 when he retired, but he'd been in the league nine long, hard years, helping the Cowboys rise from spare parts to the cusp of greatness. But Dallas couldn't take that final step, and fans blamed him for it.

Meredith's persona also helped shape the aura of the job "quarterback of the Dallas Cowboys."

He parlayed his NFL fame into a show business career. He was a *Monday Night Football* analyst, an actor in TV shows, a welcomed guest on the talk-show circuit, and quite the pitchman for iced tea.

Then, Dandy Don done disappeared.

He moved to Santa Fe, New Mexico, and rarely made public appearances, keeping fans from getting to know him after about the mid-1980s. The few times he emerged, the physical toll of his playing days was painful to see. But he was still toughing it out.

"I'm very thankful," Meredith told Brad Townsend of *The Dallas Morning News* in 2009. "I'm very thankful about where I'm from and who I am."

Diamond Images/Getty Images

33

Trophy–winning season for Navy, but he had a year of college left, then a five-year military commitment. In a sense, he was the ultimate "future" pick.

Renfro was a first-round talent available in the second round because teams were worried about a hand injury. The Cowboys only cared about his fleet feet. He was a speedster who could play running back or defensive back.

The Cowboys acquired another swift future Hall of Famer that offseason in receiver Tommy McDonald in a trade with Philadelphia, and they got veteran receiver Buddy Dial from Pittsburgh. In that deal with the Steelers, Dallas gave up its top overall pick, defensive tackle Scott Appleton, but it turned out to be a smart move because Appleton signed with the AFL's Houston Oilers. Gil Brandt's

COWBOY LEGENDS
BOB HAYES

"Bullet Bob" brought a new caliber of speed to pro football: world-best.

Having earned the title of "world's fastest human" at the 1964 Olympics, Hayes arrived in the NFL a year later and scored touchdowns on two of his first three catches. His best seasons were Dallas' best too.

As a rookie, he led the league in touchdowns and became the club's first 1,000-yard receiver—and the Cowboys made the postseason for the first time.

The following season, he led the league in TDs again and cracked 1,200 yards, a team record that stood for 25 years—and the Cowboys nearly made it to the first Super Bowl.

In 1970, Hayes led the NFL in yards per catch—and the Cowboys reached the Super Bowl for the first time.

In 1971, Hayes again led the NFL in yards per catch—and the Cowboys won it all for the first time, making him the first player with an Olympic gold medal and a Super Bowl ring. He's still the only one.

"This guy revolutionized the passing game and forced them to come up with the zone defense, just like Wilt Chamberlain forced them to change certain rules in basketball," said Hall of Fame defensive back Herb Adderley, who chased Hayes while he was playing for the Green Bay Packers, then became his friend and teammate in Dallas.

No matter who threw it deep, Hayes could run under it. He caught touchdown passes of 95 yards from Don Meredith, 89 yards from Craig Morton, and 85 yards from Roger Staubach.

"You thought you'd overthrown him and he'd run under it like he had to slow down," Staubach said.

Hayes was a heck of a punt returner too, leading the league in total yards in 1967 and in yards per return in 1968. He averaged 20.8 that season; nobody has come within 2 yards since.

Defenses eventually caught up with Hayes, especially after rules changes helped them. Age caught up too, and his reliance on speed worked against him.

Hayes' reputation took a beating after retirement when he pleaded guilty to delivering narcotics to an undercover police officer and spent 10 months behind bars. Although the conviction later was overturned, he didn't make it into the Hall of Fame until 2009, seven years after he died at age 59.

"It hurts because he should have been here to witness this special occasion," his son, Bob Hayes Jr., said during the induction ceremony. "He was always a big joker, so maybe he would say, 'It's about time, y'all.'"

John G. Zimmerman/Sports Illustrated/Getty Images

unique scouting system located one more receiver: Pete Gent, a basketball player at Michigan State who had never played college football.

Then there was the new triggerman, Don Meredith, in his first year in charge all by himself. Emphasis on "by himself."

The Cowboys didn't have anyone else they could trust behind center. They'd cut Sonny Gibbs, a second-round pick in 1962 whose only physical gift was height. Rookie punter Billy Lothridge had been a college quarterback the year before, but he was a mess the one time he got in. The only other option was John Roach, a guy in the final year of a forgettable career—truly a worst-case scenario. So Meredith soldiered on, taking nearly every snap despite badly torn knee cartilage.

Landry called Meredith's performance "perhaps the most courageous and gutsy season any professional quarterback ever played." He added that the offensive line was so weak it "couldn't have protected a healthy quarterback, let alone a hobbling one."

After the finale, Landry went to shake hands with Meredith. But in that game Meredith had added a right hand injury to his maladies, so he had to shake with his left hand.

"We're gonna get you more protection next year," Landry told him.

"Promise?" Meredith said.

Fans had no idea how much Meredith was hurting or how much the offensive line was to blame. They simply saw him struggling, saw the club start 1–4–1 and figured it was all his fault. Even when Dallas won three in a row, the streak came on the road, so the home crowd didn't get to cheer Meredith. Then came four more losses.

The defense certainly wasn't to blame.

Landry realized the 4–3 scheme he'd concocted while with the Giants needed a new wrinkle. He came up with what became known as "the Flex," which basically involved moving the right tackle (Bob Lilly) and left end (Maury Youmans) slightly back. This repositioning gave them an extra tick to watch a play develop. While it meant those guys would probably make fewer tackles in the backfield, they were more likely to prevent big gains. The more often a defense limits runs to one or two yards, the

more third-and-longs they force, and that's the key to any system. The 1964 Cowboys gave up the second-fewest points in the league.

In his first full season at tackle, Lilly quickly established himself as a nightmare for opposing offenses. He was a unanimous pick for All-Pro. Renfro stood out too, snagging seven interceptions and leading the league in punt return yards.

With Meredith torn to shreds, the high-scoring offense from a few years earlier seemed a distant memory. Dallas sputtered to the league's fewest yards and third-fewest points.

The Cowboys finished 5–8–1, the same as two years ago when that was considered progress.

Folks weren't sure what to make of this, but there were more folks paying attention. Attendance hiked to nearly 40,000 per game. This city searching for a new identity a year after JFK's death was ready to fall in love with the Cowboys.

FROM TEARS OF FRUSTRATION TO TEARS OF JOY

After the false hope of the previous few years, the wise thing was to be cautiously optimistic going into the 1965 season—but it wasn't easy to temper that optimism.

Not with Bob Hayes running under passes, no matter how far they were thrown. Not with Ralph Neely arriving to anchor the offensive line. Not with Danny Villanueva there to be the consistent kicker the club had always lacked. And not with Bob Lilly using his size, speed, and the Flex defense to disrupt opposing offenses.

At first, Tom Landry wasn't sure whether Hayes could help or not. Then the "World's Fastest Human" caught a seemingly uncatchable overthrow during the final preseason game. Hayes was called into the coach's office a few days later and told he was starting the opener. His first catch was a 45-yard touchdown. He scored on another 45-yarder the next game.

The Cowboys started 2–0. But the success didn't stem only from big plays on offense. The defense didn't allow a touchdown through the first seven quarters of the season.

Then Perkins dropped a potential game-tying touchdown pass in the final minute in St. Louis, and

Rookie "Bullet" Bob Hayes helped to spark the Cowboys offense in 1965, pulling in more than 1,000 receiving yards and 12 touchdowns. *Donald Uhrbrock/Timo Life Pictures/Getty Images*

Dallas lost. Landry responded by benching Meredith for being too wild, even though everyone knew he was playing through an arm injury suffered in the preseason. The demotion stung even more because Landry turned to a pair of rookies, Craig Morton and Jerry Rhome.

The Cowboys wound up losing five straight, their worst since the inaugural season. After the fifth loss, in Pittsburgh, Landry stood before the team and said the skid was his fault. He cried as he said it.

"Nobody knew what to do," Lilly said. "It seemed like it went on for about an hour, though it was more like two or three minutes."

The impact lasted much longer. Players felt a new connection to their stone-faced boss.

"We saw the real man that day," Lilly said. "He was crying because he felt he had let us down."

Two days later, Landry began rectifying his mistakes. He called Meredith into his office.

"Don, you're my quarterback," Landry told him. "I believe in you."

"And we both started crying again," Meredith recalled.

Landry told reporters Meredith would start the final seven games.

"I had to go with the man I felt everyone on the team had the most confidence in; the man I felt could make the team rise up and play well enough to make up the seven to ten points we've been losing by all season," Landry said. "I have no doubt Don can win."

Indeed, they won the next two games. Then came two demoralizing losses.

Before the first-ever sellout crowd at the Cotton Bowl, Dallas had a chance to upset Jim Brown and the Cleveland Browns, only to see Meredith throw two late interceptions. Then the Cowboys went to Washington, and Villanueva missed a long field goal that could've forced overtime.

Two wins followed, putting the team at 6–7 and raising the stakes for the season finale against the Giants in Yankee Stadium. The winner would finish second in the conference and earn a spot in the "Playoff Bowl," an extra game between the runners-up in both conferences.

The most important game yet in franchise history turned out to have the wackiest ending.

After breaking open a close game, the Cowboys were at the New York 1-yard line with 16 seconds left. Before they could take the next snap, a kid grabbed a cop's hat and ran onto the field near the Dallas huddle. A throng of angry fans followed, and the refs called it a game, sending the Cowboys home—with a 38–20 victory, a three-game winning streak, their first non-losing season, and, best of all, their first trip to the postseason.

Sure, the Playoff Bowl game was derisively called the "Toilet Bowl" because it was meaningless. But to the 1965 Cowboys, "it was almost as exciting as going to a Super Bowl," Schramm recalled.

"After five years of getting nowhere, it was a sign that we were getting somewhere," he said. "We were thrilled—and proud—to be playing in that game."

On the celebratory flight home from New York, Hayes guzzled champagne like he'd never seen it before—because he hadn't. He turned so giddy that he sang a Fats Domino song over the plane's intercom. He deserved to kick back after the season he had just had: the most touchdowns and best yards-per-catch in the NFL, and the first 1,000-yard receiving season in team history.

Thousands of fans traveled from Dallas to watch the Cowboys take on the Baltimore Colts in Miami. Hopefully they enjoyed the beach because the game was lousy. Even though the injury-plagued Colts were forced to use halfback Tom Matte at quarterback, Baltimore romped to a 35–3 win. The Cowboys were a classic example of a team that was "just happy to be there."

What mattered most was that the Cowboys now knew they were capable of bigger, better things.

THE BREAKTHROUGH

In June 1966, the NFL and AFL announced plans to merge. Tex Schramm and Lamar Hunt were the architects of the deal, which established a championship game between the leagues beginning that upcoming season. Hunt dubbed it the Super Bowl.

Dallas' roster was really coming together by now. There were quality starters all over the field on both sides of the ball and some strong backups. Through the draft, the Cowboys added offensive guard John Niland and defensive tackle Willie Townes, both of whom contributed right away, and running back Walt Garrison, a real cowboy whose signing bonus was a two-horse trailer.

Landry beefed up his defensive coaching staff too. Dick Nolan had been the only assistant, and his specialty was the secondary. Jerry Tubbs was put in charge of the linebackers, even though he was still an active player, and Landry hired Ernie Stautner, a former Steelers tough guy who'd once broken Landry's nose in a game, to guide the linemen.

"[Stautner] made us study harder, he made us work harder in practice, and he made us much more aware of our job during the game," Lilly said. "We weren't doing a bad job during that time, but he put us up another level."

Landry wanted to see what Mel Renfro could do at running back and wound up losing him for three games with a broken foot. When he returned, Renfro went back to defense, where he would become a Hall of Famer. The new lead runner turned out to be Dan Reeves, who'd made the team the year before because he could do a little at a lot of positions.

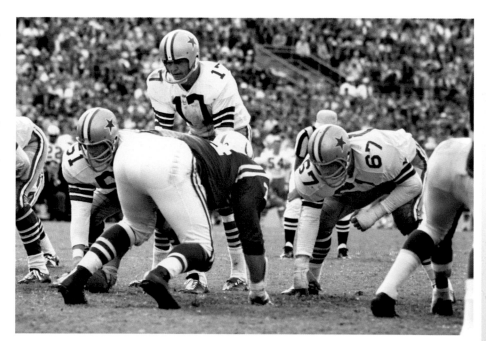

Don Meredith waits for the snap during the Playoff Bowl on January 9, 1966. The Cowboys were walloped by Baltimore in the consolation game. *NFL/Getty images*

THE KICKING KARAVAN

In the Dallas Cowboys' second season, the club's leading field-goal kicker made the Pro Bowl—at tight end.

Throughout the early years, the Cowboys struggled to find a reliable kicker. Sam Baker had the job in 1962 and 1963 and drove coach Tom Landry bonkers with his inconsistency and his attitude. They went with a rookie in 1964, then traded for Danny Villanueva in 1965.

Villanueva was pretty good that first season, then dipped in 1966. The Cowboys were close to being champions by then, so it was time to get serious about finding a kicker. So off went scouting director Gil Brandt, kicking coach Ben Agajanian, and assistant coach Ermal Allen on a trip called "The Kicking Karavan," a 28-city, 10,000-mile journey in search of untapped potential.

"We just thought we'd get all these kickers out of the way to see if they were any good," Brandt recalled.

The trip drummed up a lot of publicity, creating new fans and plenty of laughs.

In Portland, Oregon, 60-year-old Moe Levine made 15 straight 20-yarders, then shagged balls all afternoon. "He was so enthusiastic we gave him an honorary contract," scout Bob Ford said.

In Birmingham, Alabama, a bus driver got off his route, missed a kick, then drove away.

In North Carolina, a man showed up with a water-stained football and a wife complaining that she had to keep fishing it out of the creek because he didn't know how to swim.

Along the way, there was another wife who'd lost all her fingernails holding for her hubby, and a Cowboys staffer who got his hands cut up while holding for a barefoot kicker.

The Cowboys tried out about 1,300 players and brought 27 finalists to Dallas.

The winner? Villanueva.

None of the other candidates ever made the team, but some found work in the NFL, like Mac Percival, who in 1971 made two kicks for Chicago in a 23–19 victory over the Cowboys.

Villanueva lasted only one more season in Dallas. He gave up the sport after the Ice Bowl and went into television full-time. It was a brilliant move; as founder of Spanish-language networks Univision and Telemundo, he became a millionaire many times over.

In the early 1970s, Brandt and Landry took the Kicking Karavan to Europe in search of a soccer-style kicker.

"The first place we went was Vienna, and the first player we tried out was Toni Fritsch," Brandt said.

Fritsch kicked the winning field goal in his NFL debut and went on to be a reliable kicker in the league for many years.

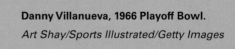

Danny Villanueva, 1966 Playoff Bowl.
Art Shay/Sports Illustrated/Getty Images

A perfect preseason sent expectations soaring, especially after the Cowboys beat the reigning champion Green Bay Packers in front of more than 75,000 in the Salesmanship Club game.

Meredith opened the season throwing for five touchdowns in a 52–7 clobbering of the Giants. Three weeks later, Dallas beat Philadelphia 56–7 to improve to 4–0. It was the best start and the longest winning streak in club history. Meredith already had 14 touchdown passes, and Reeves had scored 8. (The versatile Reeves finished the year with 8 rushing touchdowns and 8 receiving touchdowns while gaining a team-best 1,314 yards from scrimmage.)

Then came the dip: A tie at St. Louis and a loss at Cleveland. The Cowboys rang up 52 points in a win over Pittsburgh, then lost to the same Eagles club they'd dominated a month before.

COWBOY LEGENDS
DAN REEVES

Dan Reeves led the Cowboys in rushing one year. He led the club in scoring another year. He threw the only touchdown pass in the Ice Bowl.

Whatever Tom Landry needed, Danny Reeves could do it—including kicking an extra point (one-for-one in his career).

Undrafted as a quarterback out of South Carolina, Reeves made the team in 1965 and quickly embraced his role as a "football player."

"Dan Reeves didn't have the skills to compete with all the other talent at [quarterback]," Landry wrote in his autobiography, "but his determination, intelligence, adaptability and, most of all, his character impressed me so much we kept moving him around until we found a spot on the roster."

When a knee injury nearly ruined Reeves' career, Landry convinced him to remain as a player-coach. It beat Reeves' other option: going home and working with his dad in road construction, "or something like that," he said.

The Cowboys went to two Super Bowls in his three years as a player-coach. He wound up spending 16 years with the club as a player, player-coach, and assistant coach, taking part in five Super Bowls.

Fans would have loved for him to replace Landry, but once the time came he'd already guided John Elway and the Denver Broncos to two Super Bowls and was headed to a third. He reached a fourth with the Atlanta Falcons, after a stretch as coach of the New York Giants.

Tony Tomsic/Getty Images

In 2009, Reeves nearly returned as a consultant to head coach Wade Phillips. Things didn't work out, but there was still a connection: his son-in-law, Joe DeCamillis, became Phillips' special teams coach.

At 5–2–1, the Cowboys were still in good shape. But everyone wondered which direction this team was headed. Would they sink like in 1964? Or surge like in 1965?

Proving that this was a new era, they surged like never before, starting with a dramatic 31–30 win at Washington.

With 1:10 left and Dallas trailing by two, Meredith took over at his 3-yard line. He drove to the Washington 20, then Danny Villanueva atoned for his miss in D.C. the previous year by nailing the winning field goal. Meredith threw for 406 yards

that game; 246 of them went to Hayes, setting a club receiving record that stood until 2009.

The Cowboys were on their way to their second four-game winning streak of the season. It included beating the Cleveland Browns 26–14 in front of a Cotton Bowl–record crowd of more than 80,000 on Thanksgiving Day, a superb way to start that new tradition.

Dallas finished the year 10–3–1 and won the Eastern Conference. Meredith was the toast of the town, and the Cowboys were the NFL's up-and-comers. They could become league champions with a New Year's Day victory over the Packers at the Cotton Bowl.

Green Bay had a solid offense led by Bart Starr, Jim Taylor, and Elijah Pitts, but it was a defense featuring five future Hall of Famers—Ray Nitschke, Herb Adderley, Willie Davis, Willie Wood, and Henry Jordan—that made the Packers so great. They were coached by Vince Lombardi, Landry's good friend from their days as the only two assistant coaches for the New York Giants in the 1950s.

Green Bay had won three of the last five NFL titles. The winner of this game would head to Los Angeles for one more game, the NFL–AFL championship, to determine the winner of all pro football. But since the AFL was thought to be so inferior, this game was considered the *real* championship.

The main question was whether Dallas' youth could conquer Green Bay's experience. The Cowboys' spirits were lifted by playing at home, by the way they'd been rolling lately, and by the fact that they had defeated the Packers 20–3 in the preseason.

"Coach Landry has gone about this as if it were any other game," receiver Pete Gent said the day before the game. "No trace at all of nerves or doubt. I think that because he shows he really believes in us and our ability, we believe in ourselves."

Starr drove for a touchdown on the game-opening drive, then Renfro fumbled the ensuing kickoff and Green Bay returned it for a touchdown. Dallas trailed 14–0, and Meredith had yet to take a snap.

When the first quarter ended, however, the score was tied at 14, and it remained close through the middle two quarters. Then Green Bay pulled away in the fourth quarter, taking a 34–20 lead.

In the 1966 opener, Meredith threw for 358 yards and 5 touchdowns in a 52–7 thrashing of the Giants. *Walter Iooss Jr./ Sports Illustrated/ Getty Images*

POLISHING THE STAR

THANKSGIVING

Why do the Cowboys always host a game on Thanksgiving?

Because when the NFL went looking for volunteers to join Detroit in playing at home on the holiday, Tex Schramm was the only one who raised his hand.

Teams didn't want to play on three days' rest so late in the season. They didn't want their fans to pick between a game and dinner with their families. Basically, they were afraid to take a chance. Schramm wasn't, in part because of the popularity of the Texas-Texas A&M Thanksgiving game.

"People in this area," he reasoned, "are used to having football with their turkey."

The Cowboys played the Cleveland Browns on November 24, 1966, in front of a club-record crowd of 80,259, and, for the first time in club history, the game was televised in color. Dallas won 26–14, and the team has been home for the holiday all but twice since then.

"The whole nation was going to pay attention to us, whether people liked it or not," longtime defensive back Charlie Waters said. "It wasn't easy at first, having such little time to prepare for a game. But after we did it one time, we knew the formula. It was fun for us. We welcomed that Thursday game."

Other teams complained that the Cowboys had an unfair advantage, always getting the game at home then having a 10-day break after. Or maybe the complainers just hated the popularity boost Dallas got out of this plum spot on the television schedule.

Don't underestimate the importance of TV in all of this. The league took the game away from the Cowboys in 1975 and 1977 and gave the St. Louis Cardinals the

chance to play host. The ratings stunk, so back to Dallas it came. For good.

Another layer of tradition was scooped on in 1997, when Jerry Jones' daughter, Charlotte Anderson, introduced a halftime concert/fundraiser for the Salvation Army.

At the time, the Cowboys' image was suffering from off-field incidents that overshadowed the team's recent run of three Super Bowls in four years. She wanted to do something charitable and realized the Thanksgiving platform was perfect because of the spotlight and the timing at the start of the giving season. To draw attention, she decided to bring in some splashy entertainment. She convinced NBC to air the halftime show, then lined up country music star Reba McEntire as the first headliner. She also got the NFL to agree to extend halftime by a few minutes to allow for the entire production, which is capped by players dropping coins into the Salvation Army's iconic red kettles. One year, Terrell Owens donated a football into a kettle as part of a touchdown celebration.

Spending Thanksgiving with the Cowboys has been a tradition since 1966.
Wesley Hitt/Getty Images

41

Don Perkins ran for 10 touchdowns in 1966. He collected 2 of them in a 34–31 loss to Washington on December 11. *James Drake/Sports Illustrated/ Getty Images*

Meredith rallied again, hitting Frank Clarke for a 68-yard touchdown, then finding Clarke wide open again for what would have been the tying touchdown. But safety Tom Brown interfered, breaking it up yet also giving Dallas a first down at the 2-yard line with 1:52 left.

Reeves ran to the 1, but then left tackle Jim Boeke was caught moving before the snap, pushing the Cowboys back to the 6. During the play, Reeves got poked in the eye and came away seeing double. The next play was a pass to Reeves, and he saw two balls coming his way. He reached for the wrong one. While NFL Films would hype Boeke's penalty as the colossal mistake on this drive, Dallas players consider Reeves' miss the big opportunity lost.

On third down, Pettis Norman caught a short pass and was stopped at the 2. Now there was one play to get the six feet needed to force the mighty Packers into overtime for the NFL Championship and a trip to the first Super Bowl.

Meredith rolled right with the option of throwing or running. Linebacker Dave Robinson read it perfectly, charging at Meredith so quickly that he blocked the quarterback's view and his path so he couldn't throw or run. When Robinson lowered his arms to go for the tackle, Meredith threw into the end zone. It was caught, only by Brown, the Green Bay safety.

The Cowboys had erased an early 14-point deficit and nearly did it again late. Their resilience in the face of older, wiser competition showed that they really were among the best teams in pro football.

"If ever a team attained tremendous stature in defeat it was Dallas," Arthur Daley wrote in *The New York Times*. "This is a young ball club that was being pitted against wise and experienced veterans who had learned how to withstand pressures in four previous playoffs. Few expected the Cowboy kids to hold up in the face of any sort of disaster. They did though. They came bouncing back not once but twice."

Had the Cowboys won, they would've had a showdown with the old Dallas Texans in the first Super Bowl. Instead, the Packers faced the Kansas City Chiefs, and it was the rout everyone expected. The Packers were champions of all pro football. Still, the Cowboys and their fans were ready for a changing of the guard atop the NFL.

Dan Reeves finds a clear path to the end zone to give Dallas its first points during the NFL Championship Game against Green Bay in January 1967. *Russ Russell/NFL/Getty Images*

HIGH HOPES GET ICED OVER

Now that the Cowboys had some big-game experience, it seemed like only a matter of time before they would get the chance to prove it—especially when they started the 1967 season 5–1. The only loss was to another strong contender, a Los Angeles Rams squad featuring its Fearsome Foursome defensive line and quarterback Roman Gabriel.

Those guys were respectable. Their coach, George Allen, wasn't, at least not to Tex Schramm.

The week of the game, Schramm accused Allen of spying. His evidence: A yellow Chevrolet parked near the Cowboys' practice field that sped away when coach Tom Landry sent a guard over to investigate. The guard got the license plate number, and Schramm claimed it was a Hertz car rented to Johnny Sanders, the Rams' chief of scouting. Schramm brought it to the attention of the league office, while Allen arrived in town lobbing countercharges: "There was a guy sitting in a eucalyptus tree overlooking our practice field Thursday. By the time we saw him and sent someone after him, he climbed down and ran away. From the rear he looked like Bucko Kilroy." Kilroy was a Cowboys scout. He also weighed around

300 pounds, making it unlikely he was in a tree or that he could run away without being caught after climbing down the tree.

Despite the 5–1 start, it wasn't all good news in Dallas. Meredith fractured two ribs in the preseason finale and then aggravated the injury while throwing a touchdown pass in the final seconds to beat Washington. The pain was compounded by a case of pneumonia. He was put in isolation in a hospital and lost 20 pounds.

Meredith missed only three games. Craig Morton started them, and Dallas won twice; all were decided by a touchdown or less.

Upon Meredith's return, Coach Landry said, "An average man, even an above-average man, wouldn't have made it back on his feet for months, much less back to playing football."

With the number one starter back on the job, the Cowboys won two straight, then alternated losses and wins the last five games. It hardly mattered because pretty much all the other teams in their division finished with losing records. Yes, "division" is accurate.

Instead of just two conferences, the NFL was now broken into two divisions within each conference. Dallas landed in the Capitol Division along with Philadelphia, Washington, and New Orleans, an expansion team. The New York Giants replaced the Saints in the division a year later, and the foursome has been together ever since.

The new system created an extra round of play-offs, with the Capitol champ facing the Century winner for the Eastern Conference title, while the other two division champs (Coastal and Central Divisions) met to decide the Western Conference.

Tragedy struck a few days before Dallas faced Cleveland in the playoff opener. Bob Lilly found his seven-week-old daughter, Carmen, dead in her crib. The funeral was the next day. Although Lilly wouldn't miss any games, it altered his life, eventually leading to the break-up of his marriage.

The Browns came into the December 24 game talking about collecting an early Christmas present. Hardly. Meredith was a crisp 10-of-12, and Dallas rolled, 52–14. Green Bay took out Allen's Rams to win the West, so the NFL Championship game was going to be a Cowboys-Packers rematch.

These teams that had met in Dallas on the first day of 1967 met again on the last day of 1967, this time in Green Bay, on what has become known as "the frozen tundra of Lambeau Field." And, boy, was it ever frozen.

The Packers won the "Ice Bowl" on a last-minute quarterback sneak by Bart Starr. Green Bay went on to win the Super Bowl, a championship that—once again—might have been won by the Cowboys had one final play gone differently.

Bob Hayes tracks down one of his 10 receiving touchdowns of the 1967 season. *AP Images*

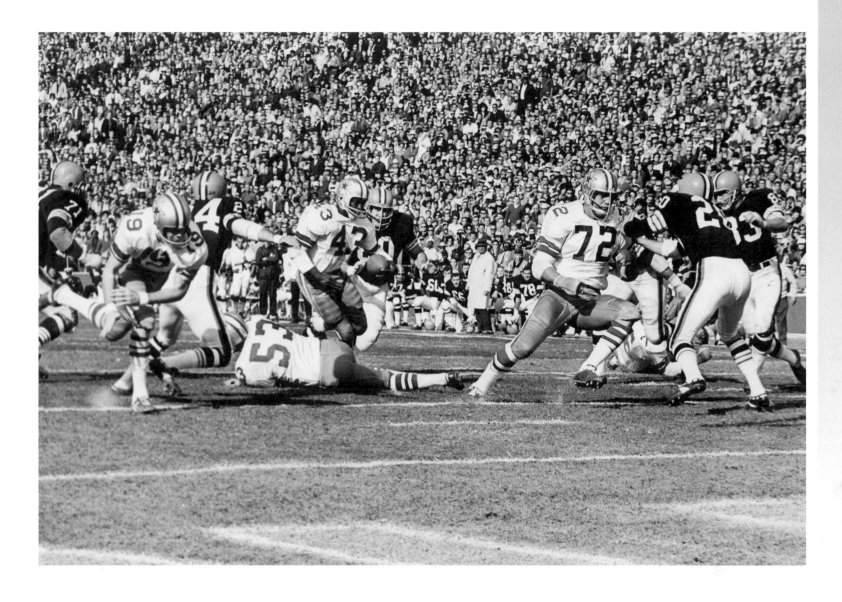

"I guess," Meredith said, "we can do everything but win the big one."

DANDY DONE

On the flight back to Dallas after the "Ice Bowl," bodies began warming up. So did the players' spirits.

"We got a lot more of these title games ahead of us," Bob Lilly said. "We are going to wipe people out next year, just clean wipe 'em out. There's no dissension on this club, we're all real close, and we've got the boys who want it."

Those lines come from the early pages of *Next Year's Champions*, a book written by Cowboys beat writer Steve Perkins that chronicled the team's 1968 season. As far as nicknames go, this one sure fit.

The Cowboys showed they were still poised to become champions by scoring a club-record 59 points against Detroit in the opener and then going on to start the year 6–0. It was the most games they'd ever won in a row.

Week 7 featured a first for Dallas: a nationally televised game on a Monday night. The Cowboys had been on television before and had even played on a Monday night back in 1965—but never the two together. Technically, this was not *Monday Night Football* because that long-running series didn't start until 1970 on ABC. This game was on CBS and was a test to see whether the viewing nation would embrace it.

The matchup was perfect for hyping: the undefeated Cowboys against the defending-champion

Don Perkins (43) heads toward the end zone for 6 of Dallas' 52 points against Cleveland in the 1967 playoff matchup. *Russ Russell/NFL/Getty Images*

GAME TO REMEMBER
THE "ICE BOWL"

GREEN BAY, WISCONSIN – **The weather in Dallas on December 29, 1967,** was a bit warm, even by Texas standards. The Cowboys players boarded the plane to Green Bay wearing only light coats.

When they arrived in Wisconsin, they needed parkas to brace themselves against temperatures that were in the teens.

And that was downright balmy compared to what happened next.

A blast of cold air from Canada shriveled temperatures into single digits, down to zero, then into negative numbers, and ultimately into the negative t-t-t-teens the morning of December 31. At kickoff, the thermometer read 13 below, with a wind chill of about minus 40.

"It hurt to breathe," Bob Lilly recalled.

The ground crackled and crunched. The $80,000 underground warming system Vince Lombardi had installed to keep his field from freezing conked out—that is, if it was even turned on.

There couldn't be enough layers of clothes to keep players or fans comfortable. The University of Wisconsin–LaCrosse marching band refused to perform, fearing their lips would freeze to their instruments. (Officials had similar problems with their whistles; after one ripped lip, they kept Vaseline smeared

AP Images

on their mouthpieces the rest of the game.) In the open-air broadcast booth, Frank Gifford said to Jack Buck, "Can I have a bite of your coffee?"

Most Dallas players went through warm-ups with their hands inside their pants. Players wrapped their feet in Saran Wrap. Don Meredith had a kangaroo pouch rigged onto his jersey so he could hide his hands from the chill between plays, although it was really only making him *think* he was keeping warm.

Ernie Stautner wouldn't let the defensive linemen wear gloves because he said real men didn't need them. The Packers were more smart than tough; they all wore gloves.

Despite the weather, there was a game to be played, a championship to be determined.

The Packers took the opening kickoff and skated 82 yards across the ice-rink-like surface for a quick 7–0 lead. They scored again in the second quarter. Just like the 1966 game, Meredith was down 14–0.

The defense produced Dallas' first touchdown, when Willie Townes forced Bart Starr to fumble and George Andrie took it seven yards into the end zone. Another fumble recovery set up a short field goal to get Dallas within 14–10 at halftime.

After a scoreless third quarter, the Cowboys went ahead 17–14 on a 50-yard halfback pass: Meredith pitched the ball to Reeves, and the former college quarterback threw to Lance Rentzel, who caught it around the 20 and beat everyone to the end zone.

The Packers went for a tying field goal on their next drive but missed. That gave the Cowboys a chance to go ahead by two scores, likely putting the game out of reach, but they couldn't do it. Green Bay got the ball back on its 32-yard line with 4:50 left in the game.

As Starr got the Packers moving, the Cowboys were often in position to make tackles, only to slip on the ice. Green Bay managed to move all the way to the Dallas 1-yard line with less than a minute left.

Dick Daniels (21) and Bob Hayes (22) do their best to keep warm during the "Ice Bowl," on December 31, 1967.
Vernon Biever/NFL/Getty Images

Donny Anderson tried plowing up the middle on the next two snaps, but he couldn't get his footing and was stopped on both tries. Now there were 16 seconds and about two feet left.

Starr used his final timeout to discuss the next play with Lombardi. If they ran and were stopped, there wouldn't be time to kick a field goal. They could kick now and probably make it, although the conditions made even a short kick risky. Besides, that would only force overtime.

So Lombardi called for "31 Wedge"—a quarterback sneak.

Starr took the snap and dove toward the goal line behind a block from center Ken Bowman and right guard Jerry Kramer. (Dallas fans still believe Kramer moved before the snap.) Jethro Pugh tried lunging into them, but when he dug his cleats into the turf for traction, his foot slipped on the ice. Starr reached the end zone with 13 seconds left.

Green Bay won, 21–17. Dallas went home disappointed. Devastated, really.

"You can tell the real Cowboys," coach Tom Landry later said. "They're the ones with the frozen fingers and broken hearts."

Dan Reeves stumbles into the end zone during the Cowboys' win over the Lions in the 1968 season opener. *AP Images*

Packers, who were 2–3–1 and looked ripe for a whipping. It wouldn't quite be payback for the last two postseason games, but it sure would feel good. Dallas had never beaten Green Bay outside of the preseason, so a lot of demons could be exorcised on this night.

They weren't.

The Cowboys led 10–0, then fell apart. Meredith threw three interceptions and broke his nose, for a second straight year, as Dallas lost 28–17.

"We're still 6–1," Landry said. "I'll take that second half of the season."

He did. The Cowboys matched their first-half performance and steamed into the playoffs with a 12–2 record, easily claiming the Capitol Division crown. The offense produced 431 points, by far the most in the NFL, and the defense allowed the second-fewest, just 186.

Meredith had gone into the finale needing only a decent game to win the passing title, which was then based on passer rating. On a snowy afternoon in New York, he started 1-of-9 and took himself out in the second quarter, telling Landry it just wasn't his day. He wound up second to Baltimore's Earl Morrall,

albeit with a career-best rating of 88.4. The flight home was an adventure too. The plane shut down on takeoff and skidded across the runway. Maybe they should have considered it all a sign.

Cleveland won the Century Division again, so the Browns and Cowboys again met to decide the winner of the Eastern Conference. It was in Cleveland this time, and Dallas players were extremely confident. They had beaten the Browns in the playoffs the year before and crushed them 28–7 earlier this season. They had beaten Cleveland four straight times dating to Thanksgiving 1966.

This game played out just like the overconfident midseason flop against Green Bay, with Dallas jumping ahead 10–0 and then losing control.

The defense gave up a 45-yard touchdown pass in the final minute of the first half to tie it, then the Browns went ahead when Meredith opened the third quarter with an interception that was returned for a touchdown. On the next series, Meredith hit Lance Rentzel in the hands with a pass, but Rentzel tipped it right to a defensive back. Cleveland scored on the next play, and, only two and a half minutes into the second half, Landry benched Meredith.

Mel Renfro (20) breaks up a pass intended for Cleveland receiver Paul Warfield during Dallas' playoff loss to the Browns on December 21, 1968. *AP Images*

Craig Morton brought Dallas back a little but not enough. The Cowboys lost 31–20. Landry called it "one of the worst days in Cowboys history."

"Right now," Ralph Neely said, "I feel like I never want to see a football helmet again."

There would be no trip to the NFL Championship Game. No chance of making the Super Bowl. There was one piece of business left to handle—another trip to Miami for the Playoff Bowl.

Dallas beat Minnesota 17–13, but it was a hollow victory, especially after Joe Namath and the New York Jets knocked off the NFL champion Baltimore Colts in the Super Bowl. That championship was supposed to be Meredith's, not Namath's; the Cowboys were supposed to enjoy the rewards of their sustained success, not the upstart Jets of the supposedly inferior AFL.

Meredith had not flown home with the team after the Cleveland loss but instead went to New York with Pete Gent to drown his sorrows. That spring, Meredith's life took another difficult turn when his wife delivered a daughter who was mentally challenged.

In June, Meredith was dealt another blow when Landry said he would have to beat out Morton in training camp to keep his starting spot. Meredith understood, recalling when he'd been the backup long enough and was ready to replace Eddie LeBaron. Then he thought about it some more and decided he was done.

Meredith announced his retirement on Saturday, July 5, 1969. He said he was worn out mentally, unable to muster the enthusiasm needed to go through another grueling season.

"To describe how I feel is like a man going to play golf and not taking all his clubs," Meredith said. "I do not want to play with half a bag. If I play, I want to use every club in my bag."

Folks were shocked. Not only that Meredith would retire, but also that he'd do it eight days before the start of training camp, and six weeks after the Cowboys had traded their third-string quarterback, Jerry Rhome.

Now there were only two quarterbacks on the roster: Morton and a 27-year-old military man who had never played a down of pro football.

THE ROGER STAUBACH ERA, PART I

THE CRAIG MORTON YEARS: 1969–1974

In the mid-1960s, the Cowboys needed a little more time than expected to hit their stride. Yet once they did, they soared to the top of the league.

Well, near the top.

Don Meredith got them close but couldn't get past the mighty Packers. Dallas came back with the

Craig Morton (14), seen here handing off to Walt Garrison, took over as the starting quarterback after Don Meredith retired. He led the franchise to its first Super Bowl, following the 1970 season, but lost his job to Roger Staubach the next year, when Dallas became Super Bowl champions for the first time. *Diamond Images/ Getty Images*

best regular season in club history, only to be followed by a first-round playoff loss—and the retirement of Meredith and Don Perkins, the last links to the inaugural team from 1960.

The sentimental bond that broke was trumped by the practical fact that the Cowboys needed an entirely new starting backfield.

Good thing reinforcements already were in place.

MORTON TAKES OVER

Craig Morton was the fifth overall pick in the 1965 draft and was groomed from the start to be Meredith's successor. When his turn finally arrived, the Cowboys had another intriguing candidate show up at training camp: Roger Staubach.

While Morton had been apprenticing under Meredith for four years in Dallas, the former Heisman Trophy winner from Navy was fulfilling his military obligation.

Staubach enjoyed his time in the service, but being away from football made him realize how much he loved it, especially after coming to training camp in 1967 and a rookie camp in 1968. He wanted to see how he stacked up if for no reason but to prevent "what ifs" from haunting him the rest of his life.

What Staubach lacked in experience compared to Morton, he made up for in talent, leadership, and smarts. He actually was a year older than Morton (they share a birthday, February 5), and that gave Staubach a sense of urgency to get his career going. Coach Tom Landry called it maturity, and he liked it.

"The only thing he really needs is to learn our system," Landry said about Staubach the day Meredith retired. "The greatest asset a man can have to become a good quarterback is dedication. And I've seldom seen such dedication in an athlete as Roger has."

Landry noted how raw the quarterback had looked at his first training camp, in 1968, and how much work he had to do, particularly in basics like setting up over the ball and getting back to throw. When Staubach returned to camp in 1969, Landry said, "I couldn't believe it was the same man, and he did it just working by himself in every spare minute. I don't think we need to worry about Roger."

Staubach and Morton got along well, having met first as teammates at the 1965 college all-star game. But they also knew what was at stake: Only one man gets to be the starting quarterback. (Well, usually. Details on that later in this chapter.)

The running back problem was solved in the draft. Near the end of the first round, the Cowboys stunned everyone by selecting Calvin Hill of Yale, a school known for producing leaders in many fields, but not football.

Morton dislocated a finger during the preseason, so Staubach got to start the opener. He completed only seven passes, but they went for 220 yards, including a 75-yard touchdown to Lance Rentzel. He also ran for a touchdown in a 24–3 victory over St. Louis. Morton returned the next week, and the Cowboys won again, but the star was Hill. In just the second pro game of his career, he set the franchise single-game rushing record with 138 yards.

Morton dislocated his throwing shoulder in the fourth game. He needed surgery, but after waiting so long to get the quarterback job, he wasn't about to give it away, especially since doctors said he could keep playing as long as he could tolerate the pain. The next week, he tied the club record with five touchdown passes in a 49–14 pounding of Philadelphia.

Following an easy victory over the Giants, Dallas was 6–0, and the new era sure looked a lot like the old one. Too much, as it turned out, because for the second straight year the Cowboys were not

able to parlay a strong start and a thirst for revenge into a victory against the team that had knocked them out of the playoffs.

Cleveland clobbered Dallas 42–10, reviving talk that Landry couldn't win the big one, and that his icy personality failed to adequately motivate his guys. The Cowboys had even brought in tight end Mike Ditka to add grit to the locker room this season, but on this day it wasn't enough.

The rest of the season also was 1968 all over again. A minor difference was that instead of going 6–1 the rest of the way, Dallas went 5–1–1. Being 11–2–1 was still enough to win the Capitol Division and set up another playoff opener against Cleveland, this time at the Cotton Bowl.

There were so many reasons to believe this would be the breakthrough postseason.

The Cowboys had one of the best offenses and one of the stingiest defenses, with lots of All-Pros.

Mike Ditka, seen here running with the ball in a game against St. Louis, was a key addition for Dallas in 1969. *Russ Russell/NFL/Getty Images*

MEL RENFRO

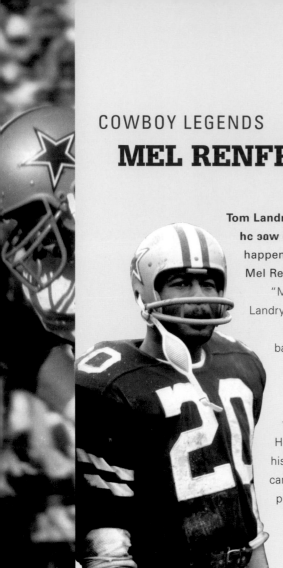

Tom Landry knew a great athlete when he saw one, and that's exactly what happened the first time he sized up Mel Renfro.

"Mel, I want to see you move," Landry said.

After watching the rookie backpedal, cut in both directions, and run forward, the coach's only question was how to use him.

Renfro played safety for six years and cornerback for eight. He also played running back during his third season. Throughout his career, he excelled at returning punts and kickoffs.

Tony Tomsic/Getty Images

"It was like he knew where you were going," said receiver Frank Clarke, who went head-to-head with Renfro in practices for several years. "You just could not shake this guy."

Renfro made the Pro Bowl each of his first 10 seasons and is enshrined in the Ring of Honor and the Pro Football Hall of Fame. He's still the club's career leader in interceptions, interception return yards, and kickoff return average.

His impact on the team and the city goes beyond football.

In 1968, a year in U.S. history filled with racial tensions following the assassination of Martin Luther King Jr., Renfro and his wife wanted to rent a duplex near the Cowboys training facility. The owner withdrew the offer once they were ready to sign a lease. Renfro accused the owner of violating the Fair Housing Act and won a federal lawsuit.

"The black ballplayers were elated, because it opened the doors," Renfro said. "It put a spotlight on the problem."

Rentzel led the league in touchdown catches, and Mel Renfro was tops in interceptions. Hill was second in rushing, behind only Gale Sayers. His 942 yards were just 3 yards shy of Perkins' single-season record; if he hadn't played on a broken foot the final month, he probably would have had the club's first 1,000-yard season.

Before the playoff game against Cleveland, Landry moved Renfro from safety to cornerback in an effort to contain receiver Paul Warfield. Players considered it a sign of weakness. They thought they were good enough to win doing things their usual way, despite two straight losses to the Browns.

On a rainy late-December day at the Cotton Bowl, an early punt nicked Dallas' Rayfield Wright; Cleveland recovered and quickly jumped ahead. In the third quarter, the Browns were up 24–0. Morton scored on a 2-yard run to put Dallas on the board, but then he threw a fourth-quarter interception that

was returned 88 yards for a touchdown. Staubach came in with the Cowboys trailing 38–7, but there was no salvaging this game.

Dallas was forced into the Playoff Bowl against the Rams the following week. Suffice it to say the Cowboys didn't want to be there. It showed as they lost 31–0 in what turned out to be the final one of these pointless matchups between teams already kicked into the offseason.

But there were bigger issues at hand.

The Cowboys now had back-to-back losses to Cleveland to go with the back-to-back playoff losses to Green Bay.

"We began to doubt ourselves," Lilly said. "We started thinking that maybe we couldn't win the big one. Maybe everybody else was right about us."

Landry looked and felt awful. Critics were after him. It was so bad that Meredith went to his old coach's house and advised him to retire.

RAYFIELD WRIGHT

If Rayfield Wright had gotten to choose his pro sport, it would've been basketball.

If he'd gotten to choose his football position, it would've been tight end.

The Cowboys tried him there and at defensive end. Then Tom Landry put him at offensive tackle just in time for a game against Deacon Jones, the most menacing pass rusher in the NFL.

Lining up for their first collision, Jones asked whether Wright's mother knew that he was doing this. Then Jones ran over Wright before he could answer.

"Mr. Jones had a tough day after that," Wright proudly recalled.

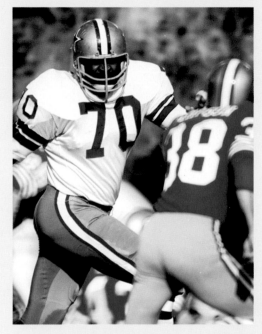

George Long/NFL/Getty Images

Wright blossomed into one of the best blockers in football. Dubbed "Big Cat" for his size and quickness, he paved the way for the first five 1,000-yard rushers in team history and helped the Cowboys rank among the 10 highest-scoring teams in the NFL every year in the 1970s.

"An all-day fight with Rayfield Wright definitely is not my idea of a pleasant Sunday afternoon," Minnesota's Carl Eller once said.

Wright was named All-Pro four times and made the NFL's All-Decade Team for the 1970s. He became the first lineman in the Ring of Honor in 2004 and entered the Pro Football Hall of Fame in 2006.

The mood in Dallas wasn't helped by the fact that the NFC's representative in the Super Bowl that year was the Minnesota Vikings, a team that came into the league a year *after* the Cowboys. And the Super Bowl champions were the Kansas City Chiefs, the club formerly known as the Dallas Texans.

NOT REALLY THE ULTIMATE GAME

A big season for the Cowboys began with all sorts of change, around the club and the NFL.

With the merging of the National Football League and the American Football League, the leagues became conferences, the NFC and AFC. A new division structure was instituted—from four down to three per conference—and a wild-card playoff berth was created for the best of the rest. Dallas' Capitol Division was renamed East, with the Giants, Eagles, and Redskins sticking around and the St. Louis Cardinals joining the mix. Another

Calvin Hill's rookie season came to a disappointing end with a second straight Cowboys postseason loss at the hands of the Cleveland Browns.
AP Images

53

CLEVELAND BROWNS

As much of a pain as the Green Bay Packers were in the 1960s, the Cleveland Browns were worse.

It's one thing to lose to a team like Green Bay, which had won a bunch of NFL titles before squeaking past the Cowboys on the way to the first two Super Bowls.

But getting KO'd the next two years by the Cleveland Browns really stung.

Jim Brown was retired by then. Paul Brown was gone too. From 1965 to 1985, the *only* playoff wins the Browns had were against Dallas in 1968 and 1969.

Cleveland was one of the teams Dallas played twice a year in the early days, and the Browns won 11 of the first 12 meetings. The pendulum finally swung back in the Cowboys' direction, however, when Dallas won the next four meetings—until those disastrous first-round playoff clashes.

The teams rarely met after that because the Browns switched to the AFC in 1970.

Another Dallas-Cleveland connection worth mentioning predates the birth of the Cowboys.

In 1949, Tom Landry was a rookie defensive back on the New York Yankees of the All-America Football Conference when he was humiliated by quarterback Otto Graham and the aptly named receiver Mac Speedie. While supposedly being covered by Landry, Speedie set an AAFC single-game record with over 200 receiving yards. Landry pondered what he'd done wrong and figured out what he later described as "the very foundation of my philosophical approach to playing and coaching pro football."

"I conceded that it was impossible to succeed solely on skill, on emotions, or even on determination," Landry wrote in his autobiography. "Any success I ever attained would require the utmost in preparation and knowledge. I couldn't wait and react to my opponent, I had to know what he was going to do and before he did it."

So at least something good happened for the Cowboys at Cleveland Municipal Stadium.

---

new development was ABC's launching of *Monday Night Football*.

Labor issues surfaced too. Tex Schramm became the lead negotiator between management and the players' association. A strike delayed training camp by a few days. Bitterness lingered once Dallas players realized how much less they were making than guys on other teams.

Tom Landry, meanwhile, was tired of underachieving, so he decided to shake things up.

Jim Myers was named offensive coordinator, and Dan Reeves became a player-coach. The offense would scale back on the deep passes to Bob Hayes, and Lance Rentzel would run more, especially since Dallas again spent its top draft pick on a running back. This time, it was Duane Thomas.

The team's vaunted scouting computer ranked Thomas as the third-best player in the draft, but because he already had a reputation as a head case, NFL teams ignored him. When it was the Cowboys' turn to pick at No. 23, they couldn't resist—even with Hill coming off a terrific rookie season. Dallas found several more valuable players that draft: cornerback Charlie Waters, center John Fitzgerald, cornerback Mark Washington, and defensive end Pat Toomay. Undrafted safety Cliff Harris made the team in training camp, and a trade for Herb Adderley gave the secondary a further boost.

Over the offseason, Landry sent players a questionnaire asking what they wanted to see done differently. He changed practice routines, increased discipline, and demanded more focus. A residual benefit of the questionnaire was that players appreciated being asked. Intentional or not, Landry showed he valued their input and acknowledged he might not have all the answers.

Landry showed from the start that he was serious about enforcing the changes.

Hayes wasn't working out or following all the rules, so he was benched. Ralph Neely lost his starting job. And then there was the big move: Roger Staubach was named starting quarterback over Morton because the incumbent didn't come back in good enough shape following shoulder surgery.

After winning the opener, Staubach struggled in the first half of the second game. Landry wanted to take him out, but Staubach talked the coach out of it. The Cowboys won, but Staubach still struggled. When he threw two interceptions in the first quarter of the third game, Landry sent in Morton. He didn't do much better, getting only a late touchdown to avoid a shutout loss to the Cardinals.

Landry decided that Staubach's lack of experience was starting to show. He had skipped his apprenticeship, and Landry figured it was time for him to sit and watch Morton. Landry justified his new stance by noting that no quarterback had won a championship in his first, second, or third year.

It was the worst thing Staubach could've heard. He was only in his second season and already 28 years old. He would be too old by the time his turn came.

Besides, Morton wasn't necessarily the answer at quarterback, either.

In the wake of his shoulder problem, Morton altered his throwing motion. That led to elbow problems. Dallas won only three of the next six games, enduring two of the most humiliating losses in franchise history.

In October, the Cowboys were smacked around 54–13 in Minnesota. It was the most points they had ever allowed, and it matched their most lopsided loss. And that wasn't even the worst performance.

The big stinker came on November 16, in the Cowboys' first appearance on *Monday Night Football*. The St. Louis Cardinals, who had already beaten Dallas once, came to the Cotton Bowl and took charge from the start. They were up 17–0 midway through the third quarter when Dallas fans who used to boo Don Meredith saw him in the broadcast booth and started yearning for him.

"We want Meredith!" they chanted. "We want Meredith!"

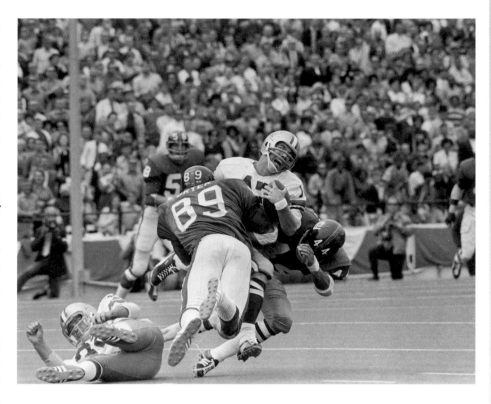

"I ain't going back down there, I tell you that, folks!" Meredith told the TV audience.

The final score was 38–0. Bob St. John of *The Dallas Morning News* referred to the loss as the Cowboys' funeral. He needed something harsh because after the loss to Minnesota he'd already proclaimed this Landry's worst team since 1965.

Dallas left the field with a 5–4 record, two games behind St. Louis, and having been drubbed in consecutive weeks. In the locker room, Landry's postgame talk sounded to players like a concession speech. Once reporters and coaches were gone, team leaders gathered the players, and everyone agreed to ignore all the doom and gloom.

"There is no one pulling for us but us, the guys right here in this room," linebacker Lee Roy Jordan told his teammates. "Hell, the coaches aren't pulling for us. They've already given up. Most of the wives have given up. We know damn well the press has been against us forever so they're not pulling for us. And most of the fans are not excited about us anymore. . . . We're going to do it for *us*."

Added Lilly: "We got 'em right where we want 'em now."

Roger Staubach, who was battling Craig Morton for the Cowboys QB job, gets a rough welcome from two New York Giants defensemen in the second game of the 1970 season, the third start of Staubach's NFL career. *AP Images*

CLIFF HARRIS AND CHARLIE WATERS

At a rookie minicamp in March 1970, an undrafted cornerback from Ouachita Baptist and a quarterback from Clemson drafted in the third round met for the first time.

Cliff Harris and Charlie Waters turned into one heck of a safety tandem and the closest of friends.

"We both knew the other one had a lot of competitive drive," Waters said, "and we just got along with each other."

Harris—the free safety whose crunching tackles earned him the nickname "Captain Crash"—played 10 years and was named to the All-NFL team for the 1970s. A six-time Pro Bowler, he joined the Ring of Honor in 2004.

Waters lasted through 1981, although he missed 1979 with an injury. He had 41 career interceptions—same as his jersey number, and third-best in club history—plus

Russ Russell/NFL/Getty Images

a team-record 9 pickoffs in 25 playoff games.

As rookies, Harris was the starter and Waters his backup. Then Harris got called to the military and his buddy took over, even getting to start in the Super Bowl. Waters was a backup strong safety and a cornerback until 1975, when Tom Landry finally made them the starting safety duo.

"Best pair of safeties I ever saw," said Gene Stallings, who coached Dallas defensive backs from 1972 to 1985 during a distinguished career that also included stints as head coach at Texas A&M, at Alabama, and with the NFL's Cardinals. "Charlie was smart, a student of the game. Cliff was aggressive, just an intimidating hitter.

"They were the perfect complement to each other. Each by himself was very good. Together, they were the best."

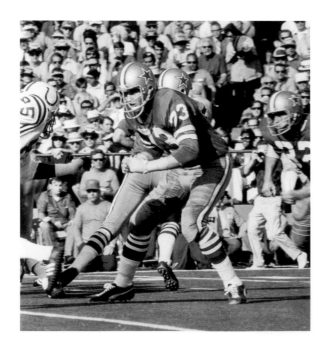

Ralph "Rotten" Neely (73) was a block of granite on the Dallas offensive line for 13 years, starting at right tackle as a rookie and later moving to right guard and left tackle. He was named All-Pro three times and made the NFL's All-Decade Team for the 1960s.
NFL/Getty Images

Amazingly enough, they did.

The Cowboys drilled the Redskins 45–21 the following week, then wouldn't give up that many points again the rest of the season. Combined.

Dallas gave up just 15 points over the last four games, with the lone touchdown in that span coming on a fumble return. The "Doomsday Defense"—as they were now being called—went into the playoffs on the heels of 17 straight quarters without allowing a touchdown.

Along the way, the Cowboys squeaked out a 6–2 win in Cleveland and crushed Houston 52–10 in the finale. Beating the Browns meant less now that they were in the AFC, but it still felt good after the two playoff losses. Against the Oilers, Morton overcame a cut hand to throw five touchdown passes, four to Hayes.

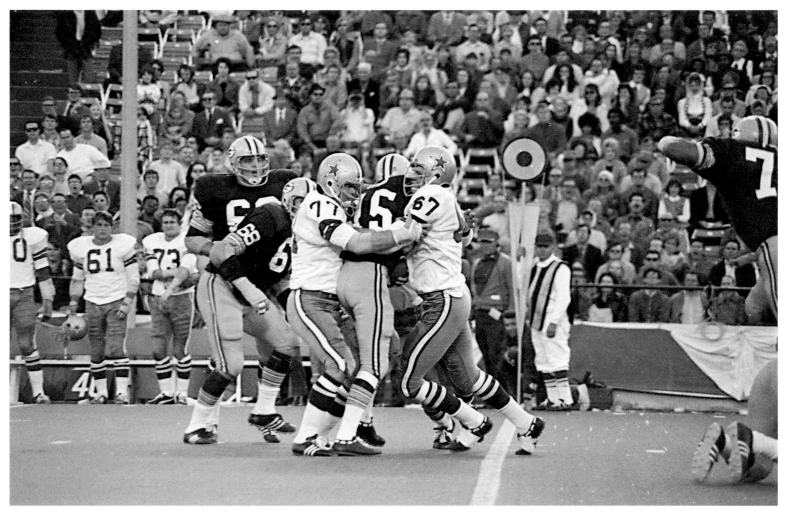

Defensive linemen Ron East (77) and Pat Toomay (67) wrap up Packers quarterback Bart Starr on Thanksgiving Day 1970. Dallas won, 16–3, just four days after trouncing the Redskins, 45–21. *AP Images*

The Cowboys closed the season with five straight wins to finish 10–4 and claim the inaugural NFC East title. The Cardinals sunk from 7–2 to 8–5–1, dropping all the way to third.

How could a team supposedly ready for the morgue go into the playoffs on such a roll?

The speeches by Jordan and Lilly set the tone. Then came practices that featured the first teams going hard after each other—and occasional games of touch football. The suggestion actually came from Landry; nobody was really sure if he was being serious or sarcastic, but they tried it anyway and had a blast. Landry also became more open to suggestions about which plays would and wouldn't work, and he cut back on meetings.

He wouldn't relent on his decision at quarterback. Even though Morton completed less than 50 percent of his passes, Landry stuck with him.

Also during the late-season surge, the club lost Rentzel under ugly circumstances.

Rentzel was arrested for indecent exposure to a minor. He had driven to a Catholic girls school and exposed himself to a 10-year-old girl. People within the organization knew he'd been troubled for years but hadn't properly addressed it. Now they had no choice. Rentzel never played for the Cowboys again.

When the playoffs began, Cowboys fans weren't sure whether to believe this would be *the* year or to be petrified that the team would find a new way to blow it.

They almost did in the opener against Detroit, winning only 5–0. Mike Clark kicked a 26-yard field goal in the first quarter, George Andrie and Jethro Pugh sacked Lions quarterback Greg Landry in the end zone for a safety in the fourth quarter, and Mel Renfro intercepted a pass on the 17-yard line with 35 seconds left to clinch the win. It was the first NFL playoff game without a touchdown since 1950.

The Dallas offense was brutal. The cut on Morton's hand pestered him into going 4-of-18 for 38 yards, but Landry refused to use Staubach.

Next up was a game in San Francisco against a 49ers club coached by Dick Nolan, Landry's old pal from the Giants and his former player and assistant coach on the Cowboys.

The 49ers were led by John Brodie, the NFL MVP and the leader in most passing categories, making this a classic showdown of a great offense versus a great defense.

The game was tied at three at the half, then Morton broke it open with two nice, long drives. The

Cowboys had to hold on at the end, and they did. They were finally headed to the Super Bowl.

"Next Year's Champions" were getting their chance to be this year's champions under the most unusual circumstances, having risen from the ashes of two midseason losses that could've torn them apart, and from a 5–4 record that had them left for dead by fans, media, and perhaps some of their inner circle. Instead of taking the easy way out, this team catapulted itself to a new height by winning seven straight games, the most in club history.

The only bad news was that the Cowboys were headed to Miami, a place where they'd lost twice in the Playoff Bowl. They were facing the Baltimore Colts, who were still smarting from the Super Bowl loss to the Jets two years before.

Dallas' first Super Bowl also was the first game officially called the "Super Bowl." (The past four years it was technically the "AFL–NFL World Championship Game.") During the build-up, several reporters saw Thomas on the beach, watching the

Rookie Duane Thomas ran for 143 yards and one touchdown, spearheading Dallas' 17–10 win over San Francisco in the NFC Championship Game on January 3, 1971. *George Long/NFL/Getty Images*

waves roll in and out. Asked what he thought about the Super Bowl scene, he responded, "If it's the ultimate game, why are they playing it again next year?"

The Cowboys already were developing an aura about them. In the *Miami Herald*, Edwin Pope wrote that the Cowboys were "football's *Peyton Place*," referring to the popular book, movie, and television soap opera. He continued:

"They've got everything: sex scandals, player-management bitterness, bankruptcies, divorces; plus a Super Bowl football team. . . . All the inner strife doesn't sound like the kind of organization that would be put together by a 130-pound former halfback at Massachusetts Institute of Technology, which is what owner Clint Murchison happens to be."

Murchison was offended. He wrote to Pope to set the record straight.

"I weigh 142 pounds," he said.

But there was no happy ending to this story. In a game that would be remembered as the "Blunder Bowl," the Colts had a chance to win in the end, and they did. Rookie kicker Jim O'Brien booted a 32-yard field goal with five seconds left to give Baltimore a 16–13 victory. The Cowboys were bridesmaids again.

"We beat ourselves," Landry said.

Only two players on the Dallas roster didn't get into the game: offensive lineman Tony Liscio, who was injured, and Staubach.

On the flight home, Staubach wondered whether this was it for him in Dallas. Landry must have sensed it because he went over to his backup and said, "You will get your opportunity to be a starting quarterback this coming season."

Mel Renfro on the bench following the Cowboys' loss in Super Bowl V. *NFL/Getty Images*

SUPER BOWL V
BALTIMORE COLTS 16,
DALLAS COWBOYS 13

MIAMI, FLORIDA – The Dallas Cowboys had never seen anything like a Super Bowl atmosphere. Then again, the NFL had never seen anything like this either.

By January 1971, the Super Bowl was starting to become the national sensation it is today. There were parties and press conferences and a parade. A heavyweight boxing match featuring former world champion Floyd Patterson was held the night before the game.

More than 80,000 fans filled the Orange Bowl on Super Sunday. More than 62 million people watched on television. And, boy, would they regret it.

The teams combined for 11 turnovers, with the winners committing 7. The Cowboys had 10 penalties for 133 yards, still the most in Super Bowl history. Baltimore scored a touchdown on a ricochet that didn't ricochet the way refs said it did. Dallas had a touchdown taken away because of a fumble that wasn't fumbled.

"Both teams bumbled through a laugher of a Super Bowl," Tex Maule wrote in *Sports Illustrated*. "But in the end the joke was on the Cowboys, who made the biggest mistake of all—losing."

Dallas scored first, getting a 14-yard field goal in the first quarter. The Colts tried to help the Cowboys crack things open, yielding an interception to Chuck Howley and a fumbled punt, but the Cowboys refused to comply. They eventually got within 12 yards of the end zone, only to move backward and settle for a 30-yard field goal and a 6–0 lead early in the second quarter.

On the next series, Colts quarterback Johnny Unitas threw a pass that receiver Eddie Hinton tipped. Dallas defenders Mel Renfro, Cornell Green, and Charlie Waters all reached for it, and all missed. Baltimore's John Mackey snared it at midfield and ran into the end zone without anyone chasing him. The Cowboys insisted it was an illegal catch because, under the rules at the time, a Dallas player had to touch it before Mackey could, and none of them did. But officials said Renfro touched it. The Cowboys got some measure of revenge when

Super Bowl MVP Chuck Howley.
Walter Iooss Jr./Sports Illustrated/
Getty Images

Mark Washington blocked the extra point, keeping the score tied at six.

A fumble by Unitas led to a touchdown catch by Duane Thomas and a 13–6 Dallas lead. Then Unitas threw another interception and broke a rib in the process. Earl Morrall replaced him and had the Colts at the Dallas 2-yard line just before halftime. After the Doomsday Defense turned back three straight runs, Baltimore opted not to kick the short field goal. Morrall threw and it fell incomplete.

So, at halftime, the Cowboys had a one-touchdown lead over a team that had lost its Hall of Fame–bound quarterback.

Dallas kicked off to open the second half, and Baltimore returner Jim Duncan fumbled. The Cowboys recovered and had another chance to break things open. It looked like they had when Thomas crossed the goal line, but then the Colts claimed they recovered a fumble in the end zone—even though Dallas center Dave Manders ended up with the ball on the bottom of the pile.

"The official nearest the play couldn't see it," Tex Schramm said. "He was stupid."

Regardless, the Colts were given a touchback, though they failed to capitalize on the turnover once again.

The Cowboys had the ball in the fourth quarter when Craig Morton threw a pass to fullback Walt Garrison. He deflected it, and the ball landed in the hands of safety Rick Volk, who returned it to the Dallas 3. Baltimore's Tom Nowatzke ran it in two plays later, and the extra point tied the score at 13.

With less than two minutes to go, the game seemed headed for overtime when, after the Cowboys took over near midfield, a penalty pushed them back into their own territory. On second-and-35, Morton threw a pass that went through the hands of Dan Reeves and was caught by Colts linebacker Mike Curtis. A few plays later, rookie Jim O'Brien came out to try a 32-yard field goal with five seconds left. The straight-ahead kicker nailed it for the title.

At game's end, Bob Lilly was so angry that he threw his helmet as if it were a softball. Using a big, left-handed windup, he gave that sucker an underhanded heave. He probably wished it had broken to pieces. Instead, a well-meaning rookie linebacker for Baltimore named Robbie Nichols fetched it and said, "Mr. Lilly, here's your helmet."

"It made me feel like a heel," Lilly said.

He had a right to be angry, though. The Doomsday guys gave their offense the ball at the Baltimore 9-, 29-, 31-, 47-,

Dan Reeves' dropped pass in the fourth quarter led to a game-changing interception. *AP Images*

and 48-yard lines, yet Morton and crew managed only one touchdown out of it.

Howley was named the game's MVP, the first and still only time the recipient came from the losing team. He earned it with two interceptions, a forced fumble, and the play that forced Morrall's incompletion just before halftime.

Years later, Ditka was still grumbling about the fumble that wasn't a fumble.

"It was a terrible call," he said. "Duane really let the ball go when he heard the whistle blow. . . . If we had scored then, it wouldn't have mattered what happened later because the game would have been over."

Perhaps the most wistful spin came from owner Clint Murchison Jr., who considered this loss progress from the Ice Bowl.

"At least we're close," he said. "We got it down to 5 seconds from 13."

Defensive linemen Bob Lilly (74), Jethro Pugh (75), and Larry Cole (63) formed a formidable front line for Dallas' Doomsday Defense in 1971. *Focus on Sport/ Getty Images*

THIS YEAR'S CHAMPIONS

The Dallas Cowboys went into the 1971 season with Craig Morton at quarterback, the Cotton Bowl as their home, and taunted by the label of being "Next Year's Champions."

The Cowboys came out of the season with Roger Staubach at quarterback, Texas Stadium as their home, and proud to answer to the title of "Super Bowl Champions."

Quite simply, this was the turning point in team history, the season that would launch them toward becoming "America's Team."

But there was nothing simple about it.

Start with money issues: Morton filed for bankruptcy during the offseason, and Duane Thomas demanded a raise. When the team refused, he held a news conference and declared Landry "a plastic man, no man at all"; called Gil Brandt "a liar"; and said Tex Schramm was "sick, demented, and completely dishonest." Replied Schramm, "That's not bad. He got two out of three."

Then there were the roster changes: Pettis Norman and Tony Liscio were sent to San Diego for receiver Lance Alworth. He took over the spot that had belonged to Lance Rentzel, who was dealt to the Rams for Billy Truax. Truax took Norman's place at tight end, sharing the job with Mike Ditka, who lost 25 pounds and would have his best season

since his All-Pro days with Chicago. Brandt flew to Austria in search of the club's first soccer-style kicker and found him right away in Toni Fritsch. Chuck Howley threatened to retire but returned during training camp.

Schramm then traded Thomas to the New England Patriots for running back Carl Garrett and a first-round pick. New England coach John Mazur greeted Thomas by saying he wouldn't tolerate any free spirits. So when Thomas refused to accept something as minor as how to line up for a play, the trade was nullified. Thomas was gone all of three days.

After rejoining the Cowboys, Thomas refused to speak the rest of the season—to teammates, as well as to media. He became known as "the Sphinx" because he was such a riddle. Told he'd be fined if he did not wear a suit coat and tie, Thomas wore exactly that—with no shirt. Another time he wore a sports shirt and wrapped a tie around his neck without tying it.

But Thomas' saga was more of a sideshow. The main drama starred the quarterbacks.

Roger Staubach outplayed Morton in the preseason, but Landry still felt more comfortable with Morton's experience. Morton had led them to the brink of a championship—although plenty of folks believed Dallas got that close despite him.

Before the opener, Landry tried pleasing everyone by saying he had "two No. 1 quarterbacks" and would rotate them. That plan pleased no one.

A final preseason issue was the status of the team's new state-of-the-art stadium going up in Irving. It wasn't ready at the start of the year—and, a writer taunted, neither were its tenants.

The Cowboys started 3–2, with the quarterbacks swapping starts and often replacing each other in the second halves. Landry pulled Staubach at halftime of a game against the Giants, with Dallas leading 13–6.

"I went crazy," Staubach said. "I said to him I needed to be traded, to get out of here."

Texas Stadium was finally ready for the sixth game of the season, which happened to be Staubach's turn to start.

With former President Lyndon Baines Johnson, his wife Lady Bird, and former First Lady Mamie

GOODBYE, COTTON BOWL; HELLO, TEXAS STADIUM

Clint Murchison Jr. was never a big fan of the Cotton Bowl. He liked it even less after the Astrodome opened in 1965, and the folks down in Houston could brag about their "Eighth Wonder of the World."

"The Cotton Bowl, a grand lady in her day, suffered from terminal illness," Murchison wrote in a team newsletter. "I had to resort to mild trickery to have the restrooms whitewashed; later, a high school band member was to suffer heatstroke before water fountains were installed; and on and on and on."

Murchison took his complaints about the place to Dallas mayor Erik Jonsson. He didn't get very far. The two never really got along, mainly because Jonsson didn't like it that Murchison threw around money everywhere but to the city where he lived.

Jonsson considered renovating the Cotton Bowl but said the city wouldn't build a new stadium. He wanted Murchison to pay for that himself.

In January 1967, Murchison declared he would build "the finest football stadium to date in the world"—if the fine folks in the suburb of Irving would pay for it. On Christmas Eve, Irving leaders announced they could sell enough revenue bonds to pull it off.

Murchison wanted an outdoor stadium but also wanted a way to block the elements. He decided on a roof with a hole over the field, theoretically protecting the fans but not the players. He also wanted fans to enjoy the lap of luxury—none of those splinter-spitting seats at the Cotton Bowl and other such annoyances.

For better or worse, Murchison brought luxury suites to the masses. Texas Stadium wasn't the first to have them, but it was the first to have so many.

They were called Circle Suites because, well, they encircled the field. Each was 16 feet by 16 feet and included 12 seats. The suites were marketed to Dallas' elite and to businesses as a "personalized penthouse at Texas Stadium, similar to a second residence, like a lake home or a ranch." They cost $50,000, and many owners spent up to three times that on carpeting, furniture, wet bars, TVs, stereos, and other amenities.

The stadium price skyrocketed to $35 million, with Murchison paying about $10 million. Ticket prices went way up, angering fans and media. Editorials demanded lower prices, but Murchison wouldn't budge. He pointed out how much he'd paid, that no one was ever taxed to build it, and that folks didn't have to buy a bond to attend a game.

A year before it opened, Murchison wrote in a fan newsletter that the new place would be like Xanadu.

Once they finally walked in, players were in awe. Several claim they raised their playing standards to make sure they were worthy of the new place; indeed, the Cowboys won their first Super Bowl the season they moved in.

However, Cowboys games took on a different feel. The crowd was more corporate, more sedate, more white collar than at the Cotton Bowl.

"Moving to Texas Stadium pushed their elitist reputation to a new zenith," John Eisenberg wrote in *Cotton Bowl Days*, his memoir of growing up a Cowboys fan in Dallas. "At the Cotton Bowl, the Cowboys had been a workingman's team on rollicking, emotional, and slightly naughty Sundays. At Texas Stadium, they took on a regal bearing as the showpiece of what amounted to a private club."

In time, fans warmed up to the place. They even began taking pride in knowing their team played in the building "with the hole in the roof, so God can watch His team."

The city of Dallas missed out. In 1974, Murchison got a good laugh about it when he and a colleague visited Jonsson's downtown, high-rise office seeking a donation on behalf of the Boys Club. Upon leaving, Murchison remarked, "Did you notice the great view Erik has of Texas Stadium?"

Roger Staubach manages to get off a pass despite being wrapped up by a Washington defender. The quarterback led the Cowboys to a 13–0 win for their seventh victory of the 1971 season. *Nate Fine/ NFL/Getty Images*

Eisenhower watching from the owner's suite, the Cowboys broke in their new home with a 44–21 victory over New England. Thomas got revenge against the Patriots, and left a nice mark on team history, by going 56 yards for the first touchdown in the new place. Staubach threw two touchdowns to Bob Hayes and ran one in. Also that weekend, the previously unbeaten Redskins lost, helping Dallas close a gap in the NFC East race.

Staubach was closing the gap between him and Morton too.

Instead of switching starts, Landry decided to return to the "messenger system" of alternating plays, as he had done back in the early 1960s with Don Meredith and Eddie LeBaron.

Everyone hated this plan, including Meredith. "It's Landry's responsibility as the head coach to pick a quarterback," he told the nation during a Monday night game. "Now after all this time he still has no idea which one is the best. Then get another coach."

The Morton–Staubach tandem generated 481 yards—and seven turnovers—in a 23–19 loss to Chicago. In retrospect, it might have been the best thing that ever happened.

Landry was once again at a midseason crossroad. His club was 4–3, two games behind Washington in the division. There was a pack of teams ahead of them in the wild-card chase. But Landry's teams always played their best in November and early December. Another sign of encouragement was that the three losses had been by a total of 18 points. Something else those losses had in common: Morton started all three.

Two nights after the loss to Chicago, Landry called Staubach at home and said, "I've made a decision, Roger. You're going to be the starting quarterback for the rest of the year."

"I won't let you down, Coach," he said.

He didn't.

The Cowboys won their last seven regular-season games to finish 11–3 and win the division. Staubach was the highest-rated passer in the league. The offense scored the most points and the defense allowed the fewest yards.

Calvin Hill leaps into the end zone for the first points in the Cowboys' 14–3 win over the 49ers in the NFC Championship Game on January 2, 1972. *AP Images*

It wasn't easy, of course. Alworth and Calvin Hill overcame injuries, and Ralph Neely was lost to a broken leg suffered while doing motorcycle stunts with teammates. Tony Liscio was retired and selling real estate when the Cowboys brought him back to replace Neely; he wound up playing better than ever.

Although Dallas tied Minnesota for the best record in the NFL, the rules of the day forced the Cowboys to open the playoffs on the road—against the Vikings.

On a relatively warm Christmas Day in Bloomington, Minnesota, the Cowboys jumped ahead 20–3 and cruised into a second straight NFC Championship Game against San Francisco, only this time in Dallas' shiny new home. The Cowboys again took an early lead and nursed it to a 14–3 victory, leaving the 49ers a win shy of a Super Bowl for a second straight year, just like Green Bay had done to Dallas years before.

In the Super Bowl, Landry had the Cowboys perfectly primed. There was nothing the Miami Dolphins could do about it.

"I don't think there was a man on the roster who even considered the possibility of losing that game," Bob Lilly said. "We had paid our dues and felt our time had come."

Staubach and the Doomsday Defense led Dallas to a 24–3 victory, crowning "Next Year's Champions" as "THIS Year's Champions."

The championship proved that Landry and the team were among the league's elite. Dallas could win the big game as well as all the little ones.

This was truly a championship roster: 11 starters wound up in either the Pro Football Hall of Fame or the team's Ring of Honor. Although Ditka, Alworth, and Adderley built their Hall of Fame credentials mostly through accomplishments on other teams, they were key cogs in Dallas' title; Ditka and Alworth each scored touchdowns in the Super Bowl, and Adderley led the club in interceptions that season. With backup Forrest Gregg on the roster, as well as Landry and Schramm, that's three more Hall of Famers on this club.

SUPER BOWL VI
DALLAS COWBOYS 24,
MIAMI DOLPHINS 3

NEW ORLEANS, LOUISIANA – **The Super Bowl spectacle was old news for the Cowboys.** Even with the lure of New Orleans' French Quarter beckoning, this was a business trip.

Dallas was favored, but the Miami Dolphins had a lot going for them. Bob Griese was the highest-ranked passer in the AFC. His favorite target was Paul Warfield, a Cowboys killer in his days with the Cleveland Browns. Larry Csonka was a 1,000-yard rusher, with Jim Kiick and Mercury Morris adding more punch.

The Dolphins also had President Richard Nixon on their side.

Nixon had a winter home in Florida, so he followed the local team. He even called Dolphins coach Don Shula and offered some advice: "Now, the Cowboys are a good football team, but I still think you can hit Warfield on that down-and-in pattern against them. You know the one."

Nixon's predecessor, Lyndon Johnson, heard about that conversation and sent Landry a telegram: "Tom, my prayers and my presence will be with you in New Orleans, although I have no plans to send in any plays."

The game was played outdoors at Tulane Stadium on an unexpectedly cold 39-degree day, the coldest ever for a Super Bowl.

The Doomsday Defense set an early tone by forcing Csonka to cough up his first fumble of the season. Dallas got a field goal out of it, then Doomsday struck again.

On the final play of the first quarter, Bob Lilly and Larry Cole broke through the line and went straight at Griese. He started running for his life—away from the line of scrimmage. Cole got a hand on the Dolphins quarterback after a couple of yards but couldn't hold on. The chase continued until Lilly brought him down 29 yards from where they'd started.

The Dolphins never recovered from that sack.

Roger Staubach upped the lead to 10–0 by capping a long drive with a 7-yard touchdown pass to Lance Alworth. Miami got a field goal just before the half, then a long, slow Dallas drive ended with Duane Thomas scoring on a 3-yard run. The Cowboys kept running and burning the clock, stretching the score when Staubach hit Mike Ditka for another touchdown.

Dallas ran for 252 yards and limited Miami to its fewest total yards and fewest yards rushing all season. These Dolphins were the first team not to score a touchdown in the Super Bowl, obviously making their three points a record low. Yet this Dolphins team was no joke; the Dolphins would go undefeated the following season and win the next two Super Bowls.

"I remember being so thoroughly prepared that it was unbelievable," defensive tackle Jethro Pugh said. "It was like taking a final exam and being allowed to use the textbook."

At game's end, Lilly and Rayfield Wright lifted Landry onto their shoulders for a victory march. Lilly couldn't see Landry's face, but he knew the stone facade had cracked and the coach was smiling.

"I don't think I'm really conscious of my feelings yet," Landry said during the celebration. "This is certainly my biggest thrill." A year before, Landry had told Staubach that no quarterback had ever won a Super Bowl in his first three years. Well, now one

AP Images

Duane Thomas. *Focus on Sport/Getty Images*

Dolphins quarterback Bob Griese (12) fleeing the Doomsday Defense. *Pro Football Hall of Fame/NFL/Getty Images*

had—and he was the game's MVP. Staubach's steady, error-free performance earned the honor even though Thomas (19 carries, 95 yards) had been more valuable. Staubach himself said so. The difference was that everyone knew Staubach would be gracious about it, and there was no telling how "The Sphinx" would respond.

As it turned out, Thomas was so thrilled to win it all that he agreed to an interview, his first of the season.

Landry took a call from Nixon, who, according to Landry, "complimented us on playing almost perfect football, especially our offensive line."

What about the down-and-in to Warfield, which Shula indeed called and resulted in an incompletion?

"That never came up," Landry said, smiling slightly.

The last word on this victory goes to the man who got this franchise started, owner Clint Murchison Jr.

"This," he mused, "is a very successful culmination of our 12-year plan."

Rayfield Wright (70) helps give Tom Landry the ride of his life after the coach and the Cowboys shed their label of not being able to win the big one. *AP Images*

Dallas went 13–0 in Staubach's starts for the 1971 season, including the playoffs, and the quarterback was 16–1 over his career.

"This is just the beginning," Schramm said. "We have a young team. I can see the Cowboys becoming a dynasty. . . . We have many championships in front of us."

THE HANGOVER

Dallas' hopes for a second straight title took a blow right away.

In the second preseason game in 1972, Roger Staubach made the mistake of trying to get a few extra yards on a run down the sideline. Instead of just going out of bounds, he turned back inside and went right into a defender charging at him. The collision separated his throwing shoulder.

Duane Thomas was gone too, traded to San Diego, with a no-return policy.

Other star players were back but a year older. Chuck Howley was 36. Bob Lilly and Herb Adderley were 33. Lance Alworth, Mike Ditka, George Andrie, Cornell Green, and Dave Edwards were 32.

Landry brought in Sid Gillman to help run the offense, but with Morton behind center, things didn't exactly click. In fact, he was booed during every home game. Loudly.

"Certainly I hear it," he said. "A deaf man could hear those people."

Calvin Hill (35) capped off a 1,036-yard rushing season with a 125-yard performance against San Francisco in the divisional round of the 1972 playoffs, a thrilling 30–28 Dallas win. *George Long/NFL/Getty Images*

Calvin Hill had folks cheering. Without having to share time with Thomas, and aided by some rules changes, Hill became the club's first 1,000-yard rusher. Walt Garrison contributed another 784 yards, helping ease the load on Morton.

The Cowboys managed to go 5–2 during the first half of the season, which is when they usually struggled. They also went 5–2 in the second half, which is when they usually surged.

Being 10–4 wasn't enough to top Washington's "Over the Hill Gang" for the division title, ending a six-year streak of first-place finishes for Dallas. Still, it was good enough to get the reigning Super Bowl champs into the playoffs as a wild card, setting an NFL record with a seventh straight postseason trip.

Once again, Landry squared off against San Francisco and his pal Dick Nolan. The 49ers had beaten the Cowboys 31–10 on Thanksgiving, and they carried the extra motivation of wanting revenge for two straight playoff beatings.

San Francisco was getting it too, leading 28–13 late in the third quarter, when linebacker Dave Wilcox snarled, "How do you guys feel losing?"

Landry benched Morton in the second half. Staubach had been rusty in four mop-up appearances since recovering from his shoulder injury, but there was nothing to lose. Morton went over to Staubach, hugged him, and said, "I have confidence in you. You can win."

And he did, launching the legend that Staubach's games are never over until the final gun.

The Cowboys made it 28–16 on Toni Fritsch's field goal early in the fourth quarter. Then Staubach threw a 20-yard touchdown pass to Billy Parks, cutting the deficit to 28–23 with 1:30 left.

Then came a play you had to see to believe: Fritsch, a former soccer player, ran up to the ball for the kickoff, planted his kicking foot, and swung back with his *other* foot for an onside kick, which was recovered by Mel Renfro. The stunt worked so perfectly that Staubach later said, "You have to wonder if he could do it again, even if he had a million chances."

Staubach followed with a 21-yard run, a 19-yard pass to Parks, and a 10-yard pass to Ron Sellers in the end zone. In just 38 seconds, Staubach had thrown two touchdown passes to give the Cowboys the lead in the final minute of a playoff game on the road. The 49ers still had 52 seconds left, but Charlie Waters stopped them with an interception.

"This is unreal," Landry said afterward. "I think it was one of the best comebacks we ever made. It was one of the greatest moments in our history."

Alworth called it the greatest victory he'd ever seen.

"We made believers out of everyone," Staubach said after the game.

Back in the NFC Championship Game, the Cowboys were facing the Redskins for the third time this season. Each team already had won at home. On New Year's Eve in D.C., that trend held. Washington beat Dallas 26–3, shutting down the Cowboys' running game and pretty much everything else. Staubach made his first start of the season, despite the flu keeping him from practicing all week.

"After last season, the Dallas folks talked about a dynasty," Redskins linebacker Jack Pardee said. "But that's done now."

Offensive linemen Rayfield Wright (70), Blaine Nye (61), John Fitzgerald (62), John Niland (76), and Ralph Neely (behind Niland) shown during the 1973 opener against the Bears, formed a tough front line for Dallas' potent offense. *Diamond Images/ Getty Images*

STILL COMING CLOSE

The spoils of success were starting to catch up to the Cowboys.

Roger Staubach said he wanted to be the outright starter—or to be traded. His mother was dying of cancer and had moved into his house; dealing with that while also trying to accept being the backup wasn't part of his plans.

George Andrie, Lance Alworth, Herb Adderley, and Mike Ditka retired. Ditka joined the staff as an assistant coach, but Sid Gillman and Dan Reeves left. (Reeves would return a year later.)

Center Dave Manders quit over a contract dispute. Tex Schramm ended up bringing him back, a move unveiled when Manders popped out of a birthday cake during a surprise party for owner Clint Murchison Jr.

Lee Roy Jordan waited until the Cowboys made the final cuts before demanding his raise. He outsmarted Schramm and got more money. Schramm got revenge by keeping Jordan out of the Ring of Honor. (Jerry Jones eventually rectified that.)

The Cowboys got a nice infusion of youth by drafting Harvey Martin, Billy Joe DuPree, and

Golden Richards. They also signed an undrafted quarterback from Tulsa with plans to try him at receiver, a guy named Drew Pearson. Green Bay and Pittsburgh offered Pearson more money, but he signed with the Cowboys for a $150 bonus and a side job loading 18-wheelers for "six, seven bucks an hour, which I thought was great," he recalled.

Pearson was the eighth receiver on the depth chart when he arrived. He started staying after work to get in extra practice with Staubach. The quarterback liked what he saw from the kid, both in ability and work ethic, and he went to Schramm to see about getting Pearson out of that moonlighting job. Schramm plunked down $500, and Pearson agreed to become a full-time football player.

Landry chose Staubach to be the starter. And, as the coach had promised both quarterbacks during training camp, he let them call their own plays.

The Cowboys won their first three games, then went into a funk. They were 4–3 at midseason and in need of their old second-half magic.

They seemed to capture it, notching three straight wins. Then came the big test: the 9–1 Miami

AMERICA'S SWEETHEARTS

With the Cowboys upgrading homes from the Cotton Bowl to Texas Stadium, Tex Schramm decided it was time to upgrade the cheerleaders too.

From 1960 through the first championship season in 1971, Dallas fans were encouraged to yell by the CowBelles and Beaux, six boys and six girls from local high schools who spewed the traditional sis-boom-bah type of cheers.

"Fans at pro games didn't want to cheer college-style," Schramm said. "I finally said, 'The hell with it. Let's entertain 'em with our cheerleaders instead of trying to lead them in cheers. Dress 'em up pretty and let 'em entertain.' So they were sexy, but they weren't lewd. . . . Little did we know that we were starting something that one day would become what is now considered an American phenomenon."

Schramm hired dancer Texie Waterman to be the choreographer, and she led the gals in New York–style jazz dancing. They dressed for the part too—a tasseled, star-spangled vest that hung open over royal blue, long-sleeved halter tops, short white shorts, and white boots.

The cheerleaders were a hit at Texas Stadium. Television turned them into a worldwide sensation.

There's a question whether "the wink" that started the craze happened on a Monday night game in November 1975 or at Super Bowl X a few months later. Maybe both. Regardless, there was mutual affection between these gals and the cameras.

The response was overwhelming, and there was no way Waterman could handle both the managing and choreography duties. So Schramm asked his secretary, Suzanne Mitchell, to take

Dallas Cowboys cheerleaders at Wild Card Playoff Game, January 2010. *Al Messerschmidt/Getty Images*

Dallas Cowboys cheerleaders at Super Bowl V, January 1971.
Vernon Biever/NFL/Getty Images

Dallas Cowboys cheerleaders at Super Bowl XII, January 1978.
Focus on Sport/Getty Images

over as the group's manager. It was another perfect combination as Mitchell choreographed the business side of the operation.

The Dallas Cowboys Cheerleaders became regulars in movies, in TV shows, and in made-for-TV movies, on USO tours with Bob Hope, on posters, on calendars, and in every other measure of fame imaginable. They even got their own Barbie doll and, in 2006, their own reality TV show.

"I think Roger Staubach is a real-life hero, and I honestly believe the cheerleaders are real-life heroines to a lot of people in this country," Mitchell said in the mid 1970s. "I understand that where little girls used to dream of being Miss America, now they dream about becoming a cheerleader for the Cowboys."

They were dubbed "America's Sweethearts," although there's nothing sweet about the competition for these precious jobs.

The cheerleaders come from all sorts of backgrounds — dancers, models, and actresses, as well as homemakers, nurses, and college students; some single, some married, some

with children, some without. Looks, dancing ability, and overall athleticism are among the requirements. Brains play a part too, since candidates must take a written test on team history, referee signals, and current events.

"These girls have microphones and cameras in their faces all the time, and they need to be prepared to discuss any subject," said Kelli McGonagill Finglass, who went from being a cheerleader to director of the group.

Tom Landry wasn't a fan of the concept. He considered it sexual exploitation. After Landry referred to them as "porno queens," the image conscious Schramm called the coach into his office to show him the difference.

"This is what your name for them meant," Schramm said as the tape began to roll.

Then, Schramm recalled, "Tom got up and walked out the door and never said anything about cheerleaders again."

Nearly three decades later, these girls are almost as iconic as the 'Boys.

Dolphins at home on Thanksgiving in a showdown of the last two Super Bowl champions.

Miami scored two first-quarter touchdowns and nursed it to a 14–7 victory. Staubach called a goal-line audible that failed, and Landry decided that was it; he was reclaiming play-calling duties. His excuse was that Staubach had too much on his mind with his mother's health worsening. (She died a few weeks later.) Staubach never did regain control of the plays, which always was a knock against him because other quarterbacks had the privilege.

The Cowboys beat the Redskins 27–7 the following week for a crucial split of their season series. Because both teams wound up 10–4 overall and 6–2 in division play, the NFC East title came down to the next tiebreaker, point differential in those two head-to-head matchups. Dallas had the edge (34–21).

Staubach again led the NFL in passer rating and with 23 touchdowns. Calvin Hill broke his own club record with 1,142 rushing yards, just 2 yards off the NFC lead.

The Cowboys opened the playoffs at home against the Rams. Los Angeles was 12–2 but was forced to play on the road because of those wacky rules of the era. Staubach threw an early 83-yard touchdown pass to Pearson, sparking a 27–16 victory that was never even close.

Dallas was expecting a second straight NFC Championship Game against Washington, but the Redskins lost to the Vikings. So Minnesota came to Texas Stadium, with the winner moving on to the Super Bowl in Houston.

In an ugly, turnover-filled game reminiscent of Super Bowl V, Dallas was within 10–7 in the third quarter but couldn't do anything right, especially with Hill out due to an elbow injury. The Vikings won 27–10.

Although the Cowboys had fallen a game short of the Super Bowl in consecutive years, it didn't sting as much as in 1966–1967 because they had a championship under their belts. They had proven they *could* win the big one and now were the most consistent title contenders in the NFL, having played for the conference title an amazing six times in eight years.

Of course, no one was satisfied with coming close a lot.

"You aren't really successful unless you get to the Super Bowl," Landry said. "We'll be back a lot stronger next season."

THE BOTTOM FALLS OUT

For the first time in franchise history, the Cowboys had the first overall pick in the draft. It came courtesy of the Houston Oilers, who in 1973 gave up their first- and third-round picks in 1974 for spare parts Tody Smith and Billy Parks. Then Houston won only a single game in 1973, gift-wrapping the No. 1 overall selection for Dallas.

The Cowboys took 6-foot-9 defensive end Ed "Too Tall" Jones at the top of the draft, then used the third-rounder on quarterback Danny White.

The business side of pro football dominated the rest of the offseason news.

Another rival league was on the horizon, the World Football League. The WFL would start the following summer and already was signing players—including Calvin Hill, Craig Morton, and White. White went straight to the WFL in 1974 and 1975. Hill and Morton signed for the following season; Hill spent 1975 with the Hawaii club, but Morton got out of his deal when the Houston franchise moved to Shreveport, so he returned to the Cowboys.

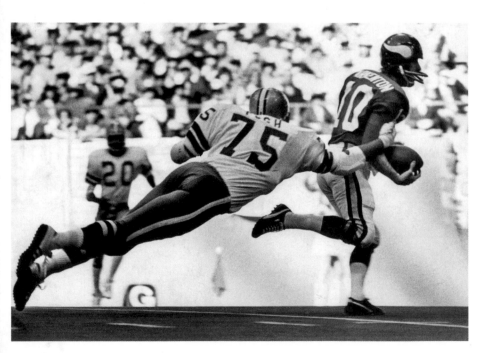

Defensive tackle Jethro Pugh makes a lunging grab for Minnesota quarterback Fran Tarkenton, but Tarkenton's Vikings ran away with a 27–10 victory in the 1973 NFC Championship Game. *Vernon Biever/NFL/ Getty Images*

POLISHING THE STAR
NORTH DALLAS FORTY

Tell-all books are so common these days that players write them while they're still playing. In the 1960s and 1970s, players lived by the code "what happens in the locker room, stays in the locker room."

Leave it to a guy like Peter Gent to blur the line.

Gent played basketball at Michigan State, but the Cowboys turned him into a receiver. He made the team in 1964 and lasted through 1968. There aren't many stories about his on-field exploits, but there are plenty about the things he did and said off the field, like this advice to a rookie studying the playbook: "Don't bother reading it, kid. Everybody gets killed in the end."

Then there was the time Landry decided to move Gent from flanker to split end against the Eagles. Landry phrased it along the lines of having him switch sides for the week, to which Gent replied, "You mean I'm going to play for Philadelphia?"

"Wait till you see the weird part."
NORTH DALLAS FORTY

And, how about this reaction when he was later told to play tight end: "Landry just wants me to sit on the bench at three positions instead of two."

Gent was a long-haired rebel, a cynic, and a wise guy. In 1973, he put his memories into a thinly veiled novel called *North Dallas Forty*. It became a movie in 1979, starring Nick Nolte in the dramatized version of Gent and Mac Davis as his carousing sidekick-quarterback, obviously patterned after Don Meredith. Even the casual fan recognized the coach as Tom Landry.

The book opens with a drunken hunting scene and features plenty about sex and drugs. Gent also explored the pain, fear, and loathing that defined his playing days.

The club obviously didn't like the portrayal. Landry didn't want to discuss it, but years later, Gent came by to interview the coach for a magazine article. And Landry agreed.

NFL players went on strike too, and it was a mess. Roger Staubach, Lee Roy Jordan, and Bob Lilly reported to training camp anyway, prompting Ed Garvey, the head of the players' group, to say of Staubach: "I'd hate to have been at Pearl Harbor with him." Lilly shot back by comparing Garvey to Jimmy Hoffa, the former Teamsters boss who'd served prison time. John Niland and Charlie Waters soon crossed the picket line. More and more followed until the strike was settled in August. One player who didn't return was Chuck Howley. He finally retired after years of threatening to do so.

Staubach was secure as the starting quarterback, even though he'd been slowed by a rib injury in the preseason. He looked just fine in a 24–0 victory over Atlanta in the season opener.

Then came the longest skid since 1965—four straight losses. The Cowboys had logged four *seasons* with fewer than four losses since then. Worse still, three of the losses were by a field goal or less, and the other was by six points.

"This team just doesn't have that right feeling," safety Cliff Harris said after the first two losses. "At different stages of the season you feel different ways.

It was a roller-coaster season for Staubach and the Cowboys in 1974, but their 17–14 win over St. Louis on November 3 brought them to .500 halfway through the schedule. *Russ Russell/ NFL/Getty Images*

It's a progressive thing leading to what you hope is your best performances. But this year . . . it still feels like we're in the preseason."

Staubach played well, and so did the running backs, but the offense just couldn't score enough. The defense couldn't salvage them, allowing more points each game, starting at 13 and rising to 31.

"We can't get over the thin line between victory and defeat when we have a chance to win at the end," Landry said.

Despite the struggles, Landry never went with Morton to shake things up. The day after Dallas ended the losing streak, Morton asked to be traded. The next day, he was sent to the New York Giants for a first-round pick in the following year's draft.

After nine and a half years—first as an apprentice to Meredith, then as a rival to Staubach—Morton was gone, headed to a fresh start in the Big Apple. In his very first game with the Giants, he lost to Staubach and the Cowboys, 21–7.

Now Dallas was starting to rally. It continued with the pleasure of winning on a last-second field goal, this one handing the division-leading Cardinals their first loss after a 7–0 start. A shutout win over Houston made it four straight wins. The Cowboys were 6–5 heading into a Thanksgiving visit by the Redskins.

To make the playoffs, Dallas had to win its final three and Washington lose its final three. A head-to-head win would be the perfect start.

Things didn't look good when Staubach was knocked woozy early in the third quarter. With Morton gone, Landry turned to rookie Clint Longley and said, "Good luck, Clint."

Known as "The Mad Bomber" for reasons including a pass that supposedly nearly hit Landry in the coaching tower during practice, the 22-year-old rattlesnake hunter from Abilene Christian made his NFL debut under the most difficult of circumstances: with his team trailing 16–3 to a ferocious Washington defense, while playing in front of a national television audience.

"He was unbelievable for a guy who hasn't played," fullback Walt Garrison said. "One time I brought in a play and started to explain things to him and he said, 'Shut up, Walt!'"

Longley threw a 35-yard touchdown pass to Billy Joe DuPree, then on a subsequent drive he handed off to Walt Garrison for a 1-yard, go-ahead touchdown. The Redskins answered with a TD by, of all people, Duane Thomas. Then Dallas lost a fumble, and with about five minutes left, Washington went for a 24-yard field goal that could have sealed a victory. "Too Tall" blocked it.

The Cowboys should have been done when Drew Pearson fumbled with 2:29 left, but Washington failed to run out the clock, and Longley got one more chance.

On second down from the 50, with 35 seconds left in the game, Longley threw into a secondary packed with seven defensive backs, aiming for Staubach's favorite deep threat, Pearson. Somehow, they connected beyond all the defenders, and Pearson stepped into the end zone for the tying touchdown. The extra point put Dallas up 24–23.

With 28 seconds on the clock, Billy Kilmer's bid for his own miracle rally ended when Jethro Pugh knocked the ball loose and Harvey Martin recovered it.

Offensive lineman Blaine Nye described Longley's heroics as "a triumph of the uncluttered mind." Longley lasted one more season, then was traded to San Diego during training camp in 1976.

White had arrived and was going to replace him as the backup, so on the final day of camp Longley sucker-punched Staubach. He later claimed it was his way of guaranteeing the Cowboys would get rid of him.

The Thanksgiving victory over Washington only delayed the inevitable as far as Dallas' play-off chances went. The Cowboys won again the next week, but so did the Redskins, eliminating Dallas from the playoff race. They lost the finale at Oakland to finish 8–6.

For the first time since 1965, the Cowboys would not be playing for a championship. For the first time since 1964, there would be no postseason trip at all.

Maybe Jack Pardee's prediction after the 1973 season was right. Maybe Dallas really was done.

Third-string rookie quarterback Clint Longley earned the game ball after leading Dallas to a dramatic 24–23 over Washington on Thanksgiving Day. *AP Images*

COWBOY LEGENDS
WALT GARRISON

Talk about being a cowboy. This real-life rodeo competitor went from the Oklahoma State Cowboys to the Dallas Cowboys, then back to the rodeo world.

"I like rodeo better than football," he once said. "It has a better class of people."

Garrison was a reliable runner, receiver, and blocker. From 1967 to 1974, he was always second or third in rushing. He didn't see many passes come his way until 1970, then he led the club with 40 catches for 396 yards.

His wit and wisdom were great to have around too.

Asked if he ever saw Landry smile, Garrison said, "No. But I was only there nine years."

As for the mental side of the game, he observed: "Psychology has won very few football games. Football is still blocking and tackling. If it was a game of psychology, psychologists would play the game. Instead of Dick Butkus, you'd have Dr. Joyce Brothers at middle linebacker."

No wonder Garrison got along so well with Don Meredith. Fittingly, Dandy Don had the ultimate zinger in describing his pal's playing style:

"If it was third down and you needed four yards, if you'd get the ball to Walt Garrison he'd get you five," Meredith said. "And if was third down and you needed 20 yards, if you'd get the ball to Walt Garrison, by God, he'd get you five."

Walter Iooss Jr./Sports Illustrated/Getty Images

CHAPTER 4

THE ROGER STAUBACH ERA, PART II

AMERICA'S TEAM: 1975–1979

Coach Tom Landry and the Dallas Cowboys headed into the second half of the 1970s looking to dominate. By the time the decade was over, the 'Boys would add three more Super Bowl trips and one championship ring to their credentials—and the label "America's Team." *Focus on Sport/ Getty Images*

The Dallas Cowboys were preparing to launch the defining years of the franchise's history. They just had no idea it was coming.

How could they?

Tex Schramm and Tom Landry were rebuilding for the first time. Sure, they'd already taken the club from start-up to contender, then from contender to elite team, and then pulled off the feat that might be hardest of all: staying near the top. So there was reason to believe in them. But, still, rebuilding was a new challenge, one that some franchises never figure out.

POLISHING THE STAR

RING OF HONOR STARTS WITH "MR. COWBOY"

On November 23, 1975, Bob Lilly pulled on his No. 74 jersey for the final time.

Lilly actually had retired months before, but he was back on the field of Texas Stadium for "Bob Lilly Day," one last chance for fans, players, and the folks who ran the organization to show their appreciation for the man who will forever be known as "Mr. Cowboy."

During halftime of a game against the Philadelphia Eagles, Lilly was driven around the field in a convertible for a well-earned victory lap. Then he received a station wagon, a shotgun, and a hunting dog. He also received a college scholarship fund for his four kids. Then, a curtain was pulled and Lilly's name, jersey number (74), and years of service (1961–1974) were displayed, permanently posted on the wall inside Texas Stadium.

With that, the Ring of Honor was born.

The membership has grown but has remained pretty exclusive, prompting plenty of debate. Only one person has any say, however. First, it was owner Tex Schramm, who came up with the idea; since 1989, Jerry Jones has served as the lone arbiter.

When the Cowboys moved into their new stadium in 2009, the Ring of Honor came too, of course.

Lilly's favorite part of being in this club is being on the welcoming committee, taking part in the ceremony every time their fraternity adds a member.

"The Cowboys have had so many other fine players through the years," he said, "I figure my job has no end."

Bob Lilly Day at Texas Stadium, November 23, 1975.
The Dallas Morning News

Then again, the Cowboys really had no choice. After missing the playoffs for the first time in a decade, they took a hard look at the roster and realized many of the guys who lifted the franchise were either retired or past their prime. It was time for a new group to take over.

Nothing emphasized the out-with-the-old, in-with-the-new concept more than the departure of Bob Lilly. The Cowboys hadn't played a game without "Mr. Cowboy" since 1960. Considering they went 0–11–1 that season, they literally had never won a game without him.

Cornell Green and Walt Garrison also retired. Bob Hayes was traded to San Francisco, and John Niland was sent to Philadelphia. All had been starters on the 1971 championship team, and all were

77

now gone. So was Calvin Hill, the team's leading rusher each of the last three seasons, headed to the World Football League.

The 1975 makeover began with the draft, a class that would become known as "The Dirty Dozen" because 12 of them made the club. That infusion of youth and talent laid the foundation for restoring the Cowboys as a championship-caliber club. If that had been all they accomplished, it would've been one heck of a rebuilding job. But this group pulled off something even more enduring.

They turned the Dallas Cowboys into "America's Team."

THE DIRTY DOZEN, THE SHOTGUN, AND THE HAIL MARY

There's something to be said about low expectations. It gives a team the leeway to take some risks, things like keeping 12 rookies and trying something radical on offense.

A youth movement was expected this season, but not this many new kids. For all the praise for Dallas' computerized scouting system and Schramm's drafting prowess, the Cowboys had never kept more than nine draft picks, and they kept that many only once. Normally, six picks made the team.

But in 1975, the first 10 guys Dallas took made the roster, as did two more late-round picks. The group was dubbed "The Dirty Dozen," a moniker they were so proud of that around midseason they all grew beards to really dirty themselves up. "They," by the way, were defensive lineman Randy White, linebacker Thomas "Hollywood" Henderson, guard Burton Lawless, linebacker Bob Breunig, offensive lineman Pat Donovan, defensive back Randy Hughes, center Kyle Davis, defensive back Roland Woolsey, linebacker Mike Hegman, punter Mitch Hoopes, guard Herb Scott, and running back Scott Laidlaw.

The infusion of fresh blood changed things right away. In training camp, Landry said this was the hardest-hitting team he could remember.

"You can hear the pads popping all the way to the other field," he said.

Also in training camp, Landry started working on his new offensive wrinkle, something he called the "spread" and fans would call the "shotgun." In fact, it wasn't all that new.

Cowboys scout Red Hickey had used the scheme with great success as coach of the San Francisco 49ers in the early 1960s. A bad stretch of games cost him his job and turned the shotgun into kryptonite for NFL coaches. They wouldn't touch it.

The premise is simple: On obvious passing downs, the quarterback takes the snap five to seven yards behind the center. By not having to drop back, he has more time to look around and has a better view of how the play is unfolding.

Landry wanted Don Meredith to use it in the 1960s, but Meredith never felt comfortable. When Landry dusted off the idea and presented it to Staubach, he bought into it right away. Why not? After getting sacked a league-high 45 times the previous season, and 43 the year before that, Staubach probably was willing to try anything.

Close to the season opener, Landry was still trying to decide what to do at running back.

Without Hill and Garrison, Dallas was missing guys who had combined for nearly 300 carries and 1,300 yards in 1974. Holdover Robert Newhouse and rookie Doug Dennison could handle much of the load, but the Cowboys still needed a third back,

Billy Joe DuPree's end-zone reception on a short pass from Roger Staubach brought Dallas a dramatic 37–31 overtime win against the St. Louis Cardinals in Week 2 of the 1975 season. The win over the division rival got the Cowboys off to a 2–0 start. *Fred Kaufman/AP Images*

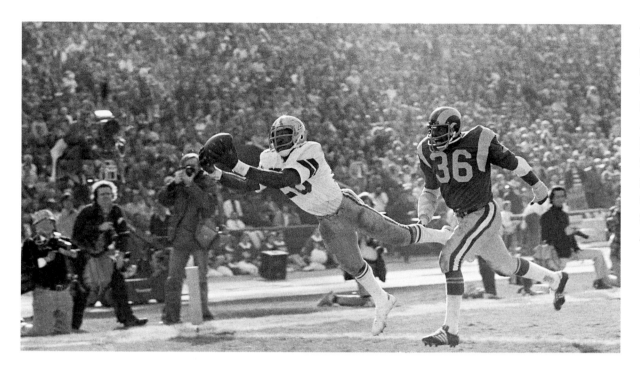

The Cowboys earned their third Super Bowl trip with a 37–7 win against the Los Angeles Rams in the NFC Conference Finals on January 4, 1976. Preston Pearson caught three touchdown passes in the game, including this diving catch in the second quarter to put Dallas ahead 21–0. *AP Images*

a fast guy with good hands. Then, voila, Pittsburgh waived Preston Pearson, and the Cowboys gladly claimed him.

Dallas started the season 4–0, and Landry was feeling pretty good about how quickly this rebuilding thing was falling into place. Then came a midseason stumble, followed by another roll at the end. The Cowboys finished 10–4, good enough for second place in the NFC East and a wild-card berth in the playoffs. They headed to Minnesota for a frigid afternoon game against NFL MVP Fran Tarkenton and the dominant Purple People Eaters defense.

The Vikings were the reigning NFC champs and winners of 11 straight at home. Bud Grant's club already had been to the Super Bowl three times (and lost them all), but folks were calling this team Minnesota's best ever.

After Tarkenton mounted a late drive to put the Vikings up 14–10, the Minnesota defense forced Dallas into fourth-and-long deep in their own territory with less than a minute left. A pass to Drew Pearson got Dallas to midfield, but time was running out, and the end zone was still 50 yards away.

On second down, Staubach threw deep to Drew Pearson. Real deep. There was a lot of contact as Pearson and cornerback Nate Wright went up for

the ball, but Pearson somehow managed to snag it. He didn't catch the pass so much as pin it to his body. Wright fell to the ground, and Pearson walked the last few feet into the end zone for the winning touchdown. Staubach later joked about having said a "Hail Mary" before throwing the pass. The term quickly became part of the sport's lexicon. (See page 80.)

Now the Cowboys were being called a Cinderella team. Landry was getting credit for one of his best coaching jobs. And everyone figured the story would end the following week against the Rams.

The Rams sure thought so.

It's easy now to say the Rams were cocky and overconfident, but think of it from their perspective. They'd lost only twice all season—to the Cowboys back in the opener when the shotgun gimmick was sprung on them, and by a single point to San Francisco eight weeks ago. Plus, Dallas needed the fluke of all flukes just to get this far. How could the Cowboys stop them?

Here's how: By Staubach throwing four touchdown passes, three to Preston Pearson, and the Cowboys scoring the first 34 points on the way to a 37–7 victory. This Dallas team that was supposed to struggle in 1975, or maybe even continue a slide that had begun the previous year, instead was going to its third Super Bowl.

GAME TO REMEMBER
THE "HAIL MARY"

MINNEAPOLIS, MINNESOTA – The crowd started heading for the exits. It was cold, and the hometown Vikings were ahead 14–10 with less than a minute left and Dallas facing fourth-and-17 from the 25-yard-line.

What could possibly go wrong? Minnesota fans thought.

Roger Staubach kept hope alive for the Cowboys by hitting Drew Pearson heading toward the right sideline. He was pushed out of bounds at the 50, a call Vikings fan still think was wrong.

Pearson had been held without a catch until this drive, and this was his third of the series. But that wasn't why he was gasping for air in the huddle. The lack of breath came from a kick to the ribs by a sideline security guard Pearson happened to roll up against after that drive-extending catch. On the next play, Staubach looked to the usually sure-handed Preston Pearson. He dropped it.

If there was ever a good drop, this was it, because Pearson was in the middle of the field far from the end zone. Dallas was out of timeouts, so the clock likely would have run out had he been tackled. Now the Cowboys had 24 seconds left and at least one more shot.

In the huddle, Staubach reminded Drew Pearson of a route they'd used in a similar situation against the Redskins the previous Thanksgiving. It was a simple deep route up the right sideline but with a juke inside to, hopefully, get some space from the defender.

Pearson ran it perfectly. Staubach almost flubbed it.

From the shotgun, Staubach looked left and pumped the ball, another stunt to try keeping the defense guessing wrong. But Staubach pumped so hard that the ball almost squirted out of his hand. His poor grip caused him to underthrow his pass, a heave down the right sideline.

Pearson had to slow down to make sure he didn't overrun it. He and cornerback Nate Wright went up for the ball together around the 5-yard line and collided in the air. Wright fell to the grass while the ball went through Pearson's arms. He was sure he had missed it.

Somehow, he didn't.

The ball nestled between Pearson's right elbow and hip. Realizing his good fortune, Pearson took the last few steps into the end zone, then the former college quarterback triumphantly hurled the ball into the stands.

To this day, the Vikings and their fans insist that Pearson should have been called for pass interference. On that day, Vikings star Alan Page drew a 15-yard unsportsmanlike-conduct penalty for complaining. Field judge Armen Terzian was knocked unconscious by a whiskey bottle thrown from the stands—and he wasn't even the one who called it a touchdown. That was linesman Jerry Bergman. Minnesota coach Bud Grant later reminded everyone about a controversial call Bergman had made in the fourth quarter of a Miami–Buffalo game a few weeks earlier.

The quote to come from that game, however, was Staubach's description of the winning pass: "I closed my eyes and said a Hail Mary."

Ever since, last-minute, long-shot bids for victory have been known as Hail Mary attempts.

Drew Pearson heads into the end zone for a touchdown as Minnesota safety Paul Krause leaps over the fallen Nate Wright. *AP Images*

In a battle between the decade's two great dynasties, the Cowboys took on the defending-champion Steelers in Super Bowl X at the Orange Bowl in Miami on January 18, 1976. *Focus on Sport/ Getty Images*

SUPER BOWL X
PITTSBURGH STEELERS 21,
DALLAS COWBOYS 17

MIAMI, FLORIDA – Nobody gave the Dallas Cowboys much of a chance to win this matchup with the reigning-champion Pittsburgh Steelers.

Then Roger Staubach threw a 29-yard touchdown pass to Drew Pearson, and for the first time all season, the Steelers had given up points in the first quarter. Suddenly they realized this was not going to be an easy coronation.

Pittsburgh soon tied it at seven with a drive boosted by one of the greatest catches in Super Bowl history—Lynn Swann reaching over cornerback Mark Washington as the two fell to the ground, the Pittsburgh receiver somehow tipping the ball to himself and grabbing it as he landed.

The Cowboys moved back ahead 10–7 at halftime, and that was still the score when the fourth quarter began.

Could Dallas really pull out another stunner?

The answer came quickly, and it wasn't a good one for the guys with the stars on their helmets.

Pittsburgh blocked a punt out of the end zone for a safety, then added a pair of field goals. When Terry Bradshaw threw a 64-yard touchdown pass to Swann, the Steelers' lead jumped to 21–10.

Defensive tackle Larry Cole knocked Bradshaw out on that play, which meant Pittsburgh was probably done scoring. And these were the never-count-'em-out Cowboys, with "Captain Comeback" in charge.

When Staubach answered with a touchdown pass that made it 21–17 with 1:48 left, chests tightened on both sidelines. An onside kick failed, but a defensive stand put the ball back in Staubach's hands 61 yards from the go-ahead score with 1:22 left on the clock.

Alas, Staubach was out of fancy finishes. He moved the ball a little, but not enough.

The Steelers held on for a victory, but the seeds for a rivalry were planted.

AP Images

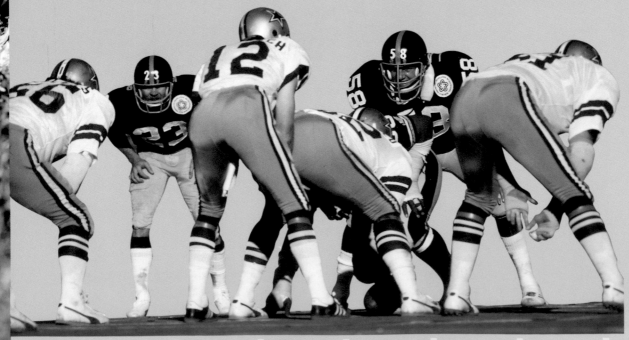

Vernon Biever/NFL/
Getty Images

Super Bowl X was held in Miami, the big game's first time back there since Super Bowl V, when Dallas lost.

The Pittsburgh Steelers came in as the reigning champs looking for more. The Cowboys were the plucky overachievers who couldn't be counted out. They kept it close going into the fourth quarter, preventing a blowout win for Pittsburgh like everyone expected, but lost 21–17.

While that was disappointing, the season was a huge success.

The Cowboys were back.

BICENTENNIAL TEASE

There was so much to look forward to in 1976.

After all, if the Cowboys could get within a few yards of a championship during what was supposed to be a rebuilding year, they might really be something with another year of fine-tuning.

They started out 9–1, with tight end Billy Joe DuPree dropping the would-be-winning touchdown in the end zone as time ran out in that lone loss. Roger Staubach and the Cowboys finished the season 11–3, NFC East champs once again.

But there were all sorts of problems.

The running game was a mess. The committee of Robert Newhouse, Preston Pearson, and Doug Dennison that worked so well in 1975 was nowhere near as productive, mainly because Pearson and Newhouse got hurt.

All-Pro tackle Rayfield Wright and defensive tackle Jethro Pugh were playing in pain.

Then, during the game against the Bears in Week 7, someone stepped on Staubach's passing hand, and he hurt it again the next week. He was never the same, a real shame because he was having the best year of his already superb career. Over the first six games, Staubach completed 67 percent of his passes; he wouldn't top 57 percent in a single game the rest of the way.

The defense made the division title possible. They were so tough, the offense usually needed only to score a touchdown or two.

Then came the playoffs, and an opener against a strong Rams team seeking revenge for the previous year's NFC Championship Game.

In 1975, Staubach's poise, leadership, and talent made all the difference in the playoffs. But in 1976, a banged-up Staubach couldn't do it, especially without a reliable running game. The Cowboys lost 14–12, with several questionable calls going against them.

For all that was right about this club, it was too flawed to provide the thrills of 1975.

But at least everyone knew what was wrong and how to fix it.

HELLO, TONY; HELLO, TITLE

The hole the Cowboys needed to fill heading into the 1977 season was at running back. Free agency was more than a decade away, so the only way to fill a need was through a trade or the draft.

Tex Schramm did both, trading up for a better spot in the draft.

The 1977 draft wasn't particularly deep at running back, but there were two great ones at the top of the class: Ricky Bell and Tony Dorsett.

Dorsett, from the University of Pittsburgh, had won the Heisman Trophy, had set the NCAA career rushing record, and was considered by most to be the better NFL prospect. But Bell had played for Southern California under coach John McKay, until McKay went to start the Tampa Bay franchise. The Buccaneers didn't win a single game that first season,

The Cowboys started the 1976 season going 9–1, including a 20–7 win over the Redskins. Staubach also got off to a strong start, but midseason injuries slowed him down, and despite an 11–3 record, the season came to a disappointing finish with an early playoff loss. *Nate Fine/NFL Photos/ Getty Images*

THOMAS "HOLLYWOOD" HENDERSON

Of all the books written about all the teams and players in Cowboys history, the most appropriate title belongs to the autobiography of Thomas "Hollywood" Henderson: *Out of Control: Confessions of an NFL Casualty*.

Henderson was among the most athletic players and most outrageous personalities the team ever saw. Imagine a blend of Don Meredith and Duane Thomas, and that was only when he was sober.

Tom Landry recognized what a rare breed Henderson was—a linebacker who returned kickoffs and celebrated touchdowns by dunking the ball over the crossbar, which is why he tolerated Henderson's flamboyance.

Landry used Henderson mostly on passing downs in 1975 and 1976, then made him a starter in 1977. Dallas won the Super Bowl that season and returned to the big game in 1978, with Henderson having a Pro Bowl season.

The better he played, the more outrageous he became. There was the famous line questioning Terry Bradshaw's intelligence ("The guy couldn't spell 'cat' if you spotted him the 'c' and the 'a.'") and his arrival at a training camp in a limousine.

Then, Henderson flamed out.

In 1979, as his drug addiction began to overwhelm his life, he missed meetings and begged out of practices, claiming he was hurt. He played an entire game against Washington without a single tackle yet was seen clowning around on the sideline. That did it. Henderson had become more trouble than he was worth, so Landry cut him—or, according to Henderson, he retired to go off to Hollywood and become a movie star.

Life without football was rough, especially for an addict. He was accused of holding a gun while sexually assaulting two women, one of them bound to a wheelchair. The court sent him to drug rehabilitation, then to prison. Henderson likes to say that "Hollywood" died November 8, 1983.

Except, there really is a Hollywood-esque ending to his story.

After prison, Henderson repaired his relationships with Landry and his former teammates. Then, in 2000, he won a $28 million jackpot in the Texas Lottery.

In 2004, he released another book: *In Control: The Rebirth of an NFL Legend*.

AP Images

so McKay owned the top pick in the draft. And he wanted his guy, Bell.

That was good news for Seattle, the other newcomer in 1976, which owned the No. 2 pick. However, Dorsett made it clear he didn't want to play there, so the Seahawks were taking trade offers.

Sly as ever, Schramm comforted the Seattle folks by telling them about the troubles he'd had building his franchise from scratch. He recommended they go for quantity over quality—as in, the four draft picks he was offering (a first-rounder and three more in the second round) for the No. 2 pick. They bought it.

Dorsett might have been the missing piece for Dallas, but he wasn't the only change.

There were new starters on the right side of the offensive line, with Tom Rafferty and Pat Donovan replacing Blaine Nye (retired) and Rayfield Wright (hurt). That was nothing compared to the turnover on defense.

Lee Roy Jordan retired, creating a rare vacancy at Landry's treasured spot of middle linebacker. Landry wanted Randy White to have it, but his skills just weren't suited for it. Instead, there was a ripple effect: Bob Breunig slid over from the strong side to the middle, and Thomas "Hollywood" Henderson went from backup on the weak side to replacing Breunig on the strong side. White claimed Bob Lilly's old spot (weak side defensive tackle), and Aaron Kyle took over at right cornerback, bumping Mel Renfro into a role off the bench.

Four new starters is a lot for a defense, especially one that had been so solid. But there was something else at work here—another youth movement.

White and Henderson were part of the amazing 1975 draft class, and Kyle was the top pick in 1976. The unit was getting younger and, it turned out, better.

The offense got younger too. Donovan was part of the 1975 draft, and Rafferty was picked the following year. Butch Johnson, also from the class of 1976, had been a dazzling punt returner as a rookie and began seeing more action at receiver. Fans looked forward to his trips to the end zone because he would pretend to pull out six-shooters and fire off a few rounds as part of his "California Quake" celebration dance.

The mix of young and old blended so well that as the Cowboys rolled to an 8–0 record, there was talk about whether they might go undefeated. That ended with a sloppy 24–17 loss at home to St. Louis.

The next week, Dallas played Pittsburgh for the first time since Super Bowl X. It was in Pittsburgh, Dorsett's hometown. Up to that point, Preston Pearson had been starting, both to let the rookie know nothing would be handed to him, and because Landry worried that Dorsett was too small to handle the punishment of being an every-down back. He wanted to preserve Dorsett, making sure he would have him later in the season and in future seasons.

Yet, under these circumstances, Landry let the kid make his first career start and, for the first time, used him the entire game. Pittsburgh's Franco Harris, however, turned out to be the best running back on the field that day, shredding Dallas' top-ranked defense for 179 yards, the most he would ever gain in a single game during his Hall of Fame career.

The Cowboys headed home with a two-game skid and only a one-game lead in the division. They

Preston Pearson helped the Cowboys to a 16–10 win over the Vikings in the 1977 opener, but his days as the team's top running threat were numbered, with rookie Tony Dorsett waiting in the wings. *Heinz Kluetmeier/Sports Illustrated/Getty Images*

bounced back with a victory over Washington, however, and were back in a groove.

They won the last four games of the regular season to finish at 12–2, matching the best record in team history. Many individual accolades came too.

Harvey Martin thrashed his way to a club-record 23 sacks and was named the NFL's defensive player of the year. Starting opposite Ed "Too Tall" Jones, Martin earned the moniker "Too Mean"—something no quarterback would've disagreed with, certainly not to his face. As a unit, the defense was bestowed the name "Doomsday II."

Dorsett became the club's first rookie to crack 1,000 yards and was named the Rookie of the Year. On one memorable afternoon against the Eagles, he ran for a club-record 206 yards, including an 84-yard touchdown, another club record. But it wasn't all smooth, with Dorsett itching to play more. Dorsett's workload would always be a point of contention with Landry, like Staubach wanting to call his own plays.

As good as the regular season was, it was just a warm-up for the postseason.

In the first playoff game, Charlie Waters intercepted three passes, and the Cowboys dominated the

clock so easily that Staubach threw only 13 passes on the way to a 37–7 victory over NFL MVP Walter Payton and the Chicago Bears.

Next up was an NFC Championship Game showdown with Minnesota. It was the first postseason meeting between these teams since the "Hail Mary" game in 1975, and this time a Super Bowl trip was on the line.

The Cowboys were trying to match the Vikings' record of appearing in four Super Bowls, while Minnesota was aiming to make it five. But the Vikings, playing without star quarterback Fran Tarkenton, put up little resistance. The Cowboys won 23–6 and were headed to New Orleans, site of the franchise's first Super Bowl championship.

A rematch with Pittsburgh would have been great, but the Steelers couldn't make it. Instead, the Denver Broncos were there, offering the unusual plot twist of a familiar foe leading the opposition.

Craig Morton had once been Staubach's foil in Dallas, the guy who replaced Don Meredith and got the start in the team's first Super Bowl appearance. Staubach always managed to get the upper hand with Morton when both were on the Cowboys, such as bringing home Dallas' first Super Bowl triumph. Now, they were dueling in the biggest battle of all.

Morton was in his first season in Denver and was as much the Broncos' missing ingredient as Dorsett had been for Dallas. The Broncos scored the most points in the NFL, then advanced to their first Super Bowl by going through the last two Super Bowl champs—the Steelers and the Oakland Raiders. Morton had plenty of help too, especially from a defensive unit that answered to the nickname "Orange Crush."

The Cowboys crushed them, however, winning 27–10 for their second title.

Dallas wasn't the first two-time Super Bowl champion, but it was the first to go so many years (six) between titles. The roster had changed a lot in between, with only three players starting both Super Bowl victories, something no other two-time champion had done. It was further testament to the greatness of Landry and Staubach, the two main conduits between the title teams.

Now, everyone was ready for more.

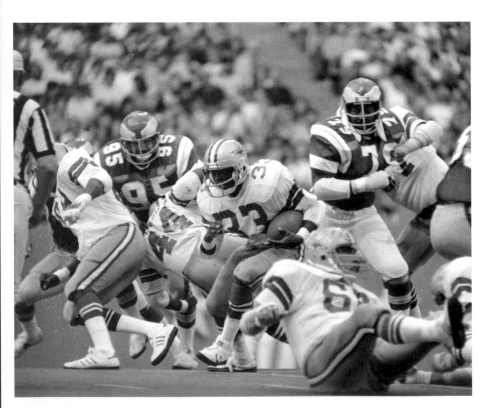

Rookie Tony Dorsett put his value to the team on full display against Philadelphia on December 4, when he ran for 206 yards, including this 84-yard touchdown run—both team records.
Joe Caneva/AP Images

SUPER BOWL XII
DALLAS COWBOYS 27,
DENVER BRONCOS 10

New Orleans, Louisiana – The Dallas Cowboys nearly blew the lid off the first indoor Super Bowl.

Playing inside the Superdome, the Cowboys jumped all over the Denver Broncos in the first half. Denver was lucky to be trailing only 13–0 after the opening 30 minutes.

The Broncos finally scored in the third quarter, but it was only a field goal. The Cowboys answered with a 45-yard touchdown pass that Butch Johnson *probably* caught without letting the ball bounce. The refs said he did, and that's all that mattered.

Then Denver scored a touchdown to make it 20–10. If this game was going to turn, it was going to happen now.

So, how did Tom Landry—the epitome of cool, calm, and collected—respond? He let fullback Robert Newhouse throw a pass. Golden Richards caught it in the end zone for the game-sealing score.

Newhouse's throw covered 29 yards, which is noteworthy because Denver's starting quarterback Craig Morton (who had been Dallas' starting quarterback in Super Bowl V) threw for only 39 yards all game.

Morton completed four passes to his current team and four to guys on his old team. Between how badly he was playing and how badly the Cowboys were beating him up, Morton also suffered the humiliation of getting benched.

Landry called this his "very best team overall," and it's hard to argue considering how easily they won the Super Bowl on a day when Dorsett ran for only 66 yards and Drew Pearson caught only one pass for a measly 13 yards.

Dallas didn't need big offensive numbers because it was the defense that led the way.

The Cowboys out-crushed Denver's vaunted "Orange Crush" so well that both Randy White and Harvey Martin were named the game's MVPs, the first and still only time the honor has been shared.

Butch Johnson's diving, tumbling catch helped extend Dallas' lead in the third quarter of Super Bowl XII. *Tony Tomsic/Getty Images*

ROGER STAUBACH

The first time Roger Staubach played football in Dallas, his 0-0 Navy team lost to SMU.

The second time he came to Big D, he'd won the Heisman Trophy and guided his team to No. 2 and a berth in the Cotton Bowl. They lost to Texas.

So the locals weren't necessarily all that impressed when the Cowboys drafted Staubach a few months later.

Eventually, they'd be smitten. All football fans would be.

Staubach was Dallas' primary quarterback for only eight seasons, but in those eight seasons the Cowboys never finished with a losing record, and they appeared in four Super Bowls. He won it all twice and lost the others by four points each.

The way he won was spectacular too—with style and flair, cunning and guile, throwing and running.

Staubach was the top-rated quarterback in NFL history when he retired, walking away after two of his best seasons. And, of course, there were all those late rallies with "Captain Comeback" at the helm—23 fourth-quarter comebacks in all, 14 in the final two minutes of regulation or in overtime.

"Roger Staubach might be the best combination of a passer, an athlete, and a leader ever to play in the NFL," Tom Landry said.

Staubach titled his 1980 autobiography *Time Enough to Win* because he never gave up in any competition. He carried

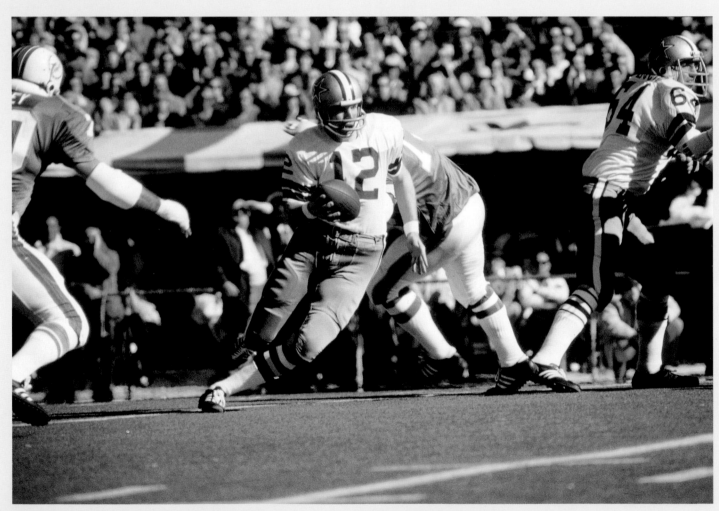

Staubach scrambles for yardage in Super Bowl VI, January 1972. *Vernon Biever/NFL/Getty Images*

that attitude into the business world; in 2008, the real-estate company he started was sold for $618 million. He also was the QB of Dallas' winning bid to host the 2011 Super Bowl in its new stadium.

"If somebody did 100 situps, Roger was going to do 101," running back Walt Garrison said. "If somebody ran a mile in six minutes, Roger would do it in 5:59. If somebody threw the ball 60 yards, he was going to throw it 61."

Staubach's path from Annapolis, Maryland, to Dallas had several twists.

After the Cowboys drafted Staubach, Chiefs owner Lamar Hunt got his AFL rights and showed up at the Naval Academy with a contract that included a signing bonus and a salary that would pay him while he was on active duty, plus another bonus for joining the team once he fulfilled his obligation.

Staubach wanted to play in the NFL because that was the dominant league, but he hadn't gotten an offer from the Cowboys. An assistant basketball coach at Navy called his buddy Gil Brandt to let him know about the Chiefs' offer. The Cowboys happened to be in Philadelphia the same weekend as the Army–Navy game, so Brandt set up a meeting that led to a signed contract.

Color blindness limited Staubach's options in the Navy, but he still worked his way up. He spent one of his four years in Vietnam overseeing more than 100 enlisted men and about 30 Vietnamese at a supply base.

Brandt sent Staubach care packages with films to watch and footballs to throw. In 1968, Staubach took two weeks' leave and headed to Cowboys training camp for a grand experiment.

"During those two weeks," Staubach said, "I made up my mind to quit the Navy after my commitment and try to play for the Cowboys."

Lieutenant (j.g.) Roger Staubach, U.S.N. (ret.) was the antithesis of Seth Maxwell, the carousing quarterback in *North Dallas Forty*. His straight-arrow personal life, contrasted with his derring-do on the field, was another part of his popularity.

Focus on Sport/Getty Images

"He's going to ruin the image of an NFL quarterback if he doesn't start smoking, drinking, cussing or something," said Don Meredith, the real inspiration for Seth Maxwell.

Bob St. John wrote in *The Dallas Morning News*, "His idea of breaking training is putting whipped cream on his pie."

Staubach thought his reputation went overboard. He tried setting the record straight in 1975, telling CBS' Phyllis George, "I enjoy sex as much as Joe Namath. Only I do it with one girl."

Then there was the time Staubach got tired of waiting while Tex Schramm was on the phone, looking out the window of his eleventh-floor office. Staubach jumped out another window and onto a three-foot-wide ledge in front of Schramm's window.

"He dropped the phone and his eyes rolled back in his head," Staubach said. "I thought maybe I'd scared him into a stroke. Anyway, he sat up and kind of shook himself all over and flagged me to come in."

When Staubach retired, NFL Films put out a show dedicated strictly to his career. Nowadays, it seems like an obvious tribute. But in 1980, it was the first time it had ever been done.

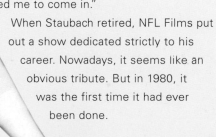

Tony Tomsic/NFL/Getty Images

Champions again! Tom Landry is carried off the field after leading the Cowboys to a 27–10 triumph in Super Bowl XII. *Heinz Kluetmeier/Sports Illustrated/Getty Images*

PAYBACK SLIPS THROUGH SMITH'S HANDS

The Cowboys were on top of the world and ready to stay there.

The only lineup changes in 1978 appeared to be improvements: Tony Dorsett's ascension to the role of featured running back, Rayfield Wright returning at right tackle, and second-year receiver Tony Hill claiming the spot opposite Drew Pearson. Doomsday II remained pretty much intact.

A 38–0 romp over the Colts in the opener sent a heck of a message to the league. Yet, in November, the Cowboys were a mediocre 6–4.

It was, quite simply, a Super Bowl hangover.

Tom Landry and Roger Staubach helped keep everyone calm by pointing out that Dallas had been 5–4 and 4–3 in seasons that ended with Super Bowl trips. Plus, this was the first year of the 16-game season, which meant Landry had two more games to work out the kinks.

Sure enough, the Cowboys snapped out of their funk and didn't lose again, finishing 12–4 and putting up their usual dazzling numbers: scoring the most points in the league and allowing the second-fewest. Staubach was the NFL's top-rated passer, and Dorsett ran for the third-most yards. Dorsett would have had more if he'd been on time for a midseason game against Philadelphia; instead, Landry left him on the bench most of the day, giving him only seven carries and a lesson in responsibility.

Not only was the regular season longer, the play-offs were too. An extra round was added, along with a first-round bye for division champs, which included Dallas. Maybe the time off left the Cowboys a little rusty because they trailed the Falcons 20–13 at half-time of their first playoff game. They looked to be in far bigger trouble when the "Grits Blitz" defense knocked out Staubach. But backup Danny White stepped in and pulled out a 27–20 victory.

Then the Cowboys headed to Los Angeles for another NFC Championship Game.

At halftime, Dallas hadn't allowed a point but hadn't scored any either. An interception by Charlie Waters led to the first touchdown, then a fourth-down stop deep in Cowboys territory kept the Rams from answering. That pretty much did it. Dallas broke loose for a 28–0 win and an unprecedented fifth trip to the Super Bowl.

Anyone who is superstitious had plenty to worry about. The game was in Miami, site of Dallas' previous two Super Bowl losses. And it was Super Bowl XIII—unlucky 13.

The Pittsburgh Steelers were back too, and perhaps better than ever. They went 14–2 in the regular season, led by their "Steel Curtain" defense and quarterback Terry Bradshaw, who was playing so well he was named the NFL's MVP.

This was a dream matchup—a pair of two-time champions who had already met in one thrilling Super Bowl just three years before. The game lived up to the hype.

The Steelers led 21–14 at halftime. The Cowboys had a chance to tie it up in the third quarter when a pass bounced off the chest of wide-open Jackie Smith in the end zone. Dallas settled for a field goal and was never tied or ahead again, but the Cowboys kept things close to the bitter end, losing 35–31.

Landry would never again get so close to winning it all.

Despite the disappointment, something good came out of this Super Bowl journey.

A few months later, as NFL Films was finishing off its annual highlight reel for the 1978 Cowboys, producer Bob Ryan was trying to come up with a title. He obviously couldn't use "Back-to-Back Champs" or "Three Rings." So he kept thinking.

Ryan noticed the Cowboys had a massive following everywhere they went, like the New York Yankees or Notre Dame football. They played in a nationally televised game nearly every week, and their roster was a collection of big-name stars. They were, he decided, "America's Team."

Fullback Robert Newhouse led the Cowboys with eight rushing touchdowns in 1978, and he joined Tony Dorsett, Tony Hill, Drew Pearson, and Billy Joe DuPree to form a versatile and dangerous offense in Dallas. *Fred Roe/NFL Photos/Getty Images*

A fatigued Harvey Martin waves a celebratory flag after Dallas dispatched the Los Angeles Rams, 28–0, in the NFC Championship Game on January 7, 1979. *Andy Hayt/Getty Images*

SUPER BOWL XIII
PITTSBURGH STEELERS 35,
DALLAS COWBOYS 31

Mike Hegman's 37-yard touchdown run on a fumble recovery early in the second quarter gave Dallas a 14–10 lead in Super Bowl XIII—but it didn't last long. *Focus on Sport/Getty Images*

MIAMI, FLORIDA – It was a publicist's dream matchup: a pair of two-time champions trying to see which could become the first three-time champ, and a rematch of what many considered the best Super Bowl yet. That clash was only three years earlier, so it was still fresh in everyone's minds, and many of the star players were the same. Both teams came away from that game not liking each other very much, and their fans didn't particularly care for each other, either.

It was also a contrast in images: The glitzy Cowboys with their coast-to-coast followers, sexy cheerleaders, and status as reigning Super Bowl champs against the guys from the Steel City, a working-man's team from a working-man's town, with a toothless linebacker, a supposedly dumb quarterback, and a little yellow towel that served as the team's rallying cry.

In the days before the game, Thomas "Hollywood" Henderson, always looking to draw some attention to himself, stirred the pot by offering this quip about Terry Bradshaw: "The guy couldn't spell 'cat' if you spotted him the 'c' and the 'a.'" *Newsweek* magazine put the two of them on the cover, while *Time* did an article about Staubach and Bradshaw.

On game day, the Cowboys got off to a slow start—from their hotel. The team bus was late getting to the Orange Bowl because of traffic, unyielding security guards, and Steelers fans who blocked roads and rocked the bus.

The game itself didn't start so great, either.

Bradshaw threw for 253 yards, more than anyone had ever thrown for in a Super Bowl—and that was just in the first half. It included a 75-yard touchdown pass to John Stallworth and several ballet-like receptions by Lynn Swann, just like he'd done the last time these teams met in a Super Bowl.

But Bradshaw also made some mistakes. He had a fumble that led to Dallas' first touchdown, then he fumbled again when sandwiched by Henderson and Mike Hegman. Hegman plucked the ball away and ran it in for a touchdown. Pittsburgh led just 21–14 at halftime.

Then came the third quarter and the play everyone remembers—the one all Cowboys fans wish they could forget.

Third-and-3 from the Pittsburgh 10. Staubach gets the play from the sideline, then calls timeout to make sure this is really what Landry wants to do.

It was a three-tight-end formation, typically used for goal-line situations. The Cowboys weren't at the goal line. Landry said he wanted to run it anyway to get the few yards needed for the first down and hopefully more.

Tony Dorsett went in motion, and Staubach faked a handoff to Scott Laidlaw. At this point, Landry's offense was going to zig when counterpart Chuck Noll's defense was going to zag. Win enough of these kinds of chess matches and you win championships—provided, of course, the players do what they're supposed to do.

Given plenty of time by the offensive line, Staubach saw Jackie Smith wide open in the middle of the end zone. The pass was a little low and a bit behind Smith, but with no defender around, he saw it all the way. Smith stumbled as he slowed, then went down to catch it . . . and didn't. The ball clanged off his chest, right between the 8 and 1 on his jersey.

"Oh, bless his heart, he's *got* to be the sickest man in America," Cowboys announcer Verne Lundquist said on the radio broadcast.

Staubach often defends Smith by saying the line of scrimmage being at the 10-yard line instead of the goal line threw the tight end's route out of whack. Staubach also points out that the throw wasn't perfect, slower than Smith expected and with a bit of a wobble to it. But anyone who has seen the replays has trouble buying any of it. The drop is even more agonizing when

you consider that Smith held the NFL career record for catches by a tight end. And he was *wide open*.

Here's where reality and memories often collide.

Folks tend to believe that Smith's catch came in the fourth quarter, not the third, and that it would have put the Cowboys ahead or even sealed a victory. It only would have tied the score, and there were more than 17 minutes left to play.

Still, the momentum of the game changed. All the Cowboys got out of the drive was a field goal that put them within 21–17.

Bradshaw knew Pittsburgh was lucky to still be ahead, and he soon broke the game open. The Steelers scored two touchdowns in a span of 19 seconds, aided by a 33-yard pass-interference call on Dallas' Benny Barnes that replays show was more Swann's fault, as well as a fumbled kickoff return.

Trailing 35–17, Staubach still had about seven minutes to pull this one out.

He moved Dallas 89 yards in eight plays, capping it with a TD toss to Billy Joe DuPree. Everyone knew an onside kick was coming, yet Cowboys rookie Dennis Thurman still recovered it. Then Staubach hit Butch Johnson for a touchdown with 22 seconds left.

Hmmm.

Dallas tried another onside kick. This time, the Steelers snagged it. The most exciting Super Bowl yet was over.

Pittsburgh was back on top of the NFL, the first three-time champs, and Dallas joined Minnesota as three-time runners-up.

Smith would never play another game, but he eventually made the Pro Football Hall of Fame, his great days with the St. Louis Cardinals not trumped by this one flub, no matter how much Cowboys fans might disagree.

Jackie Smith. *Walter Iooss Jr./ Sports Illustrated/Getty Images*

The agony of defeat. Coach Landry reacts after a wide-open Jackie Smith dropped a pass in the end zone during the third quarter of Super Bowl XIII, in what proved to be Landry's last trip to the championship game. *AP Images*

Oilers running back Earl Campbell torched the Cowboys for 195 rushing yards in Houston's 30–24 win on Thanksgiving Day 1979. It was a heartbreaking defeat to their in-state rivals. *John Iacono/Sports Illustrated/Getty Images*

ROGER'S LAST HURRAH

Coming off two Super Bowls in a row and three in four years, the Dallas Cowboys were eager for more.

But this is pro football, a violent sport that takes a toll on even the youngest, healthiest players. Those who defy the odds and enjoy a long career still wake up one day and realize they can't do it anymore. Or maybe they just don't want to.

Jethro Pugh retired, and Rayfield Wright was on his last legs. Charlie Waters tore up a knee in a preseason game and was lost for the entire season. And Ed "Too Tall" Jones left after five seasons in pro football to start a new career—as a boxer.

At first, the Cowboys seemed deep enough and talented enough to overcome it all. They started 3–0, then 7–1. Then they went to Pittsburgh for a Super Bowl rematch—and, Dallas fans hoped, a Super Bowl preview.

It couldn't have gone worse. The Steel Curtain was pulled tightly shut, allowing just a field goal. It was the fewest points Dallas had scored since 1972, and it started a tailspin of four losses in five games, the club's worst stretch since 1965.

During this rough patch, Landry cut Thomas "Hollywood" Henderson, taking yet another once-reliable performer away from a defense already missing so many, although also ridding the club of a seriously troubled player. The remaining defenders were getting run over, consistently allowing 30 points or more.

The Cowboys bottomed out on Thanksgiving.

Holding a late lead over the Houston Oilers, Dallas was about to get the ball back when 12 men went on the field for a punt return. The penalty gave Houston a first down, and the Oilers finished the drive by scoring the winning points. The loss dropped the Cowboys to third place in the NFC East, and second in the Lone Star State.

"They may be America's Team," bragged Houston coach Bum Phillips, "but we're Texas' Team."

The post-Thanksgiving break provided some much-needed time off. A week later, the Cowboys got out some frustrations in a 28–7 win over the Giants, then they beat the Eagles in Philadelphia.

All that remained was the season finale at home against the Redskins.

BECOMING "AMERICA'S TEAM"

"America's Team" is not just a nickname for the Dallas Cowboys.

It's a blanket term that covers so many aspects of the team's image and enduring popularity, the way the term *Baby Boomers* is used for an entire generation of Americans.

So let's look at how it all came together.

It started on the field, of course, with a team that rose near the top pretty quickly but struggled to break through. People can identify with that. So once the Cowboys made it, folks were happy for them. The team sustained that success too, with every victory keeping that bandwagon rolling.

In an era long before ESPN and blogs, the Cowboys roster was filled with recognizable names and colorful personalities:

- Guys whose fame went beyond the sports pages, such as Roger Staubach, the Heisman Trophy winner and all-American boy who served in the Navy before joining the NFL; and Bob Hayes, "the world's fastest human," who charged from way behind to bring home the gold in the 400-meter relay at the 1964 Olympics.
- Characters like "Dandy" Don Meredith, whose fame grew when he moved into broadcasting; Walt Garrison, the Cowboys player who was a real cowboy; Duane Thomas, known as "The Sphinx" because he was so difficult to figure out; and Thomas "Hollywood" Henderson.
- Solid, standout players like Bob Lilly, Lee Roy Jordan, Rayfield Wright, and Cliff Harris.
- Coach Tom Landry, who was always one step ahead of the competition. He designed the 4–3 defense, and when most teams started using it, he came up with some offensive schemes to beat it.
- Tex Schramm, among the most powerful men in the NFL and one of the most successful, thanks to his revolutionary computerized scouting system and a knack for gambles that paid off.

Their home field, Texas Stadium, was special too, a state-of-the-art building that featured an enormous hole in the roof "so God can watch His team."

There even was something about their helmets—that classic blue star set against shiny silver. Simple, yet distinct.

And then there was the last bit of glitz: those lovely ladies, the Dallas Cowboys Cheerleaders.

Love 'em or hate 'em, people could not get enough of the Cowboys.

They were nationally televised more than anyone else because they were better and more popular. Their Super Bowl XII victory over Denver was the second-most-watched event in television history, ahead of *Gone with the Wind* and behind only the *Roots* finale. CBS had the Super Bowl that year, and it had NFC games every year. How lucky did that make them? Network spokesman Beano Cook once said, "The two most important people to CBS are J. R. Ewing and Tom Landry. We have a rule we go by when planning NFL telecasts: Give people the best game possible and, when in doubt, give them the Cowboys."

The team's radio network covered more than 200 stations in 14 states, and that was just in English; Spanish broadcasts of *Los Vaqueros* went to more than a dozen channels in seven states. The team-run weekly newspaper had a circulation of over 100,000, going to every state and several countries. There was a Spanish version of that too.

The Cowboys sold more T-shirts, hats, and other memorabilia than any other team. Heck, the cheerleaders outsold all but a few clubs. Braniff was so proud to be the team's airline that it painted a plane Cowboys colors, with the team's logo on its tail.

And on and on it goes.

So when NFL Films producer Bob Ryan came up with the label "America's Team," it certainly was fitting.

Enduring too.

ED "TOO TALL" JONES

Ed Jones was the first No. 1 overall pick the Cowboys ever made. He was the first player to last 15 seasons. And he still holds the club record for playing in the most games.

Anything else?

Oh, yeah, he's also the only one to walk away in the prime of his career to try another violent sport, boxing.

Jones announced his career change at a New York City restaurant in June 1979. Reigning heavyweight champ Larry Holmes showed up to lend his support.

"What people have never realized is that football has always been secondary to me," Jones said that day. "Fighting is something I've always dreamed of."

It seemed like a whim, considering he'd had only one official fight, a 36-second knockout win in a Golden Gloves tournament his senior year in high school. But Jones grew up listening to fights on the radio with his dad, who died when Ed was 17.

The only reason he stayed out of the ring was because football and basketball coaches convinced him to play their sports. He told the club of his plans a year in advance, and he figured they believed him since they spent their next top draft pick on a successor, Larry Bethea.

Jones' pro boxing career turned out to be the equivalent of a technical knockout. He went 6–0, with five knockouts. All his foes were decent—no "tomato cans," but also nowhere near Holmes' caliber. His curiosity satisfied, Jones returned to the Cowboys in 1980.

The defense sorely missed him, which might explain all the care packages Jones received during his sabbatical. They included team gear and encouraging words but no clues about who they were from, just the generic signature, "The Dallas Cowboys."

Jones picked up where he left off, anchoring the left end of the defensive line and terrorizing quarterbacks. He led the team in sacks in 1981, 1985, and 1987 and made the Pro Bowl from 1981 to 1983.

To what does Jones give credit for his career lasting so long, stretching all the way from Bob Lilly's last year to Troy Aikman's first?

Boxing, of course.

"I wouldn't have been in the mental state of mind to play 15 years if I hadn't boxed," he said.

Al Messerschmidt/Getty Images

In perhaps the wildest game ever played in Texas Stadium, Staubach erased deficits of 17–0 and 34–21 to pull out a 35–34 victory. Another rally was completed that day too—capping a rise from being 8–5 and sinking fast on Thanksgiving to being 11–5 and division champions. That meant a trip to the playoffs and a first-round bye.

When the Cowboys returned to Texas Stadium two weeks later, however, the magic was gone.

Dallas spotted the Los Angeles Rams a 14–5 lead before charging ahead 19–14. Rams quarterback Vince Ferragamo threw an off-target pass that Dallas linebacker Mike Hegman could have intercepted. Instead, he accidentally knocked it right to receiver Billy Waddy for a 50-yard touchdown that put the Rams ahead. Staubach had 2:05 left to work with, but the ensuing series was such a mess that his final pass was caught by left guard Herb Scott.

It turned out to be the last pass of his career.

On March 31, 1980, Staubach announced his retirement shortly after turning 38. The highest-rated passer in NFL history had a "gut feeling" that enough was enough.

Diminishing skills certainly weren't a factor. Landry said Staubach was playing as well as he had been five years earlier. The stats backed him up, as Staubach was coming off a second straight season as the NFL's top-rated passer.

Of all the possible reasons, Staubach said it wasn't the concussions (although he'd had at least 20, 5 in that season alone). Part of it was that he thought Danny White was ready to take over.

"There is no question that Roger Staubach is this country's greatest sports hero today, maybe of our time," Schramm said. "He is unique in that his following spans all generations."

As his farewell news conference wrapped up, Staubach said to Landry, "If I do come back next year, will you let me call the plays?"

"Oh, sure," Landry said. "From the press box."

YOU MAKE THE CALL

WHO WAS THE "TEAM OF THE DECADE" IN THE 1970S?

The Cowboys, Steelers, Dolphins, and Vikings can look back at the 1970s with a lot of pride. But which team deserves the bragging rights as being the very best from the decade of disco, Watergate, and the Fonz?

The Cowboys won two Super Bowls and played in five.

The Steelers went four times and never lost. They won back-to-back titles twice, beating Dallas during each reign.

Tex Schramm knew the Steelers had the edge, which is why he was so upset when the Cowboys were knocked out of the 1979 playoffs, taking with them their chance of becoming the team of the 1970s. His dream was for the Cowboys to beat the Steelers in the Super Bowl, giving each team three titles in the decade. That probably would have been enough to end any debate because so many other factors favored Dallas.

The Cowboys made the playoffs in 9 of the 10 seasons and never had a losing record. Their regular-season overall record was 105–39, a winning percentage of .729.

Pittsburgh, meanwhile, had two losing seasons and a combined regular-season record of 99–44–1 (.687).

The Cowboys also had the most players named to the first team of the All-Decade squad, which was picked by the same folks who vote for the Hall of Fame. The selection committee chose five Cowboys: Roger Staubach, Drew Pearson, Rayfield Wright, Bob Lilly, and Cliff Harris. The Steelers had three.

Even being part of the debate about the "team of the decade" implies sustained success, and the Dallas Cowboys certainly had that in the 1970s. The players changed from 1970 to 1979, but the results didn't.

GAME TO REMEMBER
"YOU GOTTA BELIEVE!"

IRVING, TEXAS – **Leave it to Roger Staubach to have the most memorable regular-season game of his career in his very last one.**

It was December 16, 1979, and Dallas, Washington, and Philadelphia were tied for first place in the NFC East. Cowboys–Redskins games always have a little extra intensity, and the playoff ramifications ratcheted things even higher for this one. And that was only part of the back story.

When the teams met in Washington a few weeks before, the Redskins were running out the clock on an 11-point victory when they decided to kick a field goal. It was as blatant an in-your-face move as it gets in pro football. Then, before this December rematch, a funeral wreath with the inscription "From the Redskins" was delivered to Harvey Martin in the Cowboys' locker room. Whether it was really from them or not didn't matter.

Let the emotional roller coaster begin.

Dallas fell behind 17–0 early in the second quarter, doing itself in with a pair of lost fumbles. Then Staubach led two long scoring drives to tighten things up at halftime, 17–14. The first score came from rookie Ron Springs (filling in for an injured Tony Dorsett), and the second came on a diving catch by Preston Pearson with nine seconds left in the half. In the third quarter, a short touchdown run by Robert Newhouse put the Cowboys ahead 21–17.

They wouldn't stay there long.

Washington got closer with a field goal, then Staubach threw an interception, and John Riggins scored a few plays later. Riggins soon scored again, rumbling 66 yards for the longest touchdown of his Hall of Fame career. More importantly, it put the Redskins up 34–21.

When Washington got the ball with about five minutes left, fans started heading for the exits. After all, it's hard to expect a team that has already wiped out a 17-point deficit to come back from 13 down with only a few minutes left.

"You gotta believe!" injured safety Charlie Waters said on the radio broadcast. Waters' buddy Cliff Harris must have sensed it too, because he soon caused a fumble that Randy White recovered. Three plays later, Staubach threw a 26-yard touchdown pass to Springs. Now Dallas was down by just six points with 2:20 to go.

The Redskins still had a chance to drain the clock, but Larry Cole wouldn't let them. He threw Riggins for a loss on third-and-2, forcing a punt.

Although the Cowboys took over 75 yards from the end zone with 1:46 left and no timeouts, there was a good reason to believe. They still had Staubach.

He hit Tony Hill for 20 yards, then Preston Pearson for gains of 22 and 25. Dallas was on the 8-yard line when Washington decided

Jerry Hoefer/AP Images

to gamble with a blitz. Staubach had called a play for Billy Joe DuPree, but—bracing for the blitz—he also told Hill to be ready for a lob. Staubach took a couple of quick steps back, then tossed the ball into the end zone. Hill ran under it for the touchdown, and the extra point put Dallas ahead 35–34 with 39 seconds left. The way this game was going, that was way too much time.

A pass interference penalty gave Washington the ball at the 49 with nine seconds to play. The Redskins scooted a little closer, then opted to try a 59-yard field goal to win the game.

Kicker Mark Moseley ran out on the field—but the clock ran out before the snap.

With two TD passes in the final 2:20, Staubach had pulled off his latest and perhaps greatest rally. He threw for 336 yards in the game, second-best of his career. The performance gave him a club-record 3,586 yards for the season, and the three touchdown passes set another club record of 27 for the year.

"It was absolutely the most thrilling 60 minutes I ever spent on a football field," Staubach said.

For Washington, it only got worse.

Going into the day, the only way the Redskins could have missed the playoffs was if they lost and Chicago won by at least 33 points. The Bears hadn't won by more than 28 all season, but they did it this day, crushing St. Louis 42–6. As the Redskins struggled to come to grips with it all, a surprise visitor arrived in their locker room at Texas Stadium. It was Martin, and he came bearing a gift: The wreath.

"They had a rerun of the last few minutes on TV the following Saturday night," Staubach said. "I just stayed home and watched it—like a fan."

Roger Staubach hung up his cleats after the 1979 season, capping a Hall of Fame career with a league-best 92.3 passer rating on the year and an 11–5 record for the team. *George Gojkovich/Getty Images*

CHAPTER **5**

THE DANNY WHITE ERA

"NO, DANNY, NO!": 1980–1985

Shown here during Super Bowl XII with his coach and his mentor, Danny White stepped into the full-time quarterback role in 1980 with big expectations hanging over him. Although he didn't take the Cowboys all the way back to the Super Bowl, they made the playoffs in each of White's first four seasons as starter. *Vernon Biever/NFL/ Getty Images*

The afternoon that Roger Staubach retired, some teammates visited his house. They played a little two-on-two basketball. The winning team featured Staubach and Danny White.

On the football field, White was plenty ready to replace Staubach—like Don Meredith had been ready to replace Eddie LeBaron, and Craig Morton and Staubach were ready to replace Meredith.

However, there was one key difference.

LeBaron and Meredith were good quarterbacks. Staubach was one of the greatest in NFL history. The question was: How would Danny White fill those shoes?

REASON TO BELIEVE

White, a third-round pick by the Cowboys in 1974, had spent two years as a starter in the WFL and then had gotten some quality playing time in four years backing up Staubach in Dallas. He'd also been the team's punter since 1976, which had to count for something.

His first season as full-time starter was a nice, clean handoff.

Opening not only in Washington but also on a Monday night with Dandy Don in the booth, White was in control as the Cowboys beat the Redskins 17–3.

Dallas soared to 5–1 following a 59–14 victory over San Francisco. Yes, 59 points. It tied the club record and hasn't been approached since.

DANNY WHITE

Statistically, Danny White was as good of a quarterback as Roger Staubach, completing more passes for more touchdowns.

But, as Mark Twain said, there are lies, damn lies, and statistics.

White was 62–30 as a starter, an impressive ratio of better than two wins in every three games. He got the Cowboys to the NFC Championship Game each of his first three years as the starter.

Reputations, however, are made by winning big games, not just getting to them, and White lost all three of those games that could've put the Cowboys into the Super Bowl.

"It's wrong to say he didn't do a good job," receiver Drew Pearson said, "but I also have to say that sometimes Danny tried to do a little too much. We were a good team; he didn't have to carry us, he just had to play with us. At times he would try to do things that weren't necessary."

White had the physical tools but lacked the leadership. He didn't exude the same aura of Staubach, Troy Aikman, or Don Meredith. Ultimately, that's the reason they are in the Ring of Honor and his legacy is confined to the stats pages.

"It's really impossible to judge quarterbacks because it's the most independent position on the team," White said. "So much depends on the people around you. We were definitely a team in transition, and I will always be judged accordingly. But I felt good about what I did as quarterback."

For the record, he was a really good punter. White hung up his cleats with the highest net average for a career, most punts inside the 20, and longest streak without a block in Cowboys history.

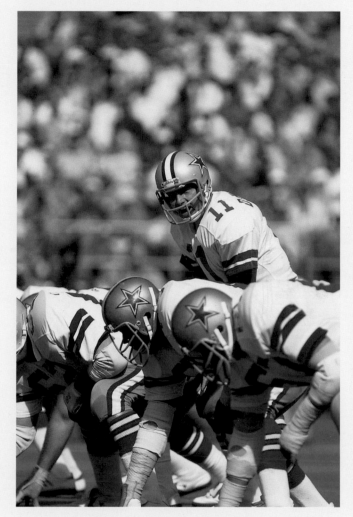

The rest of the season was amazingly smooth. In fact, Dallas' season played out exactly as coaches aim for: winning every game at home and splitting on the road. The Cowboys went 12–4, matching the most wins in club history. Alas, it wasn't enough to win the NFC East.

Dallas went into the finale needing to beat Philadelphia by at least 25 points to be division champs. The Cowboys were up 35–10 with ten and a half minutes left but ended up winning only 35–27.

Statistically, White picked up where Staubach left off, upping the club touchdown record by one to 28, while throwing for 3,287 yards, just a few hundred less than Staubach had in 1979. Dallas scored a club-record 454 points; however, the defense gave up points in bunches too. Foes scored in the 30s three times, and the Broncos put up 41 on them in the season's second game. The return of defensive lineman Ed "Too Tall" Jones helped, but the retirement of safety Cliff Harris hurt.

RANDY WHITE

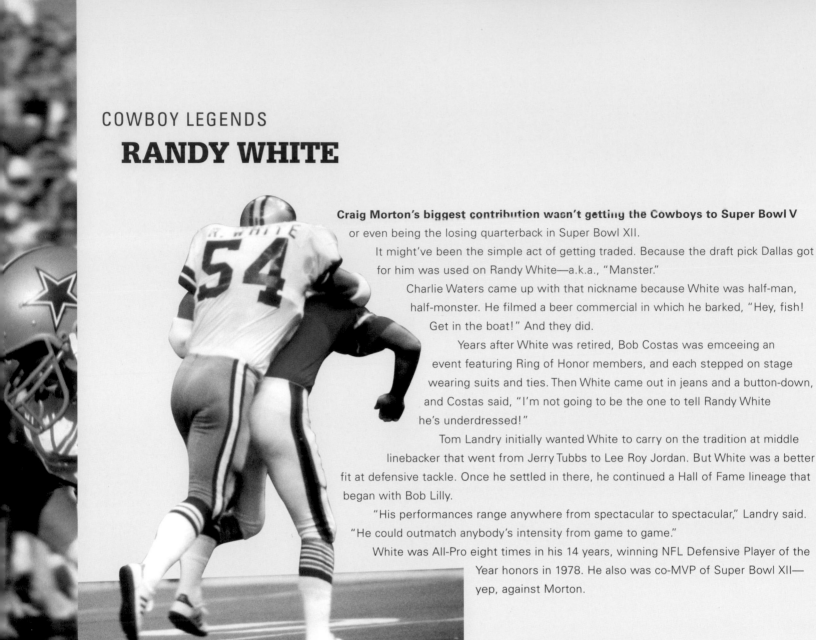

Craig Morton's biggest contribution wasn't getting the Cowboys to Super Bowl V or even being the losing quarterback in Super Bowl XII.

It might've been the simple act of getting traded. Because the draft pick Dallas got for him was used on Randy White—a.k.a., "Manster."

Charlie Waters came up with that nickname because White was half-man, half-monster. He filmed a beer commercial in which he barked, "Hey, fish! Get in the boat!" And they did.

Years after White was retired, Bob Costas was emceeing an event featuring Ring of Honor members, and each stepped on stage wearing suits and ties. Then White came out in jeans and a button-down, and Costas said, "I'm not going to be the one to tell Randy White he's underdressed!"

Tom Landry initially wanted White to carry on the tradition at middle linebacker that went from Jerry Tubbs to Lee Roy Jordan. But White was a better fit at defensive tackle. Once he settled in there, he continued a Hall of Fame lineage that began with Bob Lilly.

"His performances range anywhere from spectacular to spectacular," Landry said. "He could outmatch anybody's intensity from game to game."

White was All-Pro eight times in his 14 years, winning NFL Defensive Player of the Year honors in 1978. He also was co-MVP of Super Bowl XII— yep, against Morton.

Vernon Biever/NFL/Getty Images

The Cowboys opened the playoffs against the Rams and won easily behind 160 yards and two touchdowns from Tony Dorsett. It also was the 200th career win for Tom Landry.

Next was a trip to Atlanta. The NFC West champions also had gone 12–4, losing only once at home. The locals were riled up too. Just three days before, the University of Georgia—led by freshman sensation Herschel Walker—had won the national title. Now folks were counting on the Falcons to make the state even more proud.

Everything was looking great for the home crowd as Atlanta took a 27–17 lead late into the fourth quarter. Then White channeled his inner Staubach.

Firing pass after pass to Drew Pearson, White capped the drive with a 14-yard touchdown pass to Pearson. The defense held, and then White took over at his own 29 with 1:48 left. He found Pearson again, this time for the winning touchdown.

The Cowboys went to Philadelphia for an NFC Championship Game that would've been in Dallas had they held onto that big fourth-quarter lead over the Eagles in the regular-season finale. The Cowboys were out of their comfort zone from the start.

First, they were forced to wear their blue uniforms, which were either bad luck or truly cursed, considering all the losses in them dating to Super Bowl V. There also was a wind chill of minus 17,

COWBOY LEGENDS
DREW PEARSON

He was Roger Staubach's favorite receiver. He made big catch after big catch. He made the NFL's All-Decade Team for the 1970s.

But Drew Pearson is not in the Hall of Fame, much less the Ring of Honor.

"The honor is the achievement, not the recognition," said Pearson, who retired with more catches for more yards than any player in team history.

"When you get the respect of your teammates—people that you played with, people that are in the Ring, people that aren't in the Ring but are great teammates—that gives me the credibility to think it may happen. Hopefully I'll be around if it does come."

Raised in New Jersey, a product of the University of Tulsa, Pearson arrived as a rookie free agent in 1973. Not exceptionally fast, his motor

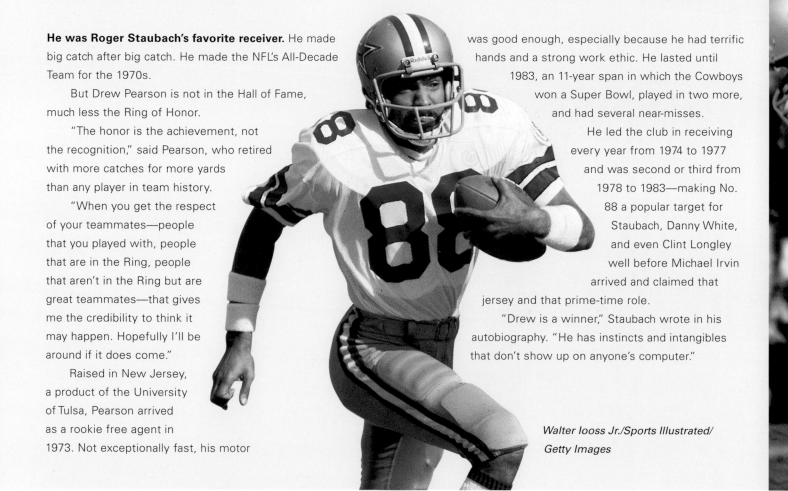

was good enough, especially because he had terrific hands and a strong work ethic. He lasted until 1983, an 11-year span in which the Cowboys won a Super Bowl, played in two more, and had several near-misses.

He led the club in receiving every year from 1974 to 1977 and was second or third from 1978 to 1983—making No. 88 a popular target for Staubach, Danny White, and even Clint Longley well before Michael Irvin arrived and claimed that jersey and that prime-time role.

"Drew is a winner," Staubach wrote in his autobiography. "He has instincts and intangibles that don't show up on anyone's computer."

Walter Iooss Jr./Sports Illustrated/ Getty Images

prompting Landry to wear a fur-lined hat instead of his trademark fedora.

The game was tied at the half, but Philadelphia pulled away to win 20–7. Wilbert Montgomery became the first rusher ever to gain 100 yards against Dallas in a playoff game.

As disappointing as it was to fall a game short of the Super Bowl again, the important thing was that the White era was off to a good start.

DROPPED BY "THE CATCH"

The Cowboys' scouting computer spit out some decent suggestions for players to draft in 1981. But the team did even better signing players nobody drafted.

The undrafted Everson Walls and Michael Downs didn't just make the team, they soared into the starting lineup. Walls would grab 11 interceptions in 1981, the most in the entire NFL.

The season played out a lot like 1980, with the Cowboys winning every game at home and splitting on the road. One difference was that they lost back-to-back games this season. A narrow loss at St. Louis was followed by a 45–14 whipping in San Francisco.

How did the 49ers—a team Dallas beat 59–14 the year before—get so good so fast? Well, there was a change of quarterbacks, with Joe Montana throwing touchdowns instead of Steve DeBerg throwing interceptions.

Butch Johnson leaps onto Drew Pearson's back after Pearson pulled in the game-winning touchdown against Atlanta in the 1980 divisional playoff round. Joining the celebration is Tony Hill. *George Brich/AP Images*

In the second game of 1981, Tony Dorsett ran for 129 yards against the Cardinals. It was his second of nine 100-yard games during the season. *Ron Heflin/AP Images*

The Cowboys lost only twice more all season—by a field goal at Detroit and in overtime at New York in the finale. In that loss to the Giants, the Cowboys committed three late turnovers in the wind and freezing temperatures at the Meadowlands. They had already clinched the division, but the loss cost them home-field advantage in the playoffs.

Dallas still wound up with the No. 2 seed. Losing home-field advantage would only matter if the Cowboys had to face the 49ers in the NFC Championship Game.

Danny White filled up the stat sheet again during the season, throwing for more than 3,000 yards and 22 touchdowns. He also cut his interceptions nearly in half, down to only 13.

Tony Dorsett had the best year of his career, running for 1,646 yards—more than 100 per game. Unfortunately, George Rogers of New Orleans had 29 more yards, keeping Dorsett from becoming the club's first rushing champion. It was the closest Dorsett would ever come to being No. 1.

Dallas had a bye in the first two rounds of the playoffs—sort of. After a week off, the Cowboys were at home against a Tampa Bay club making its franchise playoff debut. The Buccaneers were so happy to be there that they didn't bother scoring. Dallas won 38–0 with a nearly flawless performance.

"We don't have many of those games—maybe every five or six years," coach Tom Landry said. Indeed, the Cowboys hadn't blanked anyone in the preseason, regular season, or postseason since the 1978 NFC Championship Game against the Rams.

The 49ers had only slightly more difficulty with the New York Giants—a shame because it meant Dallas had to go to San Francisco instead of getting to play the conference championship at Texas Stadium.

At least the Cowboys knew what they were headed into. The 49ers had spanked them once this season and were 14–3, tops in the NFL.

But for three and a half quarters, San Francisco sure didn't look the part.

Montana threw three interceptions and the 49ers had three fumbles, helping the Cowboys lead 27–21 with five minutes left. Starting at his own 11-yard line, Montana slowly, steadily moved the ball, pushing the chains forward and winding the clock

EVERSON WALLS

Despite growing up a few miles from Cowboys headquarters, Everson "Cubby" Walls didn't play high school football until he was a senior.

He led his district in interceptions that season, earning a scholarship to Grambling. He led the nation in interceptions as a senior, yet it wasn't enough to get him drafted.

Walls wasn't a fast runner, but his knack for pickoffs earned him a spot in the NFL—and a starting job as a rookie. He kept intercepting passes, snatching a club-record 11 in his debut season and a total of 44 over nine years with the Cowboys. He had 57 in his career, more than Hall of Famers Mel Renfro, Willie Brown, and Lem Barney.

Walls made the Pro Bowl in each of his first three seasons and four times overall. After leaving the Cowboys, he won a Super Bowl with the New York Giants. His joyous reaction was featured on the cover of *Sports Illustrated*, a nice counterbalance to his previous cover—reaching in

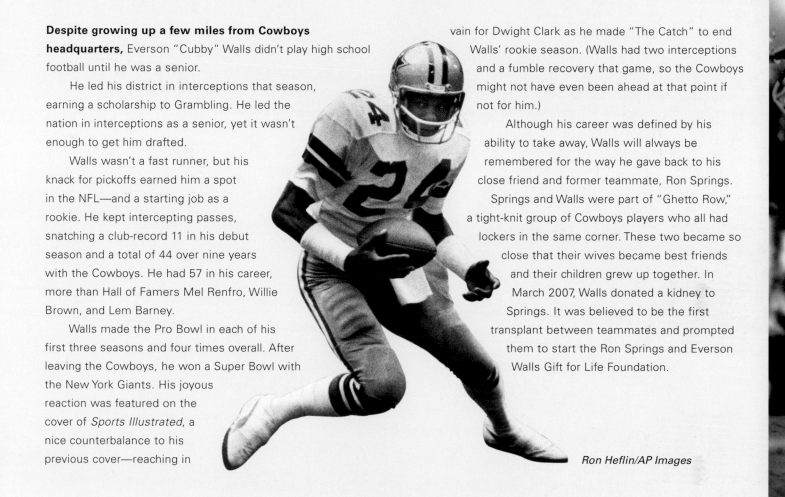

vain for Dwight Clark as he made "The Catch" to end Walls' rookie season. (Walls had two interceptions and a fumble recovery that game, so the Cowboys might not have even been ahead at that point if not for him.)

Although his career was defined by his ability to take away, Walls will always be remembered for the way he gave back to his close friend and former teammate, Ron Springs. Springs and Walls were part of "Ghetto Row," a tight-knit group of Cowboys players who all had lockers in the same corner. These two became so close that their wives became best friends and their children grew up together. In March 2007, Walls donated a kidney to Springs. It was believed to be the first transplant between teammates and prompted them to start the Ron Springs and Everson Walls Gift for Life Foundation.

Ron Heflin/AP Images

down. Facing third down from the Dallas 6, the 49ers called timeout.

"If you don't get what you want," coach Bill Walsh told Montana on the sideline, "just simply throw the ball away."

On the snap, Dallas' Larry Bethea broke into the backfield and chased Montana toward the right sideline. Montana then took a couple steps backward. By then, Ed "Too Tall" Jones and D. D. Lewis had joined Bethea in the pursuit, all ready to crunch Montana. He pumped once, then heaved the ball—either throwing it away or because he thought Dwight Clark would be there. He was. Clark leaped

up and caught the ball over Walls, who had covered Clark off the line then lost him in the middle of the end zone. Once the pass was in the air, Walls darted over to where Clark was, but he arrived too late. A photo taken from behind the play made the cover of *Sports Illustrated*, immortalizing the image of Walls reaching in vain.

"The Catch"—as the play came to be known—tied the game at 27. The extra point made it 28–27, San Francisco's lead.

Often forgotten is that there were still 51 seconds left on the clock. Plenty of time for the Cowboys to regain the lead.

On Dallas' next play from scrimmage, White threw long to Drew Pearson, who broke free for a chance to get into field goal range. Rookie cornerback Eric Wright made a desperate grab at Pearson's jersey, getting just enough to pull him down at midfield.

"I thought I was gone," Pearson said. "We almost had another 'Hail Mary' pass, and then Dwight Clark's catch would have been forgotten."

There was still time to get in kicker Rafael Septien's range, but on the next play, White got hit from behind and fumbled. San Francisco recovered. White argued that his arm was coming forward for a throw, making it an incompletion, but the officials didn't buy it.

"This," Landry said, "ranks with some of the bad ones we had."

YOU MAKE THE CALL

WAS "THE CATCH" THE BEGINNING OF THE END FOR THE LANDRY DYNASTY?

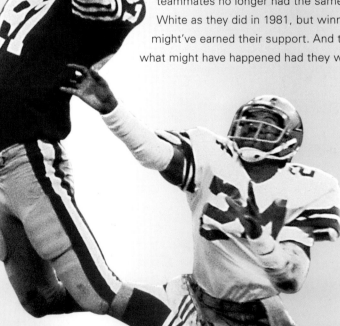

Tom Landry once looked back on the NFL Championship Game losses in 1966 and 1967 and wondered how franchise history might have changed if the Cowboys had won either of those games. They would've gotten into the habit of winning and would've had a completely different reputation.

He felt the same way about the 1981 NFC Championship Game.

"If we got to the Super Bowl in 1981, we might have won the Super Bowl a couple of more times," he said years later. "I think Danny [White] would have gotten us there again. Danny was a solid winner, and nobody recognized that too much."

History isn't always kind to White because he failed to get the Cowboys to the Super Bowl. The crushing part is that he got them one win away each of his first three seasons in charge.

In 1980, it was his first try, and the weather was terrible. A year later, the team was still very talented, and White now had the experience of playing high-stakes football. Those factors—as well as Dwight Clark's miraculous catch of a pass that Joe Montana

may have been throwing away to avoid a sack—are what make the 1981 loss such a heartbreaker.

But while it might be easy to blame that one play for being the turning point, the Cowboys did still have a chance to win that game. Drew Pearson nearly broke free for the game-winning touchdown, and although he was stopped, Dallas was still at midfield, near field-goal range—until White fumbled.

Also, remember that the Cowboys returned to the NFC title game the very next year. Maybe teammates no longer had the same faith in White as they did in 1981, but winning that game might've earned their support. And there's no telling what might have happened had they won in 1982.

Walter Iooss Jr./Sports Illustrated/Getty Images

DISAPPOINTMENT STRIKES AGAIN

Going into his third year at the helm, Danny White still hadn't completely won over Cowboys fans.

Great numbers in the regular season raised expectations for the playoffs, and White had yet to live up to them. In 1982, the quarterback would really alienate himself.

The Cowboys opened the season with a loss to Pittsburgh, making them 0–1 for the first time since the year the Beatles came to America, 1964. Remarkably, the Cowboys had won 17 straight season openers.

White threw two interceptions that day and heard plenty of boos from the hometown crowd. Dallas followed with a lopsided win at St. Louis—then the league players went on strike. It lasted 57 days and wiped out eight games. It hardly accomplished anything, with owners making only a few minor concessions. Yet, during the layoff, White sabotaged his popularity in the locker room by trying to talk things out with Tex Schramm.

"In the middle of negotiations, all of a sudden we see that Danny's . . . trying to settle the strike himself," receiver Drew Pearson said. "And when we said things among ourselves in meetings, well, I'm not saying Danny went back and told management, but things we said got back. A lot of players resented it."

The season resumed November 21, and the Cowboys won five in a row. They were going to the playoffs even if they lost their last two games, which they did. Still, that stretch provided one of the greatest plays in NFL history.

In the fourth quarter of a Monday night season finale at Minnesota, return man Timmy Newsome muffed a kickoff, forcing Dallas to start at its own 1-yard line. White called the play "H 31 Fold," which meant the center and left guard blocked the right tackle and linebacker, creating a lane for Tony Dorsett. Fullback Ron Springs thought a different play was called, one he wasn't supposed to be on the field for, so he took off for the sideline, leaving just 10 men on the field.

The rest of the play worked to perfection. Dorsett darted through the middle, went outside to his right, and just kept going. He ran 99 yards for a touchdown, the longest run from scrimmage anyone

In the lone Pro Bowl season of his career, Danny White led Dallas to two postseason wins in 1982, beginning with a comeback triumph over Tampa Bay. *Sylvia Allen/NFL/ Getty Images*

had ever done—and, obviously, the longest anyone ever could. It was the rare record that could never be broken.

Since the strike had ruined the usual playoff system, the NFL instituted a "Super Bowl tournament" format, which allowed more teams to play for the title. In their opener, the Cowboys went into the fourth quarter trailing Tampa Bay but won 30–17, then looked shaky again the next week in a 37–26 victory over Green Bay.

That second game was significant for two reasons. Number one, it was Dallas' first victory over Green Bay in a playoff game, and while it certainly couldn't make up for the disappointments of 1966 and 1967, there was some satisfaction in the fact that Bart Starr was coaching the Packers. And number two, it proved to be Tom Landry's final postseason victory.

Appearing in a third straight NFC Championship Game, the Cowboys met their old friends from Washington, who had won the NFC East with an 8–1 record.

The Redskins and their "Smurf" receivers were ahead 14–3 when Dexter Manley knocked out White. In came backup Gary Hogeboom to try to pull out the game—and he almost did. In the third quarter, he threw the first two touchdown passes of his NFL career to get Dallas within 21–17, sparking hopes of another Staubach-like rally and a trip to another Super Bowl. Then Hogeboom reminded everyone that he was the inexperienced backup. He threw two interceptions, one setting up a Washington field goal and the other getting returned for a touchdown. The Redskins won 31–17.

"The older guys are really ticked off," Everson Walls said. "We were ready, that's what is so disappointing."

Three straight title game losses. Dallas was back to being the bridesmaid of the NFL.

TURMOIL IN TEXAS

Getting close was exasperating. Unlike the late 1960s, when the Cowboys were a franchise on the rise, the near misses of the early 1980s were an indication of a franchise on its way down.

There were other signs too.

Rumors swirled about players breaking curfew the night before last season's NFC title game. Then, in May, Harvey Martin was sent to drug rehab. He and receiver Tony Hill were subpoenaed to testify for the defense of a retired Brazilian soccer player facing drug-smuggling charges. They ended up not appearing, but the PR damage was done—especially when Martin, Hill, Tony Dorsett, Ron Springs, and

COWBOY LEGENDS
HARVEY MARTIN

Playing opposite Ed "Too Tall" Jones, Harvey Martin needed a nickname. Considering the terrorizing way he used his 6-foot-5, 250-pound frame, "Too Mean" fit quite nicely.

Yet when it came time to name his radio show, he went with *The Beautiful Harvey Martin Show*.

Martin was a walking contradiction, a huge man who was somewhat forced into football as a teenager, then blossomed and helped his hometown team become Super Bowl champions.

A third-round pick out of East Commerce State, Martin set club records for sacks as a rookie, in a season, and for a career. His best year was 1977, when he had 23 sacks in 14 games, was named the NFL's Defensive Player of the Year, and shared Super Bowl MVP honors with Randy White.

Flush with fame and fortune, trouble followed Martin. Or, as a 1983

profile in *Sports Illustrated* described it, Martin went through "that little ripple of bad luck when the IRS demanded a quarter of a million dollars in unpaid taxes and threatened to throw him in jail, and his nightclub and five restaurants collapsed and the 11 lawsuits were filed against him and he went nearly $612,000 in debt and he declared bankruptcy and he was fired from his sportscasting job on Dallas' Channel 5 and lost his defensive captaincy of the Cowboys and his engagement to Sharon Bell was broken and he was accused in print of snorting cocaine."

He went to rehab in 1983, which turned out to be his final season. He later got involved with pro wrestling and suffered more run-ins with the law. He cleaned up his life in the late 1990s but died of pancreatic cancer in December 2001. He was 51.

Al Messerschmidt/Getty Images

Larry Bethea were linked to federal investigations into the Brazilian cocaine pipeline. Nothing came of that, either, beyond tarnished reputations.

"The whole thing would never have been more than a city case if it hadn't been the Dallas Cowboys," Dorsett said. "I guess you're supposed to screen everybody you come in contact with to protect your image. When you're America's Team, you've got to stay clean."

Cowboys Haters amused themselves with jokes about the "Cocaine Cowboys" and Dallas being "South America's Team." Image-conscious Tex Schramm tried to regain control by putting a former FBI agent on the payroll.

"I don't think that's what we need to bring unity to this team," Dorsett said. "If we can't do it without a security man, we're in trouble."

Landry tried regaining control by getting tough.

He ran a strict training camp, going back to the days of enforcing curfews and bed checks plus fining players for the slightest rules violations. He told receiver Butch Johnson to end the "California Quake" shtick. He also said that incumbents would not be given the benefit of the doubt, and that included Danny White. So when White threw two interceptions in the preseason opener, Landry let Hogeboom start the second preseason game.

"Players have a lot of respect for Gary," receiver Drew Pearson said. "He exudes confidence. He gets in the huddle and he gives you this feeling, even when he's having a bad day, that he'll still be able to pull the game out at the end with a big play. There's only one other quarterback I've seen the same thing in, that mystique, and that's Roger Staubach."

Landry ended up sticking with White, and, statistically, he had the best season yet by a Cowboys quarterback: 3,980 yards and 29 touchdowns, albeit with 23 interceptions.

White guided the Cowboys to a 7–0 start and then to 12–2 when the Redskins made their annual visit to Texas Stadium. Washington was the reigning Super Bowl champs and also had a 12–2 record.

Even though Dallas had won the first meeting, in the regular-season opener, a lot was riding

Despite the off-field distractions, fullback Ron Springs led the Cowboys with 73 receptions in 1983 while chipping in more than 500 yards rushing. *Tony Tomsic/Getty Images*

on this game: the division lead, a first-round bye, the best record in the conference, and the accompanying home-field advantage.

Trailing 14–10 early in the third quarter, the Cowboys were facing fourth-and-inches from their own 49. A Washington player was injured, so White

A disappointed Coach Landry heads off the field after his 12–4 Cowboys lost to the Rams in the opening round of the 1983 playoffs. *AP Images*

sidled over to Landry and talked him out of punting. They agreed to try drawing the Redskins offsides, or for White to try a quarterback sneak if it looked like there might be an opening.

White couldn't get Washington to jump, but he noticed that the defensive line was bunched toward the middle. So he audibled for a left outside run by Ron Springs. Landry realized what was happening, and TV cameras caught him screaming, "No! No! No, Danny, no!" White went through with his plan, and Springs lost two yards. The Redskins won 31–10.

The Cowboys finished the season with a Monday night game at San Francisco. Needing a good performance simply to regain some confidence, they lost 42–17.

Fans were so fed up that the smallest crowd in Texas Stadium history showed up for the playoff opener. White threw interceptions on consecutive possessions in the second half, and the Cowboys lost 24–17 to the Rams.

RIVALRY IN REVIEW
SAN FRANCISCO 49ERS

As much as Cowboys fans like to consider the Washington Redskins their top rival, a strong argument could be made for the San Francisco 49ers.

Dallas might play the Redskins and other NFC East rivals more often, but when the Cowboys and 49ers meet, there's usually a lot more on the line.

The teams have met six times to decide the NFC's representative in the Super Bowl: 1970, 1971, 1981, 1992, 1993, and 1994.

Dallas won four times and won the Super Bowl after three of them. Both San Francisco victories were devastating defeats for the Cowboys. The first was "The Catch" in 1981, which some say changed the course of history for both franchises. The second was in 1994, which prevented Dallas from winning an unprecedented third-straight Super Bowl.

The 49ers won Super Bowls after both those games, forming the bookends in their collection of five titles.

The postseason matchups started as a friendly rivalry because of the close relationship between coaches Tom Landry and Dick Nolan. There was plenty of respect between Landry and Bill Walsh, then a memorable war of words between Jimmy Johnson and George Seifert prior to the 1993 game, sparked by Johnson's guarantee, "We will win the ballgame."

Another unforgettable moment came in 2000, when Terrell Owens celebrated a touchdown on the midfield logo at Texas Stadium—twice. Emmitt Smith mimicked him after the first one, and George Teague took out T. O. with a tackle from behind on the second one.

"Things were bigger than Danny this time," said Landry. "He was just a reflection of the whole team."

It was Dallas' earliest playoff exit since 1976 and the first season to end with three straight losses since 1976. A bigger reflection of where things were headed was that the Cowboys plummeted from a 7–0 start to a 5–5 finish.

"The Cowboys," wrote Gary Myers in *The Dallas Morning News*, "have expired."

BUM BRIGHT TAKES OVER

Founder Clint Murchison Jr. loved everything about the Cowboys. So it speaks to how much of a mess his finances were in that he had to sell the club.

He put Tex Schramm in charge of finding a buyer, with orders that the new owner must remain behind the scenes and leave Schramm and Landry alone, as Murchison had done. The winning bid was led by H. R. "Bum" Bright, a Dallas-area business-man worth an estimated $600 million.

In the spring of 1984, Bright's group paid $60 million for the team and $20 million for the lease to Texas Stadium. It was the most ever paid for a pro sports team.

Everyone wondered: How would new owner-ship handle an underachieving club?

Harvey Martin, Pat Donovan, Billy Joe DuPree, and Robert Newhouse retired. Drew Pearson's career ended after he fell asleep at the wheel driving home from a basketball game and rammed into the back of a semi parked on the side of the road; his brother died in the accident.

The Cowboys spent their first-round pick on Billy Cannon Jr., a linebacker whose dad had been coveted by the club in the start-up days. What attracted Schramm most was the kid's school: Texas A&M, the beloved alma mater supported heavily by the new owner.

The week of the season opener, Landry was sur-prisingly nervous at a news conference. First he said that the only new starter on offense would be Phil Pozderac at left tackle. Then he said, "In the quar-terback area, we've decided to go with Pozderac. I mean, Hogeboom." (Landry actually struggled to get the name out, but he always had trouble with that one, and others.)

Hogeboom won the opener but couldn't keep it up. Dallas was 4–3 when Landry turned to White. He went 3–2.

The whole division was down, though, so the Cowboys went into the last few weeks with a chance to win the NFC East.

After winning two straight to get to 9–5, they blew a 21–6 lead at home against Washington, coughing up four turnovers in the third quarter alone, and lost by two points. They went to Miami for the finale with a chance to grab a wild card spot in the playoffs. The game was tied late in the fourth quarter, then there were touchdown passes of 39, 63, and 66 yards. Only one of them was thrown by Dallas, who lost 28–21.

In their 25th season, the Cowboys finished with a 9–7 record and missed the playoffs for the first time since 1974. They endured their most losses since 1965. No Cowboys player started in the Pro Bowl, something that hadn't happened since 1963. The team's mediocrity was summed up best by the fact that over the entire season, Dallas scored as many points as it gave up.

Gary Hogeboom called the shots in the Dallas huddle for most of 1984—and the Cowboys missed the playoffs for the first time in a decade. *George Gojkovich/Getty Images*

THE OVERACHIEVERS

Missing the playoffs exposed a lot of problems that had been easy to gloss over before.

Start with the scouting woes. Dallas went into 1985 with only one starter from the previous seven drafts; just 14 players from the last eight drafts were even on the roster. Either the computer was on the fritz or other teams were using better software. For instance: Doug Cosbie and Jim Jeffcoat were good picks and solid players taken in 1979 and 1983—but the Cowboys could've taken Joe Montana and Dan Marino at those spots.

COWBOY LEGENDS
TONY DORSETT

Tony Dorsett was No. 2 on the career rushing list when he retired.

Imagine how well he might've done if he'd carried the ball as often as he would've liked.

Tom Landry limited Dorsett's carries to around 20 per game because he feared that was all his 5-foot-11, 190-pound frame could handle.

"I understood his logic," Dorsett said, "but I didn't totally accept it."

Growing up in Aliquippa, Pennsylvania, the sixth of seven children to a father who spent 30 years working in steel mills, Dorsett rose to prominence in college at Pittsburgh, where he won the Heisman Trophy in 1976. Tex Schramm pulled a fast one to get Dorsett to Dallas, and he helped the Cowboys become Super Bowl champions as a rookie.

He became the first player to gain more than 1,000 yards in each of his first five seasons, a streak interrupted not by one of the injuries Landry feared but by the 1982 strike. Dorsett was back over 1,000 yards each of the next three years, making him 8-for-9 to start his career.

He also proved to be durable, missing only 3 of 142 games those first nine seasons.

"My running style was to avoid defenders," Dorsett said.

Of course, the carry limit might have helped too. He averaged 17.5 carries per game over his Dallas career.

With his flat-out speed and elusive moves, Dorsett had a knack for turning nothing into something and something into something special. Perhaps you remember what happened when he found a crease 99 yards from the end zone in Minnesota. Yet, for all his success, Dorsett never won a rushing title and only made four trips to the Pro Bowl.

He also led a star-crossed life in the public eye.

He drove a car with a *TD33* license plate and *TD* engraved on the doors. There was a bar fight soon after he arrived in town and a benching in his second season for oversleeping and arriving late to a game. There were several contract battles, the death of a fiancée and his father, a divorce, an FBI investigation, and trouble with the IRS. He called Randy White "Captain Scab" for crossing a picket line, then did so himself a week later. He called out Herschel Walker for getting a huge contract to join the team, even though he made four times as much as Roger Staubach his rookie season.

Dorsett was traded to Denver in June 1988, becoming the first major figure in team history to end his career elsewhere. He played one season with the Broncos before a knee injury forced him to retire. He was voted into the Pro Football Hall of Fame as soon as he became eligible.

Focus on Sport/Getty Images

The club's star player was Tony Dorsett, and he held out in training camp before signing a two-year extension with a 20-year annuity worth $6 million and $750,000 in real estate. (Dorsett needed all the help he could get after a messy divorce and IRS problems that publicized bad investments and loans from the team.)

Dorsett was closing in on 10,000 career yards, but that also meant he was getting up in age. Tex Schramm took an interesting gamble in the 1985 draft, spending a fifth-round pick on running back Herschel Walker; although Walker was playing in the USFL, Dallas now owned his rights should he ever want to play in the NFL or if the rival league went under.

Not too much to get excited about, is it? Well, years later, Tom Landry would look back at this team as the one he enjoyed coaching the most.

Freed from high expectations, Landry stuck with Danny White and was rewarded with a 5–1 start. Then came a roller-coaster ride, alternating losses and wins pretty much the rest of the season. Some of the losses were brutal: 44–0 at home to Chicago (albeit to the "Super Bowl Shuffle" Bears that went 15–1 and won it all) and 50–24 at Cincinnati right after the Cowboys had won back-to-back games.

The secondary was the team's driving force. Led by Everson Walls' league-high 9 interceptions, the Cowboys picked off 33 passes as a team; only Da Bears had more, with 34.

Dallas opened the season with six picks against Washington, prompting White to say, "They are like thieves, Thurman's Thieves," in honor of the group's elder statesman, Dennis Thurman. The secondary appeared in a poster dressed up as gangsters, and 90 minutes before a Monday night game in St. Louis, they were interviewed as a group with everyone wearing Indiana Jones–style fedoras. Some teammates didn't like all the attention they were getting. When that game against the Cardinals got out of hand—the Cowboys gave up 21 unanswered points in the second half—Randy White and Thurman got into a shouting match on the sideline. Problems lingered for days, until Landry called a meeting of the team captains to defuse it.

It was another down year in the NFC East, and Dallas could have won it by beating the Giants at

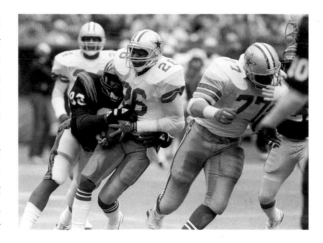

Safety Michael Downs (26) pulls in one of his three interceptions of the 1985 season, this one in a December loss at Cincinnati. *George Gojkovich/Getty Images*

home in the second-to-last game. But White had to leave with hand, rib, and shoulder injuries, and then Hogeboom suffered a concussion. Leading 21–14 early in the fourth quarter, the Cowboys needed third-stringer Steve Pelluer to protect it, and he had never taken a snap in his two NFL seasons.

Yet Pelluer led a long touchdown drive, converting a third-and-15 by recognizing a blitz and making a perfect throw to rookie Karl Powe. The Cowboys won 28–21, and the NFC East crown was theirs. In the postgame celebration, Thurman asked Landry to put up his right hand, then told him, "Higher." The cornerback then slapped palms with his coach, giving Landry his first-ever high five.

Years later, Landry said he enjoyed this season so much because the team was "so outmanned."

"There's no reason why New York or Washington shouldn't have won the division that year," Landry said. "We won it because of guys like Mike Renfro. And Steve Pelluer coming in and throwing the ball to Karl Powe. . . . That was a thrilling team. I enjoyed coaching them and seeing them perform."

Dallas lost the finale at San Francisco, then got skunked 20–0 at home by the Los Angeles Rams. Eric Dickerson ran over the Cowboys for 248 yards, an NFL playoff record. It was Dallas' first shutout in 36 postseason games and the second blanking of the season, something that had never happened before.

The high of winning the division was offset by the low of another ugly playoff loss.

But that was nothing compared to what was coming next.

CHAPTER 6

THE STEVE PELLUER ERA

SINKING FAST: 1986–1988

The dream backfield: Herschel Walker and Tony Dorsett. *Peter Read Miller/Sports Illustrated/Getty Images*

Coming off a surprising division title, Dallas got more good news when the USFL collapsed.

That meant Herschel Walker was all theirs.

Instead of trading Walker for, say, a whole bunch of players and draft picks, the Cowboys decided to pair him and Tony Dorsett in a "Dream Backfield" of former Heisman Trophy winners.

The plan was a nightmare to Dorsett, and he let everyone know it. After Walker's introductory news conference, Dorsett held his own to complain about this move. The leading rusher in club history didn't think it was fair he was making $450,000 and the unproven Walker received a $5 million, five-year deal.

Another idea that was better on paper than in reality was bringing in a bright, young offensive coach for Tom Landry to groom as his successor.

Tex Schramm thought he found his next head coach in Paul Hackett, who came with the endorsement of his previous boss, Bill Walsh of the 49ers. Landry made him passing-game coordinator, even though they held polar-opposite views. They also differed on the idea of succession, because Landry wasn't ready to go anywhere.

Yet another forced relationship was instituted in the scouting department. Gil Brandt was limited to colleges and Bob Ackles was hired for the pro side.

If it looks like trouble and sounds like trouble, you know what usually happens.

COWBOY LEGENDS
HERSCHEL WALKER

It took a smart move to get Herschel Walker on the Cowboys. It took a brilliant move to get rid of him. And then there was the unique twist of bringing him back.

All told, he was among the handful of players to have played for Tom Landry, Jimmy Johnson, and Barry Switzer.

So, what kind of a player was he while he was here?

While playing 6 of his 13 NFL seasons in Dallas, Walker ran for 3,491 yards. Only Emmitt Smith, Tony Dorsett, Don Perkins, Calvin Hill, Robert Newhouse, and Walt Garrison gained more rushing yards for the Cowboys. Among the members of that group, only Dorsett averaged more than Walker's 4.3 yards per carry.

His biggest contribution—well, other than getting traded— was on special teams.

Walker returned 77 kickoffs for 1,946 yards, an average of 25.3 yards per return. Only Hall of Famer Mel Renfro averaged more with Dallas.

Add up his rushes, receptions, and returns, and Walker produced 7,993 yards. Pretty good for a fifth-round pick.

Richard Mackson/Sports Illustrated/Getty Images

RUN OF WINNING SEASONS
HITS FINISH LINE

Danny White remained the starting quarterback in 1986, with Steve Pelluer now in the apprentice role. Gary Hogeboom was gone, traded to Indianapolis.

Dexter Clinkscale and Dennis Thurman also were dealt, which Everson Walls called "a terrible blow for this team." He was right, as interceptions were cut nearly in half from the previous season, down to 17.

The Cowboys opened the preseason with the longest road trip in club history—all the way to London's Wembley Stadium to face the Chicago Bears in an exhibition the NFL billed as the "American Bowl." They opened the real season

Coach Landry and Ed "Too Tall" Jones don a couple of Bobbies' helmets during a practice session prior to the "American Bowl" in London, July 1986. *Gerald Penny/AP Images*

TWENTY STRAIGHT WINNING SEASONS

The 1966 Dallas Cowboys were the first team in franchise history to win more games than they lost. The Cowboys did it again the next year too. And the next . . . all the way through 1985.

When the streak ended with a 7–9 record in 1986, the Cowboys had piled up 20 consecutive winning seasons.

Dallas' streak is the third longest in pro sports history, topped only by the New York Yankees (39 straight from 1926 to 1964) and the Montreal Canadiens (1951–1952 through 1982–1983). The longest streak in NBA history was 19 seasons by the Utah Jazz (1985–1986 through 2003–2004).

Perhaps the best way to put the Cowboys' accomplishment in perspective is to relate it to current times.

The longest active streak at the time of this publication began in 2005, meaning it would take a team at least nine wins every year through 2024 to tie Dallas' mark.

with a 31–28 victory over the New York Giants on a Monday night, with Herschel Walker scoring the winning touchdown.

Dallas went 6–2 the first half of the season. There was even a three-game stretch in which the Cowboys allowed a total of 26 points.

Everything changed in the ninth game.

White broke his wrist, forcing Pelluer into action. He clearly wasn't ready. Some would say he never would be ready. (The naysayers included Hackett, who while with the 49ers had scouted Pelluer in college and came back saying he wasn't impressed.)

Pelluer finished the season with 17 interceptions and 8 touchdowns. He showed a statue-like pocket presence, getting sacked 47 times, including 12 in one game. His line was to blame too. And the vaunted running backs behind Pelluer were far less effective against defenses that weren't worried about Dallas throwing the ball.

Dorsett missed three games with an injury and failed to run for 1,000 yards for the first time. Things got so bad down the stretch that Landry took away Hackett's play-calling duties.

The Cowboys went 1–7 in the second half of the season, averaging just 15 points per game. They dropped their final five, sinking to 7–9 for their first losing record since 1964.

The streak of consecutive winning seasons ended at 20, the run of non-losing seasons at 21.

Dallas was about to start a new streak, but in the wrong direction.

COMING APART AT THE SEAMS

Second-year receiver Mike Sherrard was running for a pass in training camp before the 1987 season when his legs got tangled and his right leg cracked in two. It looked and sounded so bad that quarterback Danny White and passing-game coordinator Paul Hackett had to leave the field and collect themselves.

Sad, gruesome, and self-inflicted, that play symbolized one of the most spectacularly bizarre seasons in Cowboys history.

Hackett was offered the head coaching job at Southern Cal, but Schramm convinced him to turn it down. The implication was obvious: Stay and you can replace Tom Landry. Landry, meanwhile, asked for a three-year contract extension, and Schramm gave it to him. Owner Bum Bright OK'd it because he thought it was three separate one-year deals, meaning one or two could be torn up without penalty. Done Schramm's way, it would have cost $1.9 million to fire Landry.

White wasn't fully recovered from his broken wrist. Steve Pelluer, though healthy, hadn't gotten any better. Tony Hill—who had passed Drew Pearson for the most receiving yards in team history and was 10 behind in catches—was cut for being overweight. That left Mike Renfro, 32 years old and in the final year of his career, as the No. 1 receiver.

Safety Bill Bates (40) had reason to celebrate after his interception of a Phil Simms pass clinched a 16–14 win over the Giants on September 20, 1987. A week later, he and most of the other players went on strike. *G. Paul Burnett/ AP Images*

Kicker Rafael Septien, the top point scorer in team history, was accused of sexually assaulting a 10-year-old girl and pleaded guilty to a charge of indecency with a child. Schramm refused to let him return. Eight candidates were invited to camp to try to replace him. Roger Ruzek was the first one cut, but he was invited back and wound up winning the job. He then made 88 percent of his kicks, the best in club history. Ruzek made four field goals in one quarter and five total—both club records—without a miss in a victory over the Rams in December.

Labor disputes also clouded the season. The Cowboys were 1–1 when the players' union went on strike again. After a one-week hiatus, the league was determined to go on, so they hired what they called "replacement" players; the union called them "scabs."

Randy White and defensive lineman Don Smerek crossed the picket line and showed up for practice right away. Danny White, who had been on the owners' side during the 1982 strike, joined them later. Tony Dorsett called Randy White "Captain Scab" for reporting to work, then he showed up too, after receiving a letter saying he could forfeit his annuity if he didn't. Ed Jones returned for the same reason. Everson Walls and Doug Cosbie, the team's union representative, got the same letters yet stayed away.

On October 4, a mishmash of real players and strike-busters wearing Cowboys uniforms beat a similar mix representing the New York Jets. In this bizarro NFL, Kevin Sweeney—who was short and had a weak arm—started at quarterback for Dallas. Randy White and Smerek also started, while Dorsett, Danny White, and Renfro suited up but didn't play. Dallas won 38–24, with the defense recording 11 sacks.

Cowboys president Tex Schramm is followed by reporters as he arrives for a meeting of the NFL Management Council in New York in October 1987, hoping to reach a settlement to end the players' strike. *G. Paul Burnett/AP Images*

The faux Cowboys won again the following week, beating Philadelphia 41–22 at Texas Stadium. For a Monday night game at home against a Redskins club made up strictly of replacements/scabs, Landry went back to White at quarterback and Dorsett in the backfield. With more than 60,000 in attendance, Dallas lost 13–7, and the fans expressed their displeasure loud and clear with chants like, "We want Sweeney!"

All the players returned the following week, but there obviously was tension between those who stuck with the union and the 21 who didn't. Soon enough, they all had a common enemy: Eagles coach Buddy Ryan.

In the first game with the "real" players, Philadelphia led by 10 points in the final minute when quarterback Randall Cunningham took a knee. It was a ruse, though, because Ryan was still angry about losing to Dallas during the strike and wanted to run up the score. So on the next play, with the Cowboys expecting another kneeldown, Cunningham threw deep, drawing a pass

interference penalty that put the ball at the 1. Keith Byars plugged it in on the game's final play.

Future Cowboys coach Wade Phillips was on Ryan's staff at the time and was as aghast as everyone else that Ryan would pull such a stunt. Ryan bragged, "The last touchdown was very satisfying. I had it planned all along."

"I wouldn't even justify that with a comment," Landry said. "Everybody has his opinion of what it was."

Speaking of opinions, Schramm and Bright had some about Landry.

A few days after a loss to Detroit, Schramm said on his radio show, "I'm not sure it's all on the players. When things aren't working, and you see the same things, it shakes your confidence. There's an old saying, 'If the teacher doesn't teach, the student doesn't learn.'"

A month later, Bright spouted off following a 21–10 home loss to an Atlanta team that had lost six straight games. "I get horrified sometimes at our play-calling," the owner said. "It doesn't seem like

POLISHING THE STAR
BROADCASTERS

In addition to great players and coaches, the Cowboys have had their share of terrific broadcast teams.

Frank Glieber and Bill Mercer were behind the microphone in the early days. Then it was Glieber and Verne Lundquist, a team that gave way to Lundquist and Brad Sham. Sham has been a constant since 1977, except for a few years in the mid-1990s, sharing the booth for long, successful stretches with Dale Hansen and then with Babe Laufenberg.

Bud Sherman was the club's first play-by-play voice, with Glieber the color analyst. Rick Weaver and Gary DeLaune were behind the microphone in 1963, when the radio signal was sent into Oklahoma, Arkansas, and Louisiana.

In the late 1960s, newspaper columnist Blackie Sherrod provided color analysis alongside Glieber. From 1985 to 1996, Hansen, a local TV anchor, joined Sham and then worked with his replacement, Dave Garrett. When Sham returned in 1998, his sidekick was Laufenberg, a former Cowboys quarterback turned local TV anchor.

A long list of former players used their popularity to land gigs talking about football on television, starting with Don Meredith's role on *Monday Night Football*.

Because of the Cowboys' popularity, the team was a regular on Monday nights, and it has since transitioned into a staple on Sunday nights,

now the league's showcase spot. Dallas routinely opened on ABC and was among the teams featured most often.

Pat Summerall called so many Cowboys games for CBS, then Fox, that fans came to expect his voice. For many years, he partnered with Tom Brookshier, then he was paired with John Madden. Now the A-team crew for Fox, which has the NFC rights, features Joe Buck and Troy Aikman.

Brad Sham and Babe Laufenberg in the Cowboys Stadium broadcast booth, December 2009. *James D. Smith/AP Images*

we've got anybody in charge that knows what they're doing, other than Tex. I don't want to do the coaching and I don't want to try to run the team, but I'm not satisfied with the results we get."

How did Landry handle this challenging season? He served ice cream to the players after one practice. He fought back tears when he announced to players the release of veteran John Dutton.

Through it all, the Cowboys finished with a 7–8 record, second place in the NFC East.

STILL GETTING WORSE

There was no teary-eyed news conference when Tony Dorsett was traded to Denver in 1988. It was just Tex Schramm announcing that one of the greatest players in club history was gone.

"I've felt all along that this is unfortunate," Schramm said when the deal was done. "I look up over my mantel and there's a picture of Tony scoring a touchdown. There are a lot of memories with Tony."

Herschel Walker was a lone bright spot for the 'Boys in 1988. *Tony Tomsic/ Getty Images*

The 1988 season marked Steve Pelluer's last as the starting quarterback in Dallas. His 19 interceptions against 17 touchdowns didn't help his cause. *George Gojkovich/Getty Images*

Dorsett was fourth on the NFL's all-time rushing list but second on Dallas' depth chart. All the Cowboys got for him was a 1989 draft pick based on how well Dorsett played. It turned out to be a fifth-rounder, which Dallas spent on a defensive tackle who never made the team.

Now the offense was going to be all Herschel, all the time. Steve Pelluer was the quarterback and top pick Michael Irvin was his new No. 1 receiver.

Walker became the tenth player in NFL history to produce more than 2,000 combined yards running and receiving. But he wasn't a dominant back, not like Dorsett had been in his prime or like Emmitt Smith would be in his. Walker was an efficient, effective weapon—and the only weapon Dallas had.

The Cowboys were dreadful. After a 2–2 start, they lost 10 straight, from clunkers like a 43–3 loss to Minnesota to the agony of letting a 20–0 lead in Philadelphia turn into a 24–23 loss. It was hard to say which was worse, the offense or defense.

Pelluer was benched for two and a half games. Landry let former scab Kevin Sweeney start two games and hardly ever turned to White.

DO HALL OF FAME VOTERS HAVE AN ANTI-COWBOYS BIAS?

The Cowboys have played in the most Super Bowls, have won among the most, and are easily the league's most popular team, according to standards like ratings and memorabilia sales.

Then how come they don't have more players in the Pro Football Hall of Fame?

The NFL started in 1929, and Dallas didn't arrive until 1960, so it's understandable that teams like the Packers, Bears, Steelers, Giants, Redskins, and Browns would have more honorees.

But the Raiders? The Lions, whose history is long but not proud?

Dallas has 12 honorees, about as many as the Vikings, Bills, and Chiefs, and not many more than the Titans/Oilers and Chargers. Those teams have fewer Super Bowl titles *combined* than the Cowboys.

The ratio was really out of whack until the mid-2000s, when the seniors committee added Rayfield Wright and Bob Hayes, and 1990s stars Troy Aikman, Michael Irvin, and Emmitt Smith went on the ballot.

It's a good start. And the numbers are likely to go up with candidates like Deion Sanders, Larry Allen, Darren Woodson, and Charles Haley ranging from slam dunks to strong contenders.

But how about Cliff Harris, Chuck Howley, Lee Roy Jordan, Don Meredith, and Don Perkins—all of whom are in the Cowboys' Ring of Honor—getting a bust in Canton, Ohio? Good arguments can be made for Drew Pearson and Harvey Martin too. And how about founder Clint Murchison Jr.?

As for the initial question about whether or not there is an anti-Cowboys bias, just remember this: Pearson, Martin, Harris, and Ralph Neely were all voted to the All-Decade Team by the same voters who decide on Hall of Fame induction. Those players were among the best of their era during their era, but apparently voters changed their opinions once those players' careers were done.

Landry was in his 29th season as head coach, matching the NFL record set by Curly Lambeau (as in, Green Bay's Lambeau Field). As the losses mounted, there were cries that he was too old. According to a *Dallas Times-Herald* poll, 64 percent of fans said they wanted Landry to hang up his hat for good.

One respite came on December 12, when Irvin caught three touchdown passes and Dallas beat the Redskins 24–17 in Washington. It ended the losing streak and proved to be the 270th and final victory of Landry's career. In the locker room, veteran center Tom Rafferty presented him with the game ball while teammates chanted, "T-L! T-L!"

"This is for a guy who stood by us, a guy who has taken a lot of [abuse]," Rafferty said.

Landry called it one of the most satisfying wins of his career.

"After losing all the tough ones we've lost, to see them come into the dressing room smiling and excited was well worth it," he said.

At season's end, Hackett and defensive coordinator Ernie Stautner were fired, and owner Bum Bright was trying to sell the team. The only bright spot was having the No. 1 overall draft pick in the 1989 draft.

Landry returned from a Caribbean cruise and said he'd definitely be back in 1989.

TOM LANDRY

Before Super Bowl X, the *Dallas Times Herald* ran a cartoon depicting "the many faces of Tom Landry."

"Ain't had th' right 'feel' lately," says the first of Landry's 11 faces, with a fedora on top, a jutting jaw, and a suit and tie visible around the neck.

The next two Landrys say, "Gotta get th' team 'up' . . . In a mean mood . . . Today—I'm really gonna put on my 'Game-Face'!"

Of course, all 11 panels are exactly the same. Even the last, when Landry says, "Wanna see me do it again?"

"The man in the funny hat," as Roger Staubach dubbed him, wasn't big on emotion because his computer-like mind always was thinking about the next play, the next series, working through decisions he might have to make.

Staying one step ahead of the competition, Landry taught everyone how to "read" an offense, to figure out what they were going to do before they did it. He devised the 4–3 defense that became standard across the NFL, then came up with the idea of putting ends and backs in motion to give those defenses something else to think about. Next came the Flex defense, a small shift that made a big difference, then the revival of the Shotgun.

"I really enjoyed the challenge of bringing a team to the game," Landry once said. "I enjoyed the challenge of that more than the actual game."

The son of a car mechanic in Mission, Texas, Landry went to World War II before college. He survived 30 missions as co-pilot of a B-17 bomber over German-occupied Europe, including some close calls—like the time all the engines died and the plane was diving, but Landry readjusted the fuel mixture and

The classic stone face and fedora of Coach Tom Landry.
Robert Riger/Getty Images

pulled out of it. Another time he ran out of fuel and crash-landed in a forest. All when he was 20.

He returned to the University of Texas as a backup to quarterback Bobby Layne and filled in elsewhere. He played seven years of pro football, becoming an All-Pro with the New York Giants the year he also became an assistant coach in charge of defense.

Landry didn't see coaching as a career. He sold insurance in the offseason and figured he'd eventually turn to his engineering degree. Then, in 1964, he received a 10-year contract extension.

"That was a great impact on my life," Landry said, "because to me as a Christian—and I was only a Christian for one year before I came to Dallas in 1960—this was God's way of saying to me, 'This is where you should be, in coaching.'"

Landry had the Cowboys within a win of 12 of the first 17 Super Bowls. They made it five times, winning two. His three Super Bowl losses were all by four points or less.

Landry's impact on the game is evident from the impressive roster of future head coaches who spent time under his wing. In 1987, five Landry disciples were leading NFL teams: Mike Ditka with the Bears (a Landry staffer from 1973 to 1981), Raymond Berry (1968–1969) with the Patriots, Dan Reeves (1970–1972, 1974–1980) with the Broncos, Gene Stallings (1972–1985) with the Cardinals, and John Mackovic (1981–1982) with the Chiefs.

"If you came to him with an idea, he'd sit you down and make you prove it would work," Ditka recalled about his one-time mentor. "You couldn't just draw up a play that looked good; you had to say why it would work against different schemes. You had to have concrete facts. That's the way he operated."

"I think the whole Cowboys image came from him," Staubach said.

Fans who wanted him gone hated the way he was forced out. There were "Landry for Governor" bumper stickers and a "Hats Off to Tom Landry" celebration—a parade and ceremony that drew 50,000 people, including the governor. President George H. W. Bush and Billy Graham sent telegrams; Bob Hope called in.

Landry made the Hall of Fame the following year, then the Ring of Honor in 1993, where he was honored with the outline of a fedora instead of a jersey number. Surrounded by his greatest players, the game face cracked.

"I thought about what they accomplished for us," Landry said. "It gave me a warm feeling."

He died of leukemia in February 2000. At the memorial service, Staubach said, "He was our rock, our hope, our inspiration. Probably there were some players that didn't love him, but they all respected him. He was committed to us, and you don't find that type of commitment in life very often."

Though known for his stoicism, Landry did show emotion when the moment called for it, such as this leap of frustration during Super Bowl X. *Rich Clarkson/Sports Illustrated/Getty Images*

Landry's lack of emotion intentionally kept him from becoming close to players for fear it would cloud personnel decisions. He ruled through a stare known as "The Look," which also set him up as an easy target of jokes.

"Once he got into a grinning contest with Mount Rushmore," comedian Don Rickles said. "Mount Rushmore won."

Only two coaches had more than his 270 wins, and nobody coached one franchise longer. His fedora-topped profile was as much a symbol of the Cowboys as the star on their helmets. Through it all, Friday nights were reserved for date night with his wife, Alicia.

A statue of Landry clutching his detailed play-calling chart stands outside of Cowboys Stadium. *Scott Boehm/Getty Images*

THE TROY AIKMAN ERA, PART I

TRIPLETS = THREE RINGS: 1989–1995

New sheriffs in town: Head coach Jimmy Johnson and owner Jerry Jones took the helm in Dallas beginning in 1989. The duo would form a rocky but ultimately successful relationship. *Allen Dean Steele/Allsport/ Getty Images*

At the Super Bowl in January 1989, Tex Schramm invited a guest—a local coach in Miami and a native Texan—to join him, Tom Landry, and Gil Brandt in their box at Joe Robbie Stadium.

The guest was a guy named Jimmy Johnson.

Johnson was from Port Arthur, and he had made a name for himself as a college coach. With Landry perhaps losing his touch, and Paul Hackett no longer next in line, Schramm wanted to get to know Johnson.

Meanwhile, one of the guys with whom Johnson played college football at Arkansas—a fellow named Jerry Jones—was getting to know Bum Bright.

Jones had been part of Arkansas' undefeated, national championship team in 1964. Alphabetical order made Jones and Johnson roommates on the road. After college, Jones gave up playing football and became an investor in real estate, poultry, and pizza, then oil and gas. He eventually sold his company for $175 million. All along, he dreamed of owning a pro football team. Jones even tried buying the San Diego Chargers in 1967, when he was 25 years old.

Back in August 1988, Bright had announced he had hired a firm to help him sell the Cowboys. A blurb appeared in the *Wall Street Journal*, and Jones stumbled across it while on a fishing trip in Mexico. He couldn't believe his luck. Five years earlier, he had kicked himself for not taking a crack at buying the club. He wasn't going to miss out again.

Jones flew back and started negotiating. There were all sorts of snags. Then Jones' father-in-law died, and he thought about his priorities. He decided to go for it and told his kids they were coming on board. He got Johnson to come along too.

Then came a final snag: $300,000 in closing costs.

Bright offered to flip a quarter for it. Jones called tails. It was heads. Jones paid the tab and then spent a few more bucks getting the quarter framed for Bright.

JIMMY JOHNSON

Jimmy Johnson still wants credit. Not so much in the Jimmy-versus-Jerry debate over who turned around the Dallas Cowboys, but for how it happened.

He hates hearing that the Herschel Walker trade built the Cowboys' dynasty in the 1990s.

"That was *one* trade," he said a few months before the 20-year anniversary of the heist. "We made 50 others in my five years! There were a lot of good trades. Trading up to get Emmitt Smith was a pretty good trade."

As proud as he is of going 43–21 with two Super Bowl titles after a 1–15 debut, Johnson considers his legacy the nucleus that was built on his watch. (Yes, that means he wants credit for having put together much of the team that won a third Super Bowl after he left.)

Johnson ruled with an iron fist—and a degree in psychology—at a time when coaches could still effectively threaten players with playing time and roster spots.

He was so demanding that even the hairs on his head knew better than to budge.

"A lot of coaches tell you winning is the only thing," offensive lineman Nate Newton said. "But when it came to winning, well, Coach Johnson was just crazy about it."

NFL/Getty Images

A native of Port Arthur, Texas, Johnson went to high school with Janice Joplin. His high school football coach was Clarence "Buckshot" Underwood, a Bear Bryant protégé who molded Johnson into such a terror that he earned a scholarship to Arkansas.

He was planning on becoming an industrial psychologist when he got steered into coaching. He was an assistant at Oklahoma, Arkansas, and Pittsburgh before becoming a head coach at Oklahoma State. He was skipped for the top job at Arkansas twice, then went to Miami and turned them into a team people loved or loved to hate. With as much attitude as talent, the Hurricanes were scorned as the "University of San Quentin" and showed up to a bowl game wearing combat fatigues. He beat Barry Switzer and the Sooners for the national championship after the 1987 season.

A year later, Johnson was settling into Tom Landry's office as the second coach the Cowboys had ever had.

"I don't expect to replace Tom Landry," Johnson said soon after being hired. "All I can ask is just let me do my thing, let me work, let me show my enthusiasm and judge me by what happens later."

Jim Gund/Sports Illustrated/Getty Images

Jones paid $140 million for the team and the lease of Texas Stadium, a whopping 75 percent return on Bright's investment. Once again, the sale of the Cowboys set a record for the highest price ever paid for a pro sports team.

The night before the deal was announced, Jones and Johnson were spotted eating dinner in Dallas—at Landry's favorite Mexican restaurant. It was a fluke they were there, even more of a coincidence that they were spotted by the college football writer of *The Dallas Morning News*. He called a photographer, and the next day everyone knew what was coming. Landry even flew to his lake house near Austin to get away.

When founder Clint Murchison Jr. had sold the team to Bright, he insisted that Schramm and Landry stay and that the new owner butt out. Bright included no such provision, and Jones seemed intent on catching up for all the years without owner intervention.

Jones and Schramm flew to Austin to break the bad news to Landry in person. After a teary 40-minute meeting, they flew back for a news conference to announce that Landry was no longer the only coach the Cowboys had ever had, along with other massive changes.

With Schramm standing behind Jones, the new owner announced: "I intend to have an understanding of the complete situation, an understanding of the player situation, of the socks and jocks." He called Johnson "the best football coach in America."

"What Jimmy Johnson will bring to us is worth more than if we had five first-round draft choices and five Heisman Trophy winners," Jones said. "History will show that one of the finest things that ever happened to the Cowboys is Jimmy Johnson."

That night, Jones went to Texas Stadium, put his back on the 50-yard line and gazed up through the hole in the roof.

In his exuberance, Jones managed to botch the whole transfer of power and turn the world against him. Plenty of people wanted a new coach, and Johnson was certainly an intriguing hire. But nobody, *nobody*, wanted Landry thrown out like that.

The backlash was brutal. Landry was canonized. The irony was that Jones' exuberance stemmed from the legacy and tradition that Landry had built. He eventually acknowledged his mistake, but that would

RIVALRY IN REVIEW
PHILADELPHIA EAGLES

Credit or blame Buddy Ryan for stirring up the Cowboys–Eagles series into something nasty.

The bad blood began with his fake-kneel touchdown scam against Tom Landry in 1987. In 1989, he went after real blood.

The Eagles drilled the hapless Cowboys 27–0 on Thanksgiving, but that wasn't enough for Ryan. He also offered a bounty of $500 for any player who could take out Troy Aikman and $200 for kicker Luis Zendejas, who'd been with the Eagles earlier that season. Zendejas indeed left with a concussion.

Zendejas had been warned the night before and again during warmups, when an Eagles coach told him, "You know how Buddy is. He's going to put somebody on you on the first kickoff that you do."

When the teams met in Philadelphia a few weeks later, CBS hyped it as "Bounty Bowl II." The commissioner showed up to patrol the scene, and there were so many snowballs thrown at the Cowboys that Jerry Jones described it as "kind of like a big pie fight."

The really ugly scene came in 1999, when Michael Irvin ended up on his back and not moving after what proved to be the final play of his career. Fans cheered as he was carted away.

Other (not-so?) memorable moments include the sweltering game at Texas Stadium in 2000 when the Eagles fortified themselves with pickle juice, Donovan McNabb's amazing 14-second scramble and deep throw to Freddie Mitchell in 2004, and Terrell Owens doing his usual antics for both teams.

come years later—once all his other moves had been validated.

BOTTOMING OUT

Jerry Jones and Jimmy Johnson didn't have long to prepare for their first draft.

Good thing their first pick—No. 1 overall in 1989—was a no-brainer: quarterback Troy Aikman out of UCLA.

As their predecessors had done in the 1960s, the new regime started building the team through the draft. Fresh from his tenure as a college football coach, Johnson happened to have kept an eye on many of these prospects since they were in high school. The coach also believed in shuffling picks as if he were an options trader on Wall Street, packaging picks to move up for someone he liked or giving up one pick for several lower ones.

Johnson's first five draft picks included Aikman, Daryl Johnston, Mark Stepnoski, and Tony Tolbert. All went on to be starters on the 1992 and 1993 Super Bowl teams.

Then Johnson confounded everyone by taking Steve Walsh in the supplemental draft. Not only was this another rookie quarterback to compete with Aikman, but Walsh had led Johnson's Miami Hurricanes to a national championship in 1987. Thus, the novice leaders of this broken-down team had just invited a quarterback controversy, with the underdog seemingly the coach's pet pupil.

Schramm resigned soon thereafter. Others left or were fired, from Brandt to national anthem trumpeter Tommy Loy. The front office was turned upside-down, and Landry's players were herded out the door. So many other players came and went in Johnson's first season, it's a wonder the team didn't run out of thread for the names on the backs of jerseys.

In training camp, Johnson infamously banished a player "to the asthma field," a message of intolerance that kept everyone on their toes. He even took preseason seriously, thinking three wins in four games indicated they might be on to something. The foolishness of that idea was revealed when the Cowboys lost the opener 28–0.

The JJs quickly realized how wide the talent gap was between their club and the rest of the league.

It was a tough debut season for Troy Aikman in 1989. The future Hall of Famer failed to win a single game in 11 starts as a rookie. *Brad Bower/AP Images*

They needed to complete a proverbial Hail Mary pass just to catch up.

Fittingly enough, their big boost came courtesy of the Minnesota Vikings, victims of the original Hail Mary.

Vikings GM Mike Lynn thought his team was a running back away from a championship, so Dallas sent Herschel Walker to Minnesota in the largest trade in NFL history, a deal that ultimately included 18 players and picks.

Lynn gave the Cowboys a gaggle of players attached to draft picks. Dallas could use the players all season, then decide whether to keep those players or take the picks. Considering how bad the Cowboys were, Lynn figured they would want the veterans.

Nope. All along, Johnson only wanted the picks. But he ended up getting some of the players too.

How quickly did Johnson realize what a steal this deal was?

"The instant Mike Lynn said 'yes,'" Johnson said with a laugh many years later. He also pointed out that at the news conference announcing the trade he had called it "the great train robbery."

The Cowboys didn't fare as well on the field.

Dallas lost all 11 games Aikman started in 1989. He missed five games with injuries, and Walsh won one of them, beating the Redskins 13–3 in Washington. That game, the Cowboys didn't have a single turnover or penalty, and a defense that had been allowing 29 points per game didn't yield a touchdown.

"We're going to have a lot of wins over the next so-many-years in Dallas," Johnson said. "It's good to get it started."

SIGNS OF LIFE

The 1990 draft carried the weight of a Super Bowl for the Cowboys. It would go farther to determine their future than any game that season.

Maybe that's true every year, but it was especially true for a Dallas club that had the worst record in the NFL two years running.

The Cowboys earned the No. 1 overall pick, but they'd already spent it on Steve Walsh. They got back a first-rounder in the Herschel Walker trade and then started putting their stash of picks from the Walker deal to good use, adding running back Emmitt Smith, receiver Alexander Wright, defensive tackle Jimmie Jones, and cornerback Kenny Gant.

Then the Cowboys went to Plan B, which is what the NFL called its early free agency system.

It basically meant players at the bottom of rosters were allowed to sign elsewhere, which was a boon to a club like Dallas, which needed all the help it could get. Jimmy Johnson wound up with some real keepers: tight end Jay Novacek, fullback Tommie Agee, linebacker Vinson Smith, and safety James Washington.

COWBOY LEGENDS
JAY NOVACEK

Of all the passes Troy Aikman threw Jay Novacek—for first downs and touchdowns, in practices and Super Bowls—there's one that defines their relationship.

"He hit me with a pass while he was going down," Novacek said. "I asked him how he did it and he answered, 'I knew you would be there.'"

Novacek played tight end and was a decathlete during his college days at Wyoming. He spent five relatively anonymous seasons with the Cardinals, then came to Dallas in 1990 as a Plan B free agent and instantly clicked with Aikman.

He had a career-best 59 catches his first season, then 59 again the next, then 68 in

1992, the year the Cowboys won their first Super Bowl. Over six seasons, he averaged 10.5 yards per catch, pretty fitting considering he was Aikman's go-to guy when he needed to move the chains for a first down.

"Jay had that magic ability to get open," Cowboys owner Jerry Jones said. "It was so routine we almost took it for granted."

Novacek had back surgery in December 1995, then returned a month later to catch a touchdown in the Super Bowl. He played one more season before retiring because of his back.

Paul Buck/AFP/Getty Images

Emmitt Smith leapt into Cowboys lore in his rookie season. In just his fifth NFL game, Smith ran over Tampa Bay for 121 yards on 23 carries in a 14–10 Cowboys win. *Ron Heflin/ AP Images*

As the roster was being revamped, the few remaining ties to the Schramm-Landry era were cut.

Training camp was moved from Cal Lutheran University in Thousand Oaks, California, to St. Edward's University in Austin. After the team had spent 27 years working out in the cool air off the Pacific Ocean, Johnson wanted his players to deal with the Texas heat, and Jones wanted to be closer to his fan base.

Johnson demanded that players attend offseason workouts, and he made them challenging too. He wanted guys in shape, and he figured the extra time spent together would help them become more of a team. If they bonded through their hatred of him, that was fine, as long as they bonded.

Smith didn't sign until five days before the regular-season opener. Johnson made him come off the bench his first two games, and he gained just 11 yards. Then Smith moved into the starting lineup, and a legend was launched. He finished the season

with 937 yards and the NFL's Offensive Rookie of the Year award.

Dallas beat San Diego in the opener, ending a 14-game home losing streak that was the longest in NFL history. The victory also gave the Cowboys a winning record for the first time since November 1987. OK, so it was only 1–0, but you've got to start somewhere.

Then it was back to the same old, same old— three straight losses, four in five games, seven in nine.

Along the way, Johnson traded Walsh for first-, second-, and third-round picks from New Orleans. Some NFL insiders consider it a bigger steal than the Walker trade because Walker was a proven player, whereas Walsh wasn't and never would be.

Even though the Cowboys were struggling, they seemed to be pointed in the right direction. After good drafts in Johnson's first two years, they had three first-round picks in 1991 and 13 picks in the first three rounds of the next two drafts. When

Sports Illustrated suggested that this plan had three or four years to come to fruition, Johnson replied: "Actually, we ought to know by 1992."

The final six weeks of 1990 turned out to be a good indicator.

Starting the Sunday before Thanksgiving, Dallas won four straight games—more wins than the previous two seasons combined and the club's best surge since early in 1985, their last playoff season. And, now, although the Cowboys were only 7–7, the playoffs were within reach.

Those odds worsened in the next game, when Aikman separated his right shoulder in a loss at Philadelphia and was done for the season.

In Aikman's place, Babe Laufenberg—who would later become a beloved Cowboys radio analyst—played like a guy ready for a second career. He threw four interceptions against Philadelphia and two more in the finale, a loss to Atlanta that was especially humiliating because the Falcons had gone into the game as the NFC's worst team.

Dallas still had a chance for the playoffs if the Rams beat the Saints. But Walsh-led New Orleans snatched away the wild card.

Maybe it was for the best. The Cowboys weren't ready to turn the corner quite that quickly. Better to be motivated by being so close.

Johnson was voted coach of the year, but he wasn't satisfied. In mid-January, he dumped Landry coaching holdovers Dick Nolan and Alan Lowry and demoted David Shula from offensive coordinator to passing coordinator.

Aikman and Smith were thrilled to be done with Shula. They would soon be even happier with his replacement, Norv Turner.

ALMOST THERE

The most anticipated season since the early 1980s got rolling in April of 1991, when Jimmy Johnson dangled 3 of the top 14 draft picks as trade bait.

Two days before the draft, he moved up to the No. 1 spot, giving him first dibs on the hot commodity, Notre Dame receiver/returner Raghib "Rocket" Ismail. What the Cowboys really wanted was a bidding war to get an even bigger return on their investment, but the Rocket took off for Canada, crushing

the trade market. Dallas kept the pick and used it on defensive tackle Russell Maryland.

Intent on avoiding another long holdout, the Cowboys only drafted players who agreed to contracts before they were picked. It worked just fine, as they added receiver Alvin Harper, linebackers Dixon Edwards and Godfrey Myles, tackle Erik Williams, defensive end Leon Lett, and cornerback Larry Brown.

Johnson also traded for Steve Beuerlein to get the solid backup quarterback Dallas desperately needed, and for defensive lineman Tony Casillas, a two-time Pro Bowler for Atlanta who had gotten crosswise with management. Plan B delivered tight end Alfredo Roberts.

All the pieces seemed to be in place, but three weeks into the season, Dallas was 1–2 and had just been shut out by Philadelphia. The Eagles sacked Troy Aikman 11 times and allowed just 90 yards.

The Cowboys responded by winning four straight, then lost three of four. With the 11–0 Redskins up next, Johnson decided to use whatever gimmick he could. Dallas went for it on fourth down three times, pulled off an onside kick in the second quarter, and pretty much had Washington wondering what was coming next the rest of the afternoon. Aikman's right knee was mashed on the final play of the first half, but Beuerlein took over, and Dallas won 24–21.

Beuerlein started the final four games, and the Cowboys won them all. They finished 11–5 just two seasons after being 1–15.

Emmitt Smith ran for 1,563 yards, becoming Dallas' first NFL rushing leader and starting an NFL-record run of 11 straight 1,000-yard seasons. Michael Irvin led the NFL in receiving yards, another Dallas first.

In the franchise's first trip to the playoffs in six years, and the first-ever trip for most of the players, the Cowboys went to Chicago and beat the Bears 17–13. The defense gave up only a single field goal out of three drives inside their 10-yard line. A blocked punt helped set up a touchdown, and Beuerlein led a long, slow touchdown drive in the third quarter.

A week later, they participated in the first playoff game in Detroit since 1957.

With Barry Sanders in the backfield, the Lions came out . . . throwing, which caught the Cowboys by surprise. Detroit led 14–3 when Johnson put in Aikman to try to spark a comeback; he only made things worse with an interception and two fumbled snaps.

The Cowboys lost 38–6, scoring only a pair of field goals. Like the previous season ending on the brink of making the playoffs, this back-to-earth loss might have been a perfect sendoff.

These guys were good, but they still needed more work.

HOW 'BOUT THEM COWBOYS!

With Troy Aikman, Emmitt Smith, and Michael Irvin in place, the Cowboys were doing just fine on offense. They still needed some help on defense, though.

Jimmy Johnson drafted cornerback Kevin Smith and safety Darren Woodson, then the San Francisco 49ers practically gave them defensive end Charles Haley.

Safety James Washington (37) makes a diving interception in the end zone against the Bears in the NFC Wild Card Playoff Game on December 29, 1991. *Tony Tomsic/ Getty Images*

COWBOY LEGENDS
CHARLES HALEY

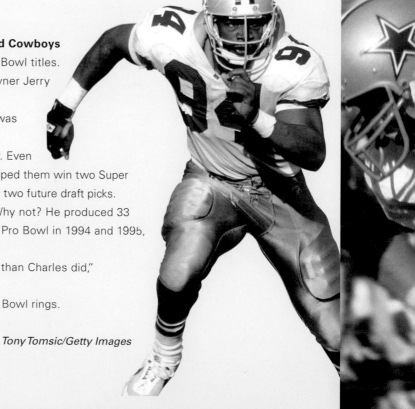

Charles Haley is widely credited as being the guy who turned a good Cowboys defense in 1991 into the league's best in 1992, launching a run of Super Bowl titles.

"We couldn't spell Super Bowl until Charles joined us," Cowboys owner Jerry Jones said. "He was our missing link."

Haley was nasty, aggressive, and practically unstoppable. And that was just how he treated his teammates.

The San Francisco 49ers couldn't tolerate his bizarre, raunchy behavior. Even though he was 28, was coming off two straight Pro Bowl trips, and had helped them win two Super Bowls, the 49ers sent him to an up-and-coming conference rival for merely two future draft picks.

The Cowboys were able to handle Haley, or, at least, tolerate him. Why not? He produced 33 sacks in 58 games from 1992 to 1995, Dallas' prime years. He made the Pro Bowl in 1994 and 1995, then retired after back problems ruined his 1996 season.

"No one came more prepared to play or played harder on game day than Charles did," Troy Aikman said.

He also had a pretty cool claim to fame: The first guy with five Super Bowl rings.

Tony Tomsic/Getty Images

Haley was a spectacular player but a spectacularly strange dude. To show how much the Cowboys valued him, Jerry Jones personally picked him up at the airport.

More help came in another steal-of-a-deal with Pittsburgh for safety Thomas Everett. And then there was the arrival of Chad Hennings, an Outland Trophy winner at Air Force who had delayed the start of his football career to fight in the Gulf War.

Haley and Hennings were terrific additions for a defensive line that relied on depth.

The Cowboys liked to rotate players to ensure that they always had fresh legs chasing quarterbacks and running backs. The new combination was so good that the Cowboys had the league's top-ranked defense for the first time since 1977, which also was the last time they won the Super Bowl.

Dallas started the season 3–0 and was feeling good going into a game against Herschel Walker and his new team, the Philadelphia Eagles. The Cowboys got steamrolled, 31–7.

From then on, they did the steamrolling.

Featuring the likes of Tony Tolbert (92), Robert Jones (55), Ken Norton (51), Thomas Everett (31), and Charles Haley (94), the Dallas defense smothered all comers in 1992. *Mike Powell/Getty Images*

They started with a 27–0 trouncing of Seattle—Dallas' first shutout win since 1978—and kept going for a 10–2 finish to the season. Those two losses were by a combined seven points.

In the season finale, the only thing at stake was a club-record 13th win. Johnson cared more about keeping up momentum for the playoffs and seemed to have it with Dallas leading Chicago 27–0 in the fourth quarter. So he took out Emmitt Smith (who'd already won another rushing title and set a club record with 1,713 yards) and put in backup Curvin Richards.

Richards fumbled, leading to a Chicago touchdown, then he fumbled again, and the Bears returned it for a touchdown. Dallas still won 27–14, but the mistakes played right into Johnson's hands. He cut Richards the next day, sending the message that he wouldn't tolerate mistakes or players who made them. So what if Richards was an inconsequential player, a backup to a guy who rarely came out?

Also that day against the Bears, Cowboys owner Jerry Jones played host to Prince Bandar bin Sultan, a Saudi Arabian ambassador to the United States. He was one of the world's richest men and a big Cowboys fan. He and his bodyguards were allowed onto the sideline, which Johnson hated—one of many points of contention beginning to stack up in the relationship between the owner and the coach.

Dallas opened the playoffs with a 34–10 victory over Philadelphia. The Cowboys held Walker to 29 yards.

Then it was off to Candlestick Park for the defining game of this generation of Cowboys, as pivotal as the 1966 NFC title game against the Packers (which Dallas lost) and the 1981 NFC title game against the 49ers (which Dallas lost).

The game was hyped as the *real* Super Bowl, Dallas' No. 1 defense against San Francisco's No. 1 offense, led by MVP Steve Young.

The Cowboys were up 24–13 in the fourth quarter and were facing fourth-and-1 from the 49ers' 7-yard line when Johnson decided to go for the kill. It backfired. Smith was stopped short, and the 49ers drove 93 yards for a touchdown that cut the lead to four with 4:22 left.

How 'bout them Cowboys! Linebacker Robert Jones (55) celebrates in the closing minutes of Dallas' 30–20 victory over the 49ers in the 1992 NFC Championship Game. *James Smith/NFL Photos/ Getty Images*

Dallas wasn't backing down. A short pass to Alvin Harper turned into a 70-yard gain, leading to a touchdown. Then James Washington intercepted a Young pass, and the raucous, Super Bowl–bound celebration was on.

TV cameras were allowed into the locker room, and they captured Johnson closing his postgame speech by hollering, "How 'bout them Cowboys!" Within days, there were hats and T-shirts bearing the slogan.

Dallas' rise was quite unbelievable.

After reaching 5 of the first 13 Super Bowls, the Cowboys had missed the last 13. They had gotten within a game many times yet couldn't make the final step. Then they went into a tailspin. Now, just three years after bottoming out at 1–15, they were back.

"[We] really didn't get caught up in the significance of each game or what the impact would be," Aikman said. "We just went out and played football, and before we knew it, we were in the Super Bowl and nobody could believe it."

Representing the AFC at the Rose Bowl in Pasadena were the Buffalo Bills, who had lost the previous two Super Bowls to NFC East teams.

Dallas took charge early and never let up on the way to a 52–17 victory that put the Cowboys atop the NFL for the first time in 15 years.

Jerry Jones and Jimmy Johnson hoist the Vince Lombardi Trophy in celebration of the Cowboys' victory in Super Bowl XXVII. *Al Messerschmidt/Getty Images*

League commissioner Paul Tagliabue made note of it all as he handed Jones and Johnson a nice, shiny Lombardi Trophy, congratulating them for "an awesome display of football and for making one of the most extraordinary turnarounds in history."

GAME TO REMEMBER

SUPER BOWL XXVII
DALLAS COWBOYS 52, BUFFALO BILLS 17

PASADENA, CALIFORNIA – Few people were allowed to watch the Cowboys practice the week leading up to the championship game against Buffalo. Those who did were amazed by how crisp the performance was.

"I don't think we dropped a pass all week," receivers coach Hubbard Alexander said.

When the Cowboys scored a pair of touchdowns within a minute of each other in Super Bowl XXVII, those observers weren't surprised. They probably weren't surprised the second time, either.

The third time? OK, at that point, even they were impressed.

The Cowboys blew out the Buffalo Bills 52–17 with an incredible performance on both sides of the ball. The defense set the tone by coming up with a Super Bowl–record nine turnovers and allowing only one field goal on two drives inside the Dallas 5-yard line.

James Washington got the party started with an interception to set up a touchdown that tied the game at seven. (Yes, Buffalo actually led 7–0.) Then Charles Haley sacked Jim Kelly and pried the ball loose before Jimmie Jones plucked it out of the air and ran for a touchdown that put Dallas ahead 14–7. Two Aikman-to-Irvin touchdowns later, it was 28–10 at halftime.

The Bills got within 31–17 after a touchdown pass by backup quarterback Frank Reich. But then the Cowboys erupted again, and the only question left was whether they would break the record for most points in a Super Bowl, 55.

It looked as if they would when defensive tackle Leon Lett picked up a fumble and began running to the end zone, 65 yards away. After about 60 yards, he held up the ball in celebration. Inches before he reached the end zone, Buffalo's Don Beebe caught up and knocked the ball out of his hands.

Oh well. Can't have everything.

Or could you? Dallas was the Super Bowl champ again. The JJs had done it their way, dammit, and it worked. Emmitt Smith became the first player to win a rushing title and a Super Bowl in the same season. Troy Aikman was named the game MVP in the city where he went to college. Those crisp practices leading up to the game were even held at his alma mater, UCLA.

"There was never any doubt we'd get to this point," said Jimmy Johnson, the first head coach to win a Division I national championship and a Super Bowl. "The [only] concern was how long it would take."

Aikman was 22-of-30 for 273 yards, threw four touchdowns, and committed no turnovers—a rarity for any quarterback in a Super Bowl, especially a first-timer.

"No matter what happens from here on out," he said, "I can say I took my team to a Super Bowl victory."

Michael Irvin's reaction was exactly what you'd expect from the flamboyant receiver: "I've already told them I want diamonds in my ring bigger than headlights. In fact, I want diamonds so big I can turn off the headlights when I'm driving down the road, stick my hand out the window, and still be able to see."

George Long/NFL/Getty Images

134

PUT IT IN THREE-INCH HEADLINES—
"BACK-TO-BACK CHAMPS"

With so much talent in so many places, talk of more titles began immediately.

So did the usual raiding of a championship organization and the demands for more money from those who stayed.

Defensive coordinator Dave Wannstedt left to coach Chicago. Steve Beuerlein and receiver Kelvin Martin left in free agency. The draft wasn't a boon, but the Cowboys did get some usable players in receiver Kevin Williams, linebacker Darrin Smith, and safety Brock Marion.

Emmitt Smith was due a big raise. He wanted a $17 million contract, nearly double the $9 million Jerry Jones was willing to pay. Smith took a gamble by stretching his holdout into the regular season. It paid off when the Cowboys lost the first two games.

The second was at home against Buffalo, with fans chanting, "We want Emmitt!" Afterward, an irate Charles Haley caved in a locker-room wall with his helmet. Then Jones caved in at the negotiating table.

A few days after a historic Mideast peace pact was signed at the White House, Jones and Smith worked out their differences with a $13.6 million, four-year contract, ending the longest holdout by a veteran in club history. (Later in the season, Aikman became the highest-paid player in NFL history, getting a $50 million, eight-year deal that included an $11 million bonus.)

With Smith back in the fold, the Cowboys were ready to start their title defense in earnest.

Dallas won its next seven games, with the defense allowing a touchdown or less in each. The stretch included:

- Smith running for a career-best 237 yards to break Tony Dorsett's single-game club record and put the Cowboys in first place.
- A 26–17 victory against rival San Francisco.
- A 31–9 victory over the Giants on the afternoon Tom Landry was enshrined in the Ring of Honor.

The winning streak ended at home against Atlanta on the Sunday before Thanksgiving. Aikman already was out with a pulled hamstring, then Smith went out with a bruised thigh.

Fullback Daryl Johnston—seen here upended after making a catch against Arizona in September—helped the Cowboys turn the rest of the NFL on its head during another championship run in 1993. *James D. Smith/NFL/Getty Images*

Four days later, the Miami Dolphins came to town. So did a snowstorm. In the worst weather anyone could remember the Cowboys playing in since the Ice Bowl, Dallas managed to hold a 14–13 lead in the final minute.

Then Leon Lett—goat of Super Bowl XXVII—made another bone-headed mistake.

Jimmie Jones had just blocked a 41-yard field goal attempt with 15 seconds left. As long as nobody touched it, the Dolphins eventually would down the ball, and the Cowboys could take a knee to end the game. Thomas Everett and Darrin Smith were among those telling their teammates to stay away, but Lett slid through the crowd and tumbled into the ball, sending it scooting across the ice. Miami's Jeff Dellenbach recovered it at the 1-yard line with three seconds left. The Dolphins tried another, shorter field goal and made it for the victory.

"There were hundreds of mistakes made in that game. It just so happens that particular one cost us the ball," Johnson said diplomatically about Lett's gaffe. "We lost two to start the season and we lost two now. But there's no reason we can't put another streak together."

They did. In fact, that would be Johnson's last loss with the Cowboys.

Dallas won the next four games to set up a tantalizing finale on the road against the Giants. With both teams 11–4, the winner got the NFC East title, home-field advantage in the playoffs, and a first-round bye. The loser got a wild-card game the next week.

Cementing his status as one of the all-time greats, Smith turned in the defining performance of his career. He produced 229 total yards and a touchdown in 32 carries and 10 receptions, the heaviest workload in team history—and most of it coming

Emmitt Smith was a true workhorse in Dallas' must-win victory over the Giants in the 1993 season finale. *Tony Tomsic/Getty Images*

after he separated his right shoulder. The Cowboys needed it all to win 16–13 in overtime.

"I don't know if it was my greatest game," Smith said years later, "but it was one of the most important and one of the best because of what I did under those circumstances."

Smith won his third straight rushing title and became the first player ever to claim the rushing crown while missing two games. He also was voted the NFL MVP, the first and still only such honor for a Dallas player.

Had the Cowboys lost to the Giants and had to play the next week, Smith probably would have been out. Given an extra week, he was ready to face Brett Favre and the Packers.

Soon, another storyline emerged.

Johnson told ESPN he would be intrigued if the incoming Jacksonville franchise wanted him to be GM and coach. Jaguars owner Wayne Weaver called to see if he was serious; he was. But Jones told Weaver he wanted two first-round picks in exchange, and Weaver backed off.

Between Smith's aching shoulder and angst over the brewing Johnson-Jones squabble, the Cowboys struggled against Green Bay. They still won, 27–17, but everyone knew a performance like that would get them whipped by the 49ers in the NFC Championship Game.

On the Thursday before the game, Johnson got their attention.

Fueled by a few Heinekens, he dialed up the radio show of *Dallas Morning News* columnist Randy Galloway and proclaimed, "We will win the ballgame. And you can put it in three-inch headlines: We will win the ballgame!"

Niners coach George Seifert responded on a San Francisco radio station the next day: "Well, the man's got balls. I don't know if they're brass or papier-mâché. We'll find out here pretty soon."

Aikman had the Cowboys up by 21 at halftime, although he doesn't remember any of it.

A few plays into the third quarter, Aikman took an accidental knee to the head. He was knocked so silly that when asked where the Super Bowl was being played, he said "Henryetta, Oklahoma," where he grew up. He also couldn't remember the name of

Things got a bit heated between the Cowboys and 49ers during the NFC Championship Game on January 24, 1994, but Dallas came away with a relatively easy 38–21 win. *Richard Mackson/Sports Illustrated/Getty Images*

last year's Super Bowl MVP. (Hint: It was on the back of his jersey.)

Backup Bernie Kosar nailed down a 38–21 victory, sending Dallas to its seventh Super Bowl.

"I thought Johnson's comment was insane," 49ers star Jerry Rice said. "But I guess it was accurate."

To win a fourth title, the Cowboys would have to win a rematch with the Buffalo Bills.

The Super Bowl was scheduled to be played the week after the championship games, so there wasn't much time for Aikman to recover.

The Cowboys weren't very sharp early, getting just two field goals and trailing 13–6 at halftime. Then James Washington returned a fumble 46 yards for a touchdown, and Dallas got rolling. The defense didn't allow another point, and Smith ran for two touchdowns on the way to a 30–13 victory—and a second straight championship.

Turmoil be damned! The Cowboys overcame Smith's holdout, Smith's injury, Aikman's concussion, and the simmering feud between Johnson and Jones.

"We have a great opportunity to do something that has never been done, and that's to win three straight Super Bowls," Jones said. "I know that Jimmy enjoys the challenges, and I know that he will be here."

He was gone 58 days later.

THREE IN A ROW? NOT WITHOUT JIMMY

The feud between Jerry Jones and Jimmy Johnson turned into a battle royale during the NFL owners meetings in 1994.

Johnson was talking and drinking with some of his closest friends—former Cowboys staffers Dave Wannstedt, Norv Turner, and Bob Ackles, and their wives—when Jones walked up and offered a toast to their roles in Dallas' success. They drank, then resumed their conversation without asking Jones to join them.

A few hours later, a still-irate Jones bumped into some reporters at the hotel bar. He said he might fire his coach and replace him with Barry Switzer.

"There are 500 coaches who could have won the Super Bowl with our team," Jones proclaimed.

SUPER BOWL XXVIII
DALLAS COWBOYS 30, BUFFALO BILLS 13

ATLANTA, GEORGIA – The big question going into Super Bowl XXVIII was whether or not Troy Aikman would be able to start. What the Buffalo Bills didn't realize was that James Washington was going to be starting too.

Washington certainly wasn't the kind of player the Bills would have paid attention to even if they had known this bit of information. However, his presence made all the difference.

Washington had an interception in the previous year's Super Bowl, but a lot of guys did. Yet his was the first of nine takeaways, so it was pretty significant. The plays he made in this game were too.

Dallas mustered only two field goals in the first quarter and was shut out in the second quarter. The Bills got a pair of field goals, as well as a touchdown on a 4-yard run by Thurman Thomas to lead 13–6 at halftime.

Could it be? In their fourth straight Super Bowl, would this be the one the Bills finally win?

They seemed to be wondering the same thing.

"I was thinking it didn't look good for us," Troy Aikman said. "But I looked over and saw their players go in, and you would have thought they were a team that just felt that something bad was going to happen, that they were snakebit in Super Bowls."

The Bills got the ball to start the second half, seeking a lead-stretching touchdown. Then Leon Lett forced Thomas to fumble, and Washington was there to recover. He took it 46 yards for a touchdown that made it 13–all.

A touchdown by Emmitt Smith put the Cowboys up 20–13. Buffalo was driving for the potential tying score when Washington struck again, intercepting a third-down pass to Don Beebe.

"I wasn't thinking touchdown on that play," Washington said. "I was exhausted and had leg cramps and I wanted to just fall on the ground and get out of there. That's why Emmitt gets so much money to run the ball. He just kept running and ran away with the MVP."

James Washington runs back an interception for a touchdown.
George Rose/NFL/Getty Images

Just two months after winning a second straight Super Bowl title, Jimmy Johnson ended his relationship with the team and owner Jerry Jones, announcing his departure as head coach. *Paul K. Buck/AFP/Getty Images*

Sure enough, Smith ran for another touchdown and became the MVP. Although there was sentiment that Washington should get it, he knew the deal. His 11 tackles and two momentum-turning turnovers were no match for the league MVP scoring two second-half touchdowns. Washington was satisfied knowing he was at his best "on the day you want to be at your best."

As time ran out on the 30–13 victory, Gatorade was dumped on Jimmy Johnson, and Smith mussed Johnson's never-a-follicle-out-of-place hairdo.

Whatever tension existed between Johnson and owner Jerry Jones evaporated as they shared a celebratory hug. Their club had just joined Green Bay, Miami, Pittsburgh, and San Francisco as the only back-to-back Super Bowl winners, and the franchise joined Pittsburgh and San Francisco as the only four-time champions.

How 'bout them Cowboys?

"Last year's Super Bowl was one of disbelief, a bunch of young, bright-eyed guys caught up in it all," Aikman said. "This is one of satisfaction because the expectations were so much higher."

The divide had grown too wide. Johnson wouldn't forgive Jones for things like bringing Saudi businessmen to the sideline. Jones wouldn't forgive Johnson for things like angling for the Jacksonville job. Both wanted credit for the Cowboys' amazing revival.

On March 30, Jones and Johnson announced they were going separate ways at a news conference that had all the hugs, smiles, and mutual praise of a rehearsal dinner, not a divorce. Then again, both got what they wanted.

Jones was thrilled to be firmly in charge, and Johnson was giddy to be free, especially since he collected a $2 million going-away gift. Jones didn't fire him, and Johnson didn't resign. They just split up after building a two-time Super Bowl champion everyone knew was poised to make a run at several more.

As stunning as Dallas' rise was from 1–15 to Super Bowl champs, this topped it. Championship formulas are so hard to come by that to willingly break it up remains as hard to believe now as it was then.

Maybe Johnson—who had never kept a job longer than five years and had just finished his fifth in Dallas—was outsmarting everyone. Leaving on top sealed his legacy. If the Cowboys kept winning, it was because he put everything in place. If they didn't, it was because he was gone.

Had they broken up right after the Super Bowl, Turner could have replaced Johnson instead of going to Washington. Perhaps to prove a point, Jones did hire Switzer.

The self-described "Bootlegger's Boy" had been out of coaching since resigning from Oklahoma in 1988, had never worked in the NFL, and had long been Johnson's adversary. Now he was being handed custody of the two-time defending champions.

"Nothing is going to change," Switzer crowed the day he was hired. "Get ready to watch the Dallas Cowboys be the best in the NFL. We got a job to do and we're going to do it, baby!"

Teams typically go from a hard-nosed coach like Johnson to a laid-back one like Switzer, or vice-versa, only when things get stale and require changing. Dallas was taking the unprecedented step of making that flip-flop in the midst of a dynasty.

Troy Aikman didn't trust Switzer. He'd already lied to him once.

Coming out of high school in Oklahoma, Aikman signed with the Sooners because Switzer promised to start passing but then changed his mind

In August 1994, the Cowboys took on the Oilers in a preseason matchup played in front of a record crowd for the "American Bowl" in Mexico City. *James D. Smith/NFL/ Getty Images*

a few days after Aikman arrived on campus. The quarterback broke his leg running the Wishbone (against Johnson's Miami Hurricanes) and transferred to UCLA. He also knew all about Switzer's wild side often taking up more of his time and attention than the playbook did.

Between free agency and salary cap trouble, the Cowboys lost key contributors like Tony Casillas and Jimmie Jones on the defensive line, linebacker Ken Norton and offensive linemen Kevin Gogan, John Gesek, and Frank Cornish. All Dallas added were Derek Kennard and Rodney Peete. The talent drain was starting.

In the preseason, the Cowboys played the Houston Oilers in Mexico City, drawing a crowd of 112,376, the biggest ever for an NFL game. (For what it's worth, the Oilers won, 6–0.)

Dallas opened the regular season 8–1, winning six straight heading into a game against the 49ers, who were 7–2. Whoever won would have a huge inside track on home-field advantage in the NFC Championship. In front of the largest crowd ever at Candlestick Park, the 49ers turned three interceptions into a 21–14 victory.

"This lets us know we're not as good as we thought," offensive lineman Nate Newton said.

Dallas bounced back with a win over Washington, but Aikman went out with a sprained knee, and Peete sprained the thumb on his throwing hand. That left third-stringer Jason Garrett to start on Thanksgiving.

In the only start thus far of his NFL career, Garrett had been pulled after a quarter. But on the 20th anniversary of Clint Longley's Thanksgiving stunner, Garrett pulled off another. The Cowboys scored five touchdowns in a span of 18:40 and scored a club-record 36 second-half points in a 42–31 victory over Green Bay.

"If this is a fairy tale, so be it," Garrett said.

The injuries started catching up, though. Dallas lost two of its last three games to finish 12–4. Emmitt Smith missed the finale with a hamstring problem, the first time in his career he missed a game because of an injury.

The Cowboys looked great in their first playoff game. Michael Irvin, Alvin Harper, and Jay

Novacek each had more than 100 yards receiving as the Cowboys beat Brett Favre and the Packers 35–9. Then it was off to San Francisco for another NFC Championship matchup.

Ask them now, and Aikman, Irvin, and Smith will call this the game they remember most from their careers. For all the great victories they enjoyed, this devastating defeat—in the muck and mud of Candlestick Park—stands out because of how quickly they fell behind and how close they came to pulling it out anyway.

An interception by Aikman, a fumble by Irvin, and a fumbled kickoff by Kevin Williams helped San Francisco spring ahead 21–0 after only five minutes. Smith later compared it to giving Carl Lewis a 20-yard head start in a 100-yard dash.

Still, there were three and a half quarters left. It was way too early for anyone to give up.

By late in the first half, the Cowboys had cut the deficit to 10, trailing 24–14. They could have run out the clock and been satisfied to be this close heading into halftime, but instead, they threw the ball. Three incomplete passes forced a punt. The muck caused John Jett to shank it, and the 49ers followed with another touchdown, stretching the lead back to 31–14. The touchdown pass came with NFL career touchdown leader Jerry Rice in single coverage against Larry Brown, and league MVP Steve Young was able to take advantage.

Dallas kept clawing. By the fourth quarter, two Aikman-to-Irvin touchdowns made it 38–28.

The Cowboys were headed for another score when 49ers cornerback Deion Sanders shoved Irvin as he went for a pass near the end zone. It was obviously pass interference and should have been an automatic first down. Instead, the only flag was against Switzer for bumping an official while arguing.

And that was it. The Cowboys would not become the first team to win three straight Super Bowls, at least not this year.

Considering everything that surrounded the season, losing the NFC title game on the road to a team that would easily win the Super Bowl was still quite a feat. So either Barry Switzer wasn't the buffoon fans feared he'd be, or this group was good enough to win despite him.

MONEY, DRUGS, RACISM, A DUMB DECISION . . . AND ANOTHER TITLE

The 1995 season was absolutely nuts, even by Cowboys standards.

The talent drain continued with Alvin Harper, Kenny Gant, Jim Jeffcoat, Mark Stepnoski, and James Washington all leaving, and Dallas doing little to replace them—not right away, anyway.

Dallas opened with a newsworthy 35–0 victory over the Giants on a Monday night in New York.

The day before the opener, Jerry Jones gave cornerback Kevin Smith an $11 million contract. Then, in the second quarter of the game, Smith tore his Achilles' tendon and was lost for the year.

Jones already was bidding on free agent Deion Sanders. Now the Cowboys really needed him.

"I told Jerry after the ballgame to go get Deion," Switzer said. "It's not showtime anymore. It's serious business."

Also serious business was the news release issued during the game—headlined "Cowboys Owner Bucks NFL Again"—announcing a seven-year contract between Nike and Texas Stadium.

NFL teams were required to share revenue, but there were no rules about stadium deals. So Jones courted rivals of companies with league deals. He

Two longtime rivals went head to head in another classic meeting in the NFC Championship Game in January 1995. This time, the 49ers came out on top, ruining Dallas' hopes for a "three-peat." *Al Bello/Getty Images*

The Cowboys acquired star defensive back Deion Sanders before the 1995 season, and the self-proclaimed "Prime Time" went on to post three straight All-Pro seasons from 1996 to 1998.

"At best, something like this is short-sighted and self-serving," commissioner Paul Tagliabue told *The Dallas Morning News*. "At worst, it's very unfair and destructive."

Five days later—flush with Nike's cash and needing a shutdown cornerback—Jones signed Sanders to a $35 million contract. (Jones and Sanders later filmed a Pizza Hut commercial in which Jones asks Sanders a series of questions—Football or baseball? Offense or defense?—and Sanders always answers, "Both!" Jones ends by asking whether he wants $15 million or $20 million, and Sanders says, "Both!")

The deal included a bonus of $12,999,999, avoiding the unlucky number 13. The bonus was more than Troy Aikman received and was the size of Emmitt Smith's entire contract. The justification was that Sanders was the reigning defensive player of the year and his arrival made the Cowboys the favorites to win the Super Bowl, especially since they were plucking him from the reigning champs.

"I know people will say I paid too much," Jones said. "My only statement is this: Any time in my life that I have ever paid too much for anything, it has been for quality."

Despite the distractions, Dallas was 6–1 when Sanders recovered from an injury and was ready for his debut. It happened to be in Atlanta, where his career began, and the Cowboys showed they were serious about using their new weapon on both defense and offense. Sanders played four snaps at receiver and caught one pass for six yards.

"Every time I was out there, they were yelling, 'Watch Deion! Watch Deion!'" Sanders said. "When you watch Deion, that's when Emmitt hits it, or Jay Novacek or Irvin."

Days later, Leon Lett and cornerback Clayton Holmes were suspended for four games for violating the league's substance-abuse policy. Said Switzer: "We turn it up a notch when adversity comes."

The Cowboys beat the Eagles the next week, and then San Francisco came to Texas Stadium for a game with all sorts of great subplots. The 49ers were reeling, however, having lost two straight and three of four. They were only 5–4 on the season and had Elvis Grbac, not Steve Young, at quarterback. Dallas was 8–1 and had Sanders.

began this end-around during training camp by putting on white boots emblazoned with the Pepsi logo, kicking up his heels, and declaring he'd be "drinking Pepsi, selling Pepsi, and promoting Pepsi," despite the league's deal with Coke. He soon added American Express.

Jones understood the history and importance of revenue sharing; he just didn't think it was fair. His team was the most popular, he worked the hardest, and he brought in the most money—but he didn't think he was keeping enough of it. The league sued him for $300 million, and he countersued for $750 million. They settled in December 1996 without ever going to court.

In the short term, however, the only owner who also was a general manager was now shaking up the foundation of the NFL's business model.

"Jerry's attitude is, 'What's mine is mine, and what's yours is ours,'" New York Giants owner Wellington Mara told the *Wall Street Journal*.

The Eagles defense stopped Emmitt Smith on a pivotal fourth-down play late in the game on December 10, 1995, allowing Philadelphia to come back and win. *Doug Pensigner/Getty Images*

The game wasn't even close—just not the way folks expected.

Eerily reminiscent of the previous year's title game, the Cowboys trailed 17–0 after only a few minutes, but there would be no dramatic comeback in this 38–20 loss.

Dallas followed with solid victories over two AFC powerhouses, then—with a chance to clinch the division title—the Cowboys lost at home to a lousy Redskins team. Things got worse a week later in Philadelphia, when Switzer made the words "Load Left" an infamous part of team lore.

A 14-point lead dissolved into a tie game with a little over two minutes left. Dallas was facing fourth-and-one-foot from its own 29-yard line. Stiff winds made it feel like minus 7 degrees and made it tough to punt.

A short punt would give the Eagles a great chance to kick the winning field goal. Switzer also knew his offense needed a boost. So, he decided to go for it, even if failure basically handed the game to Philadelphia and success still left them a long way from victory.

The play call was the bread-and-butter on short yardage: Smith going left, behind guard Nate Newton and tackle Mark Tuinei. It was so obvious the Eagles stuffed it.

But, wait! The 2-minute warning hit before the snap, so the play didn't count. Do-over. Time to send out the punt squad, right?

Nope. Arrogant or confident, stubborn or stupid, Switzer called Load Left again. The Eagles stuffed it again, then kicked the winning field goal.

The *New York Post* dubbed Switzer "Bozo the Coach." Even the usually forgiving members of the coaches-turned-broadcasters fraternity let Switzer have it. Mike Ditka called the initial decision and the second try, "The sequel to *Dumb and Dumber*." Jimmy Johnson piled on too.

Tony Tolbert's pair of sacks on Green Bay quarterback Brett Favre helped the Cowboys secure a 38–27 win in the 1995 NFC Championship Game and a third trip to the Super Bowl in four years. *Otto Greule Jr./Getty Images*

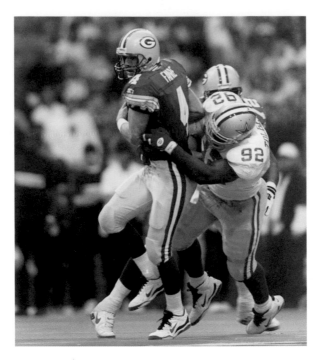

Everything Cowboys fans feared when Switzer took over seemed to be coming true.

Dallas was crumbling, and it was his fault. The Cowboys had lost two straight since having the chance to clinch the division and had given the 49ers home-field advantage in the playoffs.

"What has happened to us?" Tuinei said.

Just like Lett's snowy gaffe in 1993 didn't derail anything, this turned out to be a bump in the road too. No, it was more than that.

It proved to be a rallying point.

"You have to understand, we were in a major slump," Irvin said. "He was saying to us, 'I still believe y'all are the best in the world.'"

The Cowboys won their last two games to finish 12–4 for a third straight season. Smith won his third NFL rushing title and set an NFL record with 25 rushing touchdowns (and he saved every ball; the networks loved showing sideline staffers putting the balls away for safe-keeping).

More good news came before Dallas' next game: The Packers upset the 49ers. So when the Cowboys drubbed the Eagles 30–11—with Sanders scoring on a reverse and intercepting a pass—their last obstacle to the Super Bowl was a Packers team they had dominated in recent years.

Brett Favre was coming off his first MVP season and vowed things would be different from the last six meetings, including the last two postseasons, all Dallas victories. It sure didn't seem that way when Aikman and Irvin hooked up for touchdowns on consecutive throws in the first quarter. But Favre put the Packers ahead 27–24 in the fourth quarter and was driving for more when Larry Brown intercepted a pass. Dallas' championship pedigree emerged, with Smith scoring once to put the Cowboys ahead and then once more to send them to the Super Bowl.

"There is nobody who deserves this more than Barry Switzer," Irvin declared. Then Aikman, of all people, gave Switzer the game ball.

The good vibes were short-lived.

There was an uproar over Irvin cussing on national television during a postgame interview. Then came revelations of another crack in the Switzer-Aikman relationship, this one caused months earlier by accusations that the white quarterback was especially critical of his black teammates. Switzer said it was brought to his attention by defensive line coach John Blake, who had already left to become coach at Switzer's old school, Oklahoma. Irvin, Charles Haley, and Darren Woodson came out strongly in support of Aikman. Super Bowl week wasn't the best time for this to be happening.

As crazy as it had been getting to this point, the game itself was pretty tame.

Facing a Pittsburgh Steelers team nowhere near as good as the Steel Curtain vintage, Dallas romped to a 27–17 victory.

"We did it our way, bay-bee!!!" Switzer hollered as he received the Lombardi Trophy.

Dallas matched the 49ers as the only teams with five Super Bowl titles. But the Cowboys were the first to win three in four years and the first to win with three different coaches.

"This one is the best one of all, Mr. President," Jones told his old buddy from Arkansas, Bill Clinton, when he called the locker room. "They dwelled on the positive, Mr. President, when they could have pointed fingers at each other."

"When we go home and have a parade," Switzer said, "I'm going to stand on the curb and applaud when the players and Jerry go by."

GAME TO REMEMBER

SUPER BOWL XXX
DALLAS COWBOYS 27,
PITTSBURGH STEELERS 17

TEMPE, ARIZONA – The Roman numerals set the tone for Super Bowl XXX.
To many Cowboys, this trip to the Arizona desert was debauchery first, football second.

"The Tempe police gave us a list of places not to go," offensive lineman Nate Newton said, "and that's where I went."

Newton and several teammates got around in style too, spending $1,000 a day for each of 11 stretch limousines driven in from Dallas, many loaded with women who were, um, not the players' wives.

Coach Barry Switzer brought his ex-wife and his girlfriend; the women even shared a room. Switzer was such a gracious host to family, friends, former players, and anyone who wanted to be his friend that his liquor tab for the week topped $100,000.

Jerry Jones, meanwhile, showed up ready to plan the victory party. Days before the game, he sought a waiver to the Arizona law requiring bars to stop serving alcohol at 1 a.m.

When the game kicked off, the Cowboys were sharp enough.

Dallas scored on its first three possessions to go up 13–0 on the Steelers. A third-quarter interception by Larry Brown set up a touchdown that put Dallas ahead 20–7. Pittsburgh clawed back to within 20–17 and was moving up the

Larry Brown returning one of his two interceptions in Super Bowl XXX. *Mike Moore/NFL/Getty Images*

field midway through the fourth quarter when Brown intercepted another pass to kill the drive. Emmitt Smith scored soon after, and the Steelers were out of answers.

The victory all but clinched the title of "Team of the 1990s," with the bonus that it came against Pittsburgh, the franchise that had prevented Dallas from being the "Team of the 1970s." It was the Steelers' first loss in five Super Bowl trips.

Charles Haley became the first player to win five Super Bowls, and Aikman's three put him in a group that included only Joe Montana and Terry Bradshaw among quarterbacks. Smith broke Franco Harris' record for career yards in a Super Bowl and was three-for-three on turning regular-season rushing titles into Super Bowl titles.

In four years, the Cowboys had three titles—more than they had won in 29 years under Tom Landry.

"You can put the other two together, and this one outweighs them," Michael Irvin said. "That's because of what we went through this year, because of the times people counted us out. We got a little bit closer, tuned in a little bit more and got it done. Bottom line, we got it done."

145

THE TRIPLETS

Al Messerschmidt/Getty Images

The receiver showed up first, talking as good of a game as he played.

Then came the quarterback who could've been delivered by a Hollywood casting agent: strong arm, chiseled jaw, even a name that radiated.

Last, but not least, came the running back with the chip on his shoulder, a little guy who thrived on proving people wrong.

Michael Irvin, Troy Aikman, and Emmitt Smith joined the Cowboys as first-round picks in three straight drafts. They left as the greatest trio in team history and perhaps the best ever in the NFL. They certainly were the backbone to the greatest four-year span by any club, winning three Super Bowls and falling a game shy in their "down" year.

"You could take one of us lightly if you want to," Smith said, "but the other two are going to hurt you pretty bad."

Barry Switzer is credited for dubbing them "triplets," and it stuck.

"I loved it when they called us that," Aikman said, choking up over it during his retirement speech.

They were enshrined in the Ring of Honor together in 2005, the first season all three were out of the NFL.

As great as they were together, each was pretty special in his own right.

Here they are, presented in an unbiased order—alphabetical.

TROY AIKMAN

There was a time when folks in Dallas weren't sure about Troy Ache-man. He sure got hurt a lot.

And all that stuff about him being a winner and a leader? Well, he never even won a conference title in college.

But once the Cowboys started winning, and winning big, there was no doubt the experts were right. This guy was the prototype for a franchise quarterback.

Aikman had the vision to see the field, the brain to read defenses, and the arm to make any throw. Most of all, he was humble enough to realize his success was defined by wins and losses, not yards and touchdowns.

"My role as the quarterback was to move our team down the field and score points. Sometimes that meant passing the ball, sometimes it meant handing it off," Aikman said during his Hall of Fame induction speech. "We had a good system in Dallas. Although it wasn't one that allowed me to put up big numbers, that was fine. I did what was asked to help the team win."

Aikman went 105–75 as a starter, counting the playoffs. He won three Super Bowls and was named MVP of the first one.

So what if he never led the league in any major passing category? He was among the most efficient, often among the leaders in yards per attempt and passer rating.

His career numbers were still darn good: 2,898 of 4,715 (61.5 percent) for 32,942 yards (19th on the all-time list when he retired), 165 touchdowns, and 141 interceptions, with a passer rating of 81.6.

He also was the NFL's Man of the Year in 1997.

"He made terminally ill children have hope," Cowboys owner Jerry Jones said the day Aikman retired. "He made Cowboys fans have pride, and he made our football team a champion again. He showed why athletes can be heroes. He's a cornerstone of this franchise and a treasure of this community. He's ours to enjoy and be proud of forever."

John Biever/Sports Illustrated/Getty Images

MICHAEL IRVIN

Here's the paradox of Michael Irvin: As much as he craved attention and broke laws, no one ever was more devoted to his teammates or worked harder.

Stories of his work ethic are legendary. "First to arrive, last to leave" barely scratches the surface. By sacrificing the most, he always had the right to demand more from others. With his gift of gab, he often could convince them it was their idea.

That's how he became the heart and soul of Dallas' three Super Bowl teams.

"He practiced every day with the determination of a rookie that was hanging by a thread to make the team," Cowboys owner Jerry Jones said while presenting Irvin for his Hall of Fame induction. "Maybe that's the quality that separates the good players from the great players, the Hall of Fame players. Or maybe it's just the natural instinct of a man who had 16 brothers and sisters and knew that nothing in life was going to be given to him."

Irvin was big and strong, ran precise routes, and had great hands, all of which compensated for mediocre speed. The league even changed the rules to limit how much contact receivers could initiate against defenders because of him.

The last catch of his career was his 750th, tied for ninth in NFL history at the time. He also was No. 9 in yards with 11,904.

But Irvin should've come with a warning label: follow his lead at work, not at play.

His passion for sex and drugs is part of his legend too. Many of the worst moments in club history can be traced to him.

Andy Hayt/Getty Images

EMMITT SMITH

Among the Triplets, Emmitt Smith was the last to arrive and the lowest picked (17th).

Just more fuel for his fire.

He was supposed to be too small and too slow in high school, when all he did was set state and national records. The knock followed him in college, even after he ran for 224 yards against Alabama in his first start and was piling up the most yards in school history.

The NFL would be different, critics said. No, it won't, said Smith, who began eyeing Walter Payton's rushing record as soon as he arrived in Dallas.

Hard to bring down and too durable to keep down, Smith ran for at least 1,000 yards in 11 of his 13 seasons in Dallas.

He led the league in rushing three times, and the Cowboys won it all each of those years. Logical enough, right? Well, no other rushing champion had ever won the Super Bowl the same season, and it's only happened once since.

Some people argue that Smith was a byproduct of his environment, running behind a huge offensive line against defenses more worried about Aikman and Irvin. A popular parlor game was guessing what Barry Sanders would've done under those circumstances.

How silly. Smith had the opportunity and made the most of it. That meant staying healthy, which can never be taken for granted in football. Longevity is a badge of honor in the NFL, not a disclaimer to cheapen achievements like most carries, yards, rushing touchdowns, 100-yard games, 1,000-yard seasons, and 1,400-yard seasons.

He's probably not the best running back of all time, just the most productive.

"Look at me, I'm only 5-foot-9, 215 pounds," Smith said the day he retired. "People see guys like Charles Haley and other big guys and ask me, 'How in the world do you do it?' Sometimes I look at myself and say, 'How in the world do I do it?'

"I take a lot of pride in going out and doing it."

Mitchell Layton/Getty Images

THE TROY AIKMAN ERA, PART II

FADING GLORY: 1996–2000

The 1995 championship showed that Jimmy Johnson's departure did not ruin the Cowboys. Michael Irvin's 30th birthday party did.

During the latter half of the 1990s, this franchise would fill sports pages with stories of players arrested, suspended, and involved in all sorts of trouble. The backlash hit team owner Jerry Jones so hard that in 1998 he didn't draft Randy Moss for fear of

Emmitt Smith and the Cowboys made it look easy with a 40–15 playoff win over Minnesota in 1996. Dallas never won another playoff game at Texas Stadium—and didn't win one anywhere until 2009. *Brian Bahr/Getty Images*

adding another bad seed, even though he was the game-breaking receiver the club needed.

On and off the field, Irvin's 1996 arrest was the tipping point.

THE PARTY'S OVER

Michael Irvin was the poster child of what bad 'Boys these were. It all came crashing down shortly before midnight on March 4, 1996, when an Irving police officer knocked on room 624 at a Residence Inn hotel near Texas Stadium.

Inside, the cops found Irvin, teammate Alfredo Roberts, two "self-employed models," cocaine, marijuana, drug paraphernalia, and sex toys.

"Hey," Irvin said, "can I tell you who I am?"

In court, Irvin wore a fur coat and sunglasses. A smitten security guard asked him to autograph her Bible. Troy Aikman showed up at the trial one day to support Irvin. "The Playmaker" ended up pleading no contest to felony cocaine possession. He was fined $10,000, put on probation for four years, given 800 hours of community service work, and suspended from five games by the NFL.

"If this is America's Team, then woe is America," said William Bennett, the former U.S. Secretary of Education.

In addition to Irvin's trial, the other splashy scandal involved "the White House," a home at 115 Dorsett Drive, a few blocks from team headquarters.

WHO HAD THE BETTER FOUR-YEAR RUN, COWBOYS OR PATRIOTS?

The 1992–1995 Dallas Cowboys were the first team to win three Super Bowls in four years. And they did so while changing coaches midstream.

The 2001–2004 New England Patriots matched the feat of winning three titles in four years. And they did so well into the salary-cap era.

An easy way to judge these dynasties is by comparing what they did in the year they *didn't* win the Super Bowl.

The 2002 Patriots went 9–7 and failed to make the playoffs. The 1994 Cowboys went 12–4, won their division, and reached the NFC Championship Game before losing to the eventual Super Bowl champion San Francisco 49ers.

Using regular-season wins as a measuring stick, Dallas wins that comparison too, with 49 wins to New England's 48 over that span.

Those Patriots teams enjoyed a great run. But the Cowboys' run was better.

It was rented by Alvin Harper and served as a frat house for millionaires, loaded with drugs and women-for-hire. Some of the team's biggest stars—Irvin, Harper, Charles Haley, and Nate Newton—were among the most frequent visitors.

"We got us a little place over here where we're running some whores in and out, trying to be responsible," Newton said, "and we're criticized for that, too."

The Cowboys went 2–3 during Irvin's suspension. They went 8–3 after he returned and won the division for a fifth straight year.

Dallas beat Minnesota 40–15 in a wild-card game at Texas Stadium on December 28, 1996. The date is significant because the Cowboys wouldn't win another playoff game for 13 years and 12 days.

A few days after beating the Vikings, Irvin and the Cowboys were staring down off-field trouble again. A woman accused Irvin and Erik Williams of putting a gun to her head and sexually assaulting her, while videotaping it all. Her story turned out to be a farce; she pleaded guilty to perjury and filing a false police report. But that was months later. Dallas lost the next playoff game, in Carolina.

RECIPE FOR DISASTER

The general manager of the Cowboys never stopped the talent drain that began during the Super Bowl run, never injected enough skilled new players to support or even replace the aging veterans.

Instead, the GM just kept plunking money down for old guys, salary cap be damned, and let Barry Switzer keep running things as loosey-goosey as ever.

It was a house of cards sure to collapse. This was the year it did.

Owner Jerry Jones would have fired the GM who got him into this mess, except that it was him.

The Cowboys won three of their first four games in 1997 and then won only three of their last twelve. They lost their final five games to finish 6–10, last in the division.

"I can't explain this season to you," Jones said.

Broderick Thomas, the free agent brought in to juice up the pass rush, had more penalties than sacks. The defensive line included forgettable draft picks Shante Carver, Kavika Pittman, Darren Benson, and Hurvin McCormack. The receivers who were supposed to draw coverage from Irvin didn't. Emmitt

Deion Sanders and Michael Irvin celebrate a win against the Steelers in 1997. The opportunities for celebration would be few and far between that season. *George Gojkovich/Getty Images*

Smith couldn't finish five games because of injuries. Daryl Johnston played only six games because of a neck injury.

Switzer realized he had overstayed his welcome. He resigned in early January 1998, and it took Jones nearly six weeks to find a replacement.

Lou Holtz was briefly considered. Troy Aikman's coach at UCLA, Terry Donahue, turned the job down. Jones ended up with Chan Gailey, the relatively unknown offensive coordinator of the Steelers.

Jones insisted "Chan's the man," but Gailey was widely viewed as a "puppet" for the owner. Gailey was so happy to be an NFL head coach that he accepted one of the league's lowest salaries and was OK with not hiring his own assistants. Perhaps his

COWBOY LEGENDS
DARYL JOHNSTON

By the mid-1990s, it didn't matter where the Cowboys played. If No. 48 got the ball, *Moooooooooose* calls were sure to follow.

Daryl Johnston got the nickname from then-teammate Babe Laufenberg because when the 6-foot-2 fullback stood with the other running backs, he looked like a moose among a herd of deer.

Johnston became so popular that the league created the position of fullback in the Pro Bowl basically in his honor.

Johnston's popularity was highest within the locker room because of the kind of person and player he was. Troy Aikman and Emmitt Smith, the two guys he literally stuck his neck out for, were his biggest fans.

"Over the years, his unselfishness, his willingness to play with pain, his leadership on and off the field I think has been unparalleled," Aikman said. "He's a great football player and I don't say that loosely. He was as good playing his position as anyone has been playing their position."

The job took its toll.

Johnston needed surgery to repair a disk in his neck in 1997. He played every game the next year, but when he hurt his neck again in 1999, that was it. The rest of his life was too precious to risk.

When Smith became the NFL's career rushing leader, his one regret was that Johnston didn't open the hole for him. But Johnston was on the sideline as a broadcaster, and his wide-eyed smile made it clear how proud he was too.

Paul Buck/AFP/Getty Images

best quality, from Jones' perspective, was having a clear understanding of who was in charge.

"Everyone knows the final decision goes through this gentleman right here," Gailey said the day he was hired, pointing to Jones. "We're going to have a great working relationship, and we're going to make decisions in the best interest of this football team. It's not who's right, but what's right for the team."

DIVISION CHUMPS . . . ER . . . CHAMPS

There was a lot of Tom Landry in Chan Gailey.

A respected football mind, he was considered honorable, highly principled, and deeply religious. He was from the same Georgia town as Dan Reeves; in fact, Reeves was his Little League coach. That was reassuring to many fans, an indication of someone raised with the right values.

But Gailey wasn't an in-your-face, my way-or-the-highway kind of guy, which is what this team needed after Barry Switzer's reign. Still, Gailey was a nice enough guy—and, most of all, he simply wasn't Barry Switzer—so everyone was willing to give him a chance.

His honeymoon ended a few days into training camp in 1998.

Michael Irvin tried barging ahead of new offensive lineman Everett McIver in a line for haircuts, and a fight broke out. Irvin sliced a two-inch gash in McIver's neck with a pair of barber's scissors and a huge cover-up followed. Remember, Irvin was on probation.

Irvin remained a free man, and McIver became a richer man. This incident summed up a season in which the Cowboys did just enough right to cover the stench of something rotten.

There were a few highlights: Deion Sanders returning a punt and an interception for a touchdown in the same game, the first time in team history that had happened; and Emmitt Smith reaching two huge milestones: passing Tony Dorsett to become the leading rusher in franchise history and breaking the NFL career record for rushing touchdowns.

There also was a 46–36 loss to the Minnesota Vikings on Thanksgiving, with much of the punishment coming from Randy Moss, the receiver the Cowboys could have—and probably should

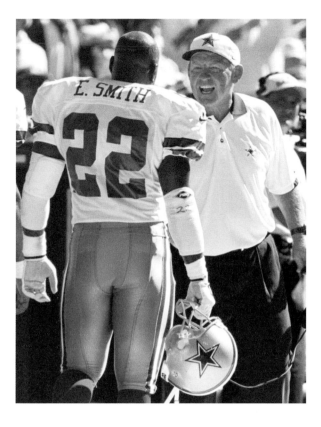

Chan Gailey congratulates his star running back during the opening game of the 1998 season. Emmitt Smith ran for 124 yards on the day. *Paul Buck/AFP/Getty Images*

have—drafted. Dallas instead took defensive end Greg Ellis, who was more productive than many first-rounders but was no Randy Moss.

The Cowboys went 10–6 and won the division. They were 8–0 against division foes and 2–6 against everyone else. While no team had ever swept NFC East play, rarely had the division been this bad, either. The only other East team with a winning record was Arizona (9–7), and the Cardinals came to Texas Stadium and knocked the Cowboys out of the playoffs.

The final score was 20–7, and it wasn't even that close. The Cardinals hadn't been to the playoffs since 1982, when they were in St. Louis, and hadn't won a playoff game since 1947, when they were in Chicago. Arizona would get blown out a week later and wouldn't make the playoffs again for another decade.

"We were asked a lot during the week, 'Is the window [of opportunity] closing?' For a lot of people, that window shut a long time ago," Aikman said. "We don't have a lot of players who were here when we had that success. We're looking through a different window right now."

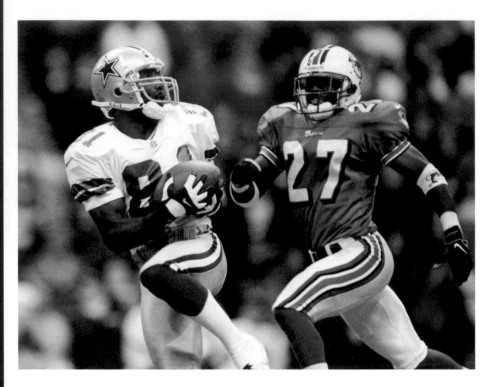

Wide receiver Raghib "Rocket" Ismail hauls in a 65-yard touchdown pass during the Cowboys' 20–0 win over the Jimmy Johnson–coached Dolphins on November 25, 1999. *Paul Buck/AFP/ Getty Images*

PLAYMAKER'S LAST PLAY

Jerry Jones decided that the future of the organization revolved around Troy Aikman, so he gave the quarterback an $85.5 million contract extension to lock him up through 2007. Jones also brought back center Mark Stepnoski and got Aikman a new deep threat: Raghib "Rocket" Ismail, who fled to the CFL the last time the Cowboys pursued him.

In the 1999 opener, Aikman pulled off the greatest comeback of his career. He wiped out a 21-point deficit in the fourth quarter at Washington to tie it, and then he won it in overtime with a club-record-tying fifth touchdown pass of the game, a bomb to Ismail that went for a 76-yard score.

"That was an awfully big show of character by our football team," Coach Chan Gailey said.

The Cowboys won the next two games, then went to Philadelphia to face a team in a 3–20 slump and whose offense hadn't found the end zone since the first quarter of the first game. Dallas blew a 10–0 lead by allowing 13 points in the fourth quarter, but that wasn't the worst part.

Early in the game, Michael Irvin caught a short pass, then on the tackle banged his head on the hard artificial turf and didn't get up. Philadelphia fans,

infamously known for booing Santa Claus, cheered as medical staffs from both teams got Irvin ready to be taken to a spine trauma center.

The injury was described as a swollen spinal cord, and there was talk of him returning later in the season. He ended up retiring because doctors discovered a narrowing of the spine that could lead to paralysis if he was hit again.

This loss started a stretch of four losses in five games. They finished 8–8, the highlights being a 20–0 victory over the Jimmy Johnson–coached Miami Dolphins on Thanksgiving and the good fortune of landing a wild-card berth.

Proving they didn't belong in the postseason, the Cowboys were wiped out 27–10 by Randy Moss and the Vikings.

As the decade ended, the Cowboys still were undoubtedly the team of the 1990s, having made the playoffs eight times while winning six division titles and three Super Bowls. Aikman won 90 games, the most of any quarterback in any decade, topping Joe Montana's 86 in the 1980s.

But as Jerry Jones looked toward the twenty-first century, he decided Chan was no longer the man and fired him. Gailey became the first Dallas coach not to win a Super Bowl, much less a playoff game; his two-season tenure was easily the shortest in team history.

Years later, Jones said he gave up on Gailey too quickly. He did win a division title and made the playoffs two straight years after inheriting Switzer's mess. That wasn't so bad—especially considering what happened next.

AIKMAN'S LAST STAND

The promotion of defensive coordinator Dave Campo to head coach reignited the "puppet" chatter. People were saying Jones might as well coach the club himself.

Campo had arrived as the last hire on Jimmy Johnson's first staff and worked his way up the ladder. Short with frizzy hair and glasses, and with a background as a folk singer and career assistant, he wasn't exactly the prototype NFL head coach.

Jones took another, bigger risk in his desperation to replace Michael Irvin and help Troy Aikman.

He sent two first-round picks to Seattle for Joey Galloway, then signed him to a $42 million, seven-year deal.

Aikman would never even complete a pass to Galloway.

The Eagles opened the season by stunning the Cowboys with an onside kick, then pestered Aikman into misfiring on his first five passes. He ended up leaving the game with a concussion, his second in 11 games. Galloway hurt his knee in the fourth quarter and missed the rest of the season. Dallas lost 41–14, matching the most lopsided season-opening loss in club history, and immediately the team was facing a *looooong* season.

"When you get blown out the way we did, everything is bad," Emmitt Smith said. "The water is nasty. The towels don't smell good. The showers don't feel warm. If there was a word for the way we played, you couldn't write it."

The Cowboys won only five games all season. The finale was in Tennessee on Christmas Day, and it was obvious the players didn't want to be there; the Titans were kind to win only 31–0.

Even the highlights of the 2000 season came under dark clouds.

In September, George Teague earned a spot in Cowboys lore with a blind-sided takedown of San Francisco receiver Terrell Owens while Owens celebrated a touchdown on the midfield star at Texas Stadium. It was his second such stunt of a game the 49ers won 41–24.

The best overall performance was a 32–13 whipping of Washington in December. But the real news of that game was Aikman taking his final snap. On a third-and-goal from the 1, Aikman scrambled to his right and was drilled into the turf by Redskins linebacker LaVar Arrington. It was another concussion to go along with the back problems that had also sidelined him this season.

On March 7, 2001, Jones decided the Cowboys could no longer build their future around a fragile quarterback. Most of all, Aikman needed to stop getting hit to preserve his quality of life. So, on the day before Aikman was due a $7 million bonus, Jones cut the first player he ever drafted, the quarterback who had brought Dallas three Super Bowl titles.

The Troy Aikman era in Dallas came to an end following a difficult 2000 season. (The patch of the fedora hat on his jersey below the left shoulder honors Tom Landry, who died in February 2000.)
Garrett Ellwood/NFL/ Getty Images

"If you're in my shoes and have been able to get up for the last 12 years and have a franchise quarterback, that's a luxury in the NFL," Jones said. "I'm going to miss that personally, and we're going to miss that as an organization."

At 34, Aikman still wanted to play. But on April 9, he called it a career.

"You watch and you think that your time will never come," said Aikman, fighting back tears. "My time has come."

When Don Meredith and Roger Staubach retired, capable replacements were ready to go.

This time, Jones could have hung a "Help Wanted" sign on the star logo.

THE SEARCH FOR A SUCCESSOR ERA

EIGHT IS ENOUGH: 2001–2005

Jerry Jones was so fortunate to have struck gold with the first quarterback he drafted that he figured he couldn't get that lucky again. So he didn't even try.

In entering life without Troy Aikman, Jones vowed not to spend a high draft pick on a potential franchise quarterback. His theory: It cost a lot to move up to the top of the draft and even more to pay the guy, without any guarantee he'd be any good.

Anyway, Dallas didn't have a first-round pick because of the trade for Joey Galloway. What's more, the salary cap was shot to pieces by the remnants of Aikman's contract. The underlying theme for 2001 was perseverance so the Cowboys could start fresh in 2002.

THE HUNT BEGINS

The post-Aikman era got off to a curious start when the first quarterback the Cowboys signed was released before the end of training camp.

Jones planned on having veteran Tony Banks hold down the fort, but the owner became so infatuated with rookie Quincy Carter that he decided to give the job to the kid right away, just like Jimmy Johnson had done with Aikman.

There were some big differences, though.

Carter was taken with the 53rd overall pick in the draft, and even that was considered a reach. He had played minor-league baseball for two years before attending the University of Georgia and joining the

football team. He was good as a freshman, decent as a sophomore, then mediocre and injured as a junior.

Yet as Jones looked around the league, he saw guys like Kurt Warner, Jon Kitna, and Jeff Garcia, who had gone from undrafted to quality starters, so he felt good about his theory of avoiding the supposed sure thing. He was counting on Carter to make him look smart. Remember, much of the fortune that Jones had built to buy the Cowboys came from "wildcatting," drilling oil in places where others wouldn't. He was hoping something similar would happen at quarterback.

The Cowboys ended up playing quarterback roulette in 2001.

Carter started only eight games because of injuries. The rest went to Anthony Wright (three games), San Diego draft bust Ryan Leaf (three), and Clint Stoerner (two).

Dallas endured a pair of four-game losing streaks and closed the season losing three of four. That was the closest thing to consistency this group could muster.

This second straight 5–11 season offered little hope, except that the salary cap was cleaned out and maybe, just maybe, Carter might learn something from this mess, the way Aikman did during his bumpy debut season.

"We're a young football team, but that excuse is over," Carter said after the finale. "That doesn't mean

Rookie Quincy Carter was given the unenviable task of replacing Troy Aikman in 2001. The Cowboys ended up using three other starting quarterbacks that season. *Ronald Martinez/ Allsport/Getty Images*

we're going to the Super Bowl next year, but it's time to make plays."

EMMITT TOPS SWEETNESS; EVERYTHING ELSE IS BITTER

There were two things on the agenda for the 2002 season: Emmitt Smith's rushing record and figuring out whether Dave Campo could be a head coach.

Between stars retiring and the salary cap mess, Campo's first two years had been doomed. This season was the closest he'd get to a decent chance at success.

Things still weren't great, especially at—where else?—quarterback. Jerry Jones had gone after another failed baseball player, bringing in Chad Hutchinson from the St. Louis Cardinals to compete with Carter. Hutchinson was in way over his head, yet Carter felt threatened.

Jones helped his quarterbacks by dropping his Randy Moss rule and taking receiver Antonio Bryant

when character issues caused him to slip in the draft. Jones also shored up the defense, getting veteran La'Roi Glover for the line and spending a high draft pick on hard-hitting safety Roy Williams.

The HBO series *Hard Knocks* brought viewers inside the Cowboys training camp. Campo came across pretty well, even while wearing a wet suit at Sea World.

Unfortunately, cameras also were rolling during the opener.

Facing the Houston Texans in the first game of that franchise's history, Dallas expected to win. The Cowboys showed the intensity of a meaningless preseason game, while this was the equivalent of a Super Bowl to the Texans. The 19–10 loss was one of the most unforgivable of this franchise's history.

The Cowboys won the next week and were 3–3 in mid-October. By then, the focus was on Smith's countdown to breaking Walter Payton's record.

Emmitt Smith finds a hole against the Seahawks and gets the yardage he needs to break Walter Payton's all-time rushing record. *Bill Frakes/Sports Illustrated/ Getty Images*

Smith went into the October 27 game at Texas Stadium against Seattle needing 93 yards. He hadn't gained that many yards in one game all season, but the Seahawks were the league's worst at stopping the run.

It was a perfect setup. And the record fell on a vintage Smith run.

Midway through the fourth quarter, Smith cut left, saw a hole, and powered through it, bouncing off several would-be tacklers. He lost his balance but put his hand on the ground to steady himself. He pitched forward for an 11-yard gain; had he kept his footing, he would have broken out for a long touchdown. Still, he had gained enough yards to claim the record he'd been chasing his entire career.

"Once I broke the line of scrimmage, I knew that had to be the one," Smith said.

Fireworks went off and fans stood cheering. Smith went to the sideline to celebrate with his family, delaying the game for several minutes. His milestone overshadowed Darren Woodson setting the franchise career record for tackles that game and Hutchinson making his first career start. It also obscured yet another loss.

Dallas was in the midst of a 2–8 freefall that would cost Campo his job. Smith provided the only other excitement that season on Thanksgiving against the Steve Spurrier–coached Redskins

The day he was hired, Spurrier promised to give team owner Dan Snyder the game ball when they beat Dallas. That riled up Cowboys fans. Smith, meanwhile, was driven by the fact that Spurrier had taken over at Florida after Smith's junior year and encouraged him to turn pro—in other words,

DARREN WOODSON

The Jimmy-Jerry, Triplet-led, three-Super-Bowls-in-four-years era ended December 29, 2004.

Darren Woodson retired.

"Woody" was the friendly, ferocious safety who took down so many receivers, runners, and quarterbacks that he broke the franchise record for tackles in 2002, then played another full season.

He wanted to play another year after that, but his body betrayed him. So at season's end he called it a career, severing the last link to the Super Bowl–winning clubs in 1992 (his rookie year), 1993, and 1995.

Woodson was part of Jimmy Johnson's final draft class and lasted on the field through Bill Parcells' first season. That also means he went from winning three Super Bowls his first four years to not even winning a playoff game his final seven seasons.

Woodson finished with 1,350 tackles. He made the Pro Bowl five times and was chosen All-Pro three times.

"The Cowboys organization is about history. It's about legends. It's about being a part of something

that's special," Woodson said. "Every time I put that uniform on, I laid it on the line for this team and my family."

Woodson hit like a linebacker, his position in college, and ran like a cornerback, which is why he made plays all over the field. Even in his later years, when he had more than enough seniority to get out of being on special teams, Woody was still chasing down kick returners.

He played at a time when some of Dallas' players were its worst citizens, but his smile always shined through.

"He had the respect of everybody, and we were here three to four years before he got here," Daryl Johnston said. "There are certain guys that have Darren's size and speed combination, but they don't have the same intangibles."

Mitchell Layton/Getty Images

pushed him out. Even though Smith was now the leading rusher in NFL history, he still felt he had a score to settle. And settle it he did, running for 144 yards, the top output of his final four seasons, in a 27–20 Dallas victory.

As the Cowboys finished up their third straight 5–11 season, Campo's fate was obvious. The question wasn't who would replace him as much as who would *want* to replace him. After three "puppets" as coaches, and with a roster in shambles, would Jerry Jones find anyone interested in the job?

Then Jones' phone rang. It was a mutual friend passing along word that Bill Parcells was interested.

Jones flew to New Jersey for a secret meeting with the "Big Tuna." The news hit before Dallas' second-to-last game, the home finale, and nobody could believe it.

Parcells? With his ego? Work for Jones? With his ego?

"Bill told me how in Las Vegas you have the lounge acts with the young comedians and singers, and then you have the big room where Sinatra and

Bill Parcells took charge of the troops in 2003 and led the team to its first playoff appearance in four years. *Bob Rosato/Sports Illustrated/Getty Images*

Presley played," Jones told *The New York Times*. "He told me the Dallas Cowboys are the big room."

On January 2, 2003, the two vowed to make their relationship work.

"I'm ready for the pitfalls and the land mines," Parcells said. "I have been around the block a few times. I think I can avoid trouble most of the time."

Said Jones, "I've made a lot of mistakes. You know I have. I am not going to grow careless with this relationship. If he fires me up, I hope I can do the same with him."

BIG BILL DELIVERS

Bill Parcells took the town and the team by storm.

He was the first coach of the Cowboys to have prior NFL experience and, boy, what a resume: two Super Bowl victories with the Giants, another trip with the Patriots, and taking the 1–15 Jets squad he inherited to the AFC Championship Game in his second year.

The new sheriff banned dominoes in the locker room and made the training room ice cold so no one would get too comfortable in there. He chose the

assistant coaches and loaded the roster with familiar faces. Nobody objected. "In Bill We Trust" might as well have been the mantra.

Emmitt Smith was released in February, a clean break that was best for everyone. Then Parcells showed his draft-day acumen by getting Terence Newman in the first round, Jason Witten in the third, and Bradie James in the fourth. The Division I-AA player of the year wasn't drafted by anyone, but Parcells and staff invited him to come to their training camp because he would have a good shot at making the team; that's how Dallas landed Tony Romo.

The first drill on the first day of training camp was baffling. Parcells had his quarterbacks throw the ball deep and out of bounds. His point was to teach them how to handle certain situations. He wanted them prepared for everything, including this obscure situation.

Parcells wasn't a fan of Chad Hutchinson. And while Parcells didn't exactly love Quincy Carter, he trusted him to be a "bus driver" who could manage games and not screw things up.

COWBOY LEGENDS
JERRY JONES

Jerry Jones insists he's not the owner of the Cowboys as much as a caretaker, and the new stadium isn't his legacy, it's a monument to the greatness of the franchise and its fans.

Believe any of that?

As owner of the Cowboys, Jones has gone from unknown Arkansas businessman to one of the most powerful men in sports. He's a *Forbes*-certified billionaire who doesn't care what you say about him as long as you're talking about him. That's one of his strengths, actually, because it has helped him persevere.

He fired Tom Landry, for heaven's sake. But, you know what? The guy he replaced him with turned out to be great too. Then Jones fired him as well.

He's burned through so many coaches that columnists have dared him to drop the middleman and just hire himself. Plenty of folks wouldn't be surprised if he did.

His first draft pick was Troy Aikman, and Jones didn't ever want anyone else at quarterback. Considering how things went in the years after Aikman, it's hard to blame him—except for the fact that the blame really is all his, because he also picked those failed replacements.

At the height of his team's success, Jones took on the NFL—kicking at the league's revenue-sharing plan with a pair of Pepsi-logo'd boots, then "bucking" them again by cutting a deal with Nike. The rub was that Coke and Reebok were league sponsors at the time. Once both sides dropped lawsuits stemming from that difference of opinion, guess who the league asked to negotiate its next television contract? Yep. And he blew everyone away with how well that turned out.

Jones stars in television commercials, many of which are self-deprecating, reminding you of his sense of humor. Then there are the halftime concerts every Thanksgiving to remind you of all the money he's helped raise for the Salvation Army and the millions more he's given on his own. He's been behind countless other, smaller acts of kindness too.

Ultimately, however, Jones is only as popular as the Cowboys' win–loss record.

During one of his immensely unpopular periods, a caller to his radio show was berating him when Jones fired back, "How'd you like those three Super Bowls?"

Decide that before you decide what you think of Jerry Jones.

*Ronald Martinez/
Getty Images*

Billy Cundiff's 52-yard field goal against the Giants in Week 2 of the 2003 season sent the game into overtime. He kicked another one in the extra session to give Bill Parcells his first win as coach of the Cowboys.
Ezra Shaw/Getty Images

"I think talent includes three or four other things besides the ability to run, jump, and catch," Parcells said, "and one of them is making intelligent decisions and good decisions under pressure."

After losing the opener, the Cowboys played a Monday night game at Parcells' old stomping grounds, Giants Stadium. Dallas led the Giants by 15 in the fourth quarter, then fell behind 32–29 with 14 seconds left.

Many viewers clicked off the TV and went to bed. Those who did missed quite a show.

Kickoff returner Zuriel Smith resisted the temptation to try to be a hero, and instead he remembered his situational drills from training camp, so he let an errant kick go out of bounds. That kept any time from running off the clock and gave Dallas the ball at the 40-yard line. Carter hit Antonio Bryant with a pass, and kicker Billy Cundiff made a 52-yard field goal to force overtime. In overtime, Cundiff made a 25-yarder, his NFL-record-tying seventh of the game, to give Parcells his first victory with the Cowboys.

"This is one of the wildest ones I've ever been involved in," Parcells said. "Our guys didn't play too well down the stretch, but they showed a lot of heart."

The performance sparked a five-game winning streak. Just six games into his tenure, Parcells already had won as many games as predecessor Dave Campo had in each of the previous three seasons.

One of the victories came against the Arizona Cardinals and their new running back—Emmitt Smith. Over the summer, Smith told *Sports Illustrated* that during his final year in Dallas he "felt like . . . a diamond surrounded by trash." Payback came in the form of a hit by safety Roy Williams that broke Smith's shoulder blade.

The Cowboys' winning streak ended with a shutout loss at Tampa Bay. They bounced back with two more wins, making them 7–2 heading into the Bill Bowl: Parcells versus Belichick, mentor versus pupil, for the first time since their Jimmy-Jerry-like split.

The Patriots—who were headed to their second of what would be three Super Bowl titles in four years, matching Dallas' run by the Triplets—slapped the Cowboys with another shutout loss. Again, Parcells brought his club back the next week, beating Carolina in a game with all sorts of ramifications.

The win put the Cowboys at 8–3, tying them for the best record in the NFC and guaranteeing that they would finish the season no worse than .500.

"You can't call them losers anymore," a teary Parcells said after the game. "Their record makes them something else besides losers. One more [win] and you have to call us winners."

POLISHING THE STAR
1-800-LOUSY-QB

Bill Parcells once got really frustrated by all the talk about Dallas' inability to develop a quarterback after Troy Aikman.

"You know what I like about the media? They think you can just dial 1-800 and get a quarterback," he said. "There are teams that have been trying to dial that for 10 years. . . . You think we don't look around?"

From 2001 to 2005, this spoiled fan base found out the hard way what it's like not to have a franchise quarterback. Here's what all that looking around got the Cowboys in the post-Aikman, pre-Romo era:

Quarterback	W–L as starter	Year(s)
Quincy Carter	16–15	2001–2003
Drew Bledsoe	9–7	2005
Vinny Testaverde	5–10	2004
Chad Hutchinson	2–7	2002–2003
Drew Henson	1–0	2004–2005
Clint Stoerner	1–1	2000–2002
Anthony Wright	1–2	2000–2001
Ryan Leaf	0–3	2001

*This list does not include Tony Banks, who was signed shortly after Aikman was released but then was cut after two preseason games, both of them losses.

Vinny Testaverde (16) and Drew Henson (7) on the sideline, September 2004. *Doug Pensinger/Getty Images*

Dallas went 2–3 down the stretch to finish second in the division, but 10–6 was enough to earn the first trip to the playoffs in four years. Credit the defense, which gave up the fewest yards and second-fewest points in the NFL.

Although the Cowboys lost in Carolina, Parcells became the first head coach in NFL history to guide four franchises into the playoffs.

Parcells' hallmark had always been huge second seasons, so Cowboys fans were giddy thinking about how Big Bill would build on his terrific start. Heck, if he could do this with Carter at quarterback and Troy Hambrick at running back, there was no telling how he'd do with more of his guys in place.

WHAT A WASTE
In his bag of motivational tricks, Bill Parcells kept a mouse trap to remind players "not to eat the cheese," his euphemism for guys reading their own press clippings and getting full of themselves.

Maybe he should've put one on his desk.

Parcells made only a few moves this off-season, bringing in his old Jets cronies Keyshawn Johnson and Vinny Testaverde. Dallas also brought in quarterback Drew Henson, yet another Jones attempt at a baseball-to-football project, and added running back Eddie George, who was well past his prime.

Quincy Carter was dumped in training camp because of substance-abuse issues. Chad Hutchinson was sent packing and so was receiver Antonio Bryant, who forced his way out by throwing his sweaty jersey at Parcells in a minicamp.

With the quarterback depth thinned to Testaverde and Henson, the Cowboys were able to keep around that I-AA kid from the previous year. What his name again? Tony Roma? Nah, that's the rib joint. Anyway, it was something like that.

The next Emmitt Smith? In 2004, rookie Julius Jones posted three games with 149 or more yards rushing, with a high of 198 yards (and three touchdowns) against Seattle on December 6. *Otto Greule Jr./Getty Images*

Parcells' second-year magic didn't work this time. The Cowboys went through a midseason stretch of six losses in seven games. Yet no matter how badly things went, Parcells refused to bench older players for young ones, especially not at quarterback.

"I'm too old to lose," Parcells often said.

He finally gave in and started Henson against Chicago on Thanksgiving, but only because the 41-year-old Testaverde had a shoulder injury. Henson was 4-of-12 in the first half and gave up an interception that was returned for a touchdown. So Parcells put in the ailing Testaverde, and he pulled out the victory.

Top draft pick Julius Jones ran for 150 yards and two touchdowns that day, motivated by squaring off against his brother, Thomas, the starting running back for the Bears.

A week later against Seattle, Jones proved it was no fluke by running for 198 yards and three touchdowns. Dallas scored two touchdowns in the final 1:45 to pull out a 43–39 victory.

At 5–7, the Cowboys were running on fumes, but the playoffs were still a possibility, so Parcells refused to consider a youth movement—even though Jones, a rookie, was a big reason for the last two wins.

But that was the last gasp. The Cowboys lost three of their final four games to finish 6–10, a flip-flop from the previous year.

In general, though, folks felt good about the organization.

The best example was in November, when Arlington voters agreed to pay up to $325 million of a $650 million stadium owner Jerry Jones was planning to build in time for the 2009 season.

HEADED BACK IN THE RIGHT DIRECTION

Jerry Jones spared no expense to restart this revival.

He signed Drew Bledsoe after Buffalo released him, then opened free agency by scooping up cornerback Anthony Henry, nose tackle Jason Ferguson, and offensive lineman Marco Rivera. The tab for those four additions: $31 million in bonuses and $80.5 million in total contracts. Jones turned his pockets inside out after announcing the last signing, joking that he was out of cash.

Then it was Parcells' turn to shine.

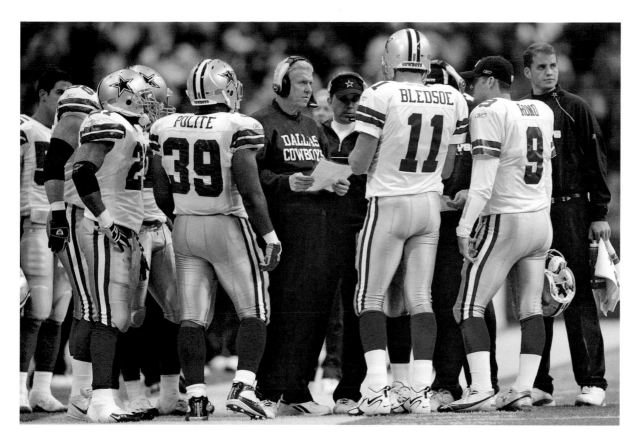

While a young Tony Romo stood patiently to the side, Bill Parcells put the ball in the hands of Drew Bledsoe in 2005. *Ronald Martinez/ Getty Images*

In the draft, he began the conversion to a 3–4 defense by taking linebacker DeMarcus Ware and defensive end Marcus Spears in the first round, linebacker Kevin Burnett in the second, and defensive end Chris Canty in the fourth. Parcells spent another fourth-round pick on running back Marion Barber III. In the late rounds, he found offensive lineman Rob Petitti—who wound up starting in place of the injured Flozell Adams—and used the 224th overall pick on a kid from Auburn named Jay Ratliff.

This was now a solid team, no smoke-and-mirrors wizardry like 2003. After a midseason spurt of five wins in six games (the only loss coming by a field goal on the road), the Cowboys went into Thanksgiving with a great chance to be the No. 1 seed in the NFC.

But the Cowboys lost to Denver in overtime on Thanksgiving and never recovered.

Keeping up their trend of falling apart down the stretch, the Cowboys lost four of their last six games. They were eliminated from the playoffs before even taking the field for the finale, then sleepwalked through it to finish 9–7.

Dallas threw 500 passes this season, and Bledsoe had 499 of them. Parcells still wasn't willing to trust his young backups, although he did let Tony Romo take two end-of-game kneel-downs and hold on field goals. It seemed strange to have a backup quarterback out there on kicks and not even let him throw a pass on a trick play. Maybe that was Parcells' way of showing he didn't really trust the guy.

Three years into Parcells' tenure, the coach and the owner were getting along just fine, but the franchise still hadn't lived up to the promise of his first season. His overall record was 25–24, counting a loss in his lone playoff appearance.

There was no doubt the Cowboys were improved. And Parcells was so intrigued by the potential of youngsters like Ware, Witten, and Barber that he decided to return for a fourth season.

Bledsoe was coming back too.

So was the holder.

THE TONY ROMO ERA

THE TRADITION CONTINUES: 2006–2009

"Getcha popcorn ready!"

That was the message from Terrell Owens when the one-time Texas Stadium star-stomper and longtime Cowboys-killer signed with Dallas in March 2006.

It was a classic Jerry Jones hiring. And Bill Parcells could only squirm, especially since Keyshawn Johnson was cut to keep the big-headed receiver count down to one. Parcells never registered his objection publicly—but he also rarely referred to Owens as Terrell or even T. O., almost always calling him "the player."

Owens had a long history as a big-play receiver and an equally long track record for destroying relationships with coaches and quarterbacks.

There was plenty of intrigue now, with Owens and Jones on one side, Parcells and Drew Bledsoe on the other.

Why was that backup quarterback wearing his baseball hat backward and smirking about all this?

EUREKA! HE WAS HERE ALL ALONG!

Bill Parcells leaked it before he came out and said it: Tony Romo might be ready.

Romo's role increased in training camp in 2006, and he played well in the preseason, as he had done the previous three years. Then Drew Bledsoe looked shaky in the opener, and a quarterback controversy began to percolate.

"Any time you have a couple of quality players at a position, that's always going to happen," said Romo, who had yet to prove himself as a quality player but already had the moxie of one.

Parcells sort of snuffed the QB question by saying he was sticking with Bledsoe . . . "right now."

"I told you I was getting Romo ready to play. And at some point in time, I'm hopeful I will be able to play him this year," Parcells said. "Now, I don't know when, where, or under what circumstances. . . . That time is not now, OK? Is that clear enough? Do you want me to repeat it?"

The following week, Owens broke a hand on one of the first plays of the game and a few days later had an operation. With a bye week coming up, he could be back without missing a game.

At home one night a few days after the surgery, Owens took some pain pills—so many that his publicist, who was also at his house, thought he was trying to kill himself. She called 911, and an ambulance responding to a suicide call whisked him to a hospital. He spent the night, then showed up at Valley Ranch in time for part of practice, catching some passes with his damaged hand and all.

The story triggered the biggest sports-media circus since Owens had worked out in his driveway hours after the Eagles kicked him out of team headquarters in 2005.

The Tony Romo Era officially began in Dallas on October 23, 2006, when he took over for Drew Bledsoe in the second half of a game against the Giants. He was named the starter a week later and led the Cowboys to three playoff appearances in his first four seasons in the huddle. *James D. Smith/NFL/Getty Images*

Parcells stormed out of his daily news conference when it became clear that the only questions were about Owens. Then Owens spoke. And then, so did his publicist, Kim Etheredge.

In trying to end the talk of a possible suicide attempt, which all traced back to her 911 call, she brought up his contract, saying, "Terrell has 25 million reasons to be alive." The police later ruled the incident an "accidental overdose."

Owens played the very next game, a win over Tennessee, and was the big story again when Dallas went to Philadelphia a week later. Fans burned his old Eagles jerseys in the parking lot, then cheered as the Cowboys lost by two touchdowns.

Back at home, Dallas beat the Houston Texans so easily that Parcells finally let Romo play. He went in midway through the fourth quarter, right after Bledsoe drove past midfield.

The first pass of his career went to rookie Sam Hurd for 33 yards. His second pass was a 2-yard touchdown throw to Owens.

Smart move, kid.

The quarterback issue was simmering when the New York Giants came to Texas Stadium the following Monday night. Bledsoe was his usual slow-moving, slow-decision-making self, and the Cowboys were losing at halftime. So Parcells put Romo in to start the second half.

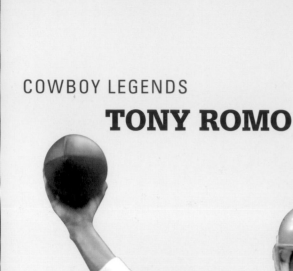

TONY ROMO

Tony Romo wears No. 9 because of Roy Hobbs, the lead character in the movie *The Natural*. Yes, it was about baseball and this is football, but the connection works in many ways.

Rise from obscurity to stardom? Check.

Win a lot and come through in stunning ways? Check.

Blonde bombshell rises in the stands and triggers a career setback? Check.

Oddly enough, Romo was never a natural until the NFL. Yes, he was the Division I-AA player of the year. But it *was* I-AA. Coming out of high school, he was lucky to even land at Eastern Illinois.

No NFL team drafted him, but several invited him to training camp. He took less money to come to Dallas, gambling on himself after looking at the competition he'd be facing with the Cowboys.

Four quarterbacks were fighting for three spots in his second training camp. As the lowest-profile guy, Romo might've been released had incumbent Quincy Carter not gotten himself tossed.

Romo treated his first few years as an internship, soaking up all he could. He practiced more on his own, working on things like throwing from awkward angles and off the wrong foot. He wanted to be ready for everything when his chance finally came.

"That's all I kept thinking. Keep getting better," Romo said.

With opportunity about to knock in 2006, team owner Jerry Jones wanted to give Romo a raise and lock him up for another year. The quarterback asked for a lot of money under the theory that the more Jones paid him, the more likely it was he'd get to play. He signed for a $2 million bonus and salaries totaling another $1.9 million—then turned it into a bargain.

Layne Murdoch/Getty Images

His breakthrough season played out like a fairytale. He really was a natural, making big play after big play. He was never in awe, though, because he always believed it would happen; to him, it was just a matter of when. Maybe that's why he was always flashing an aw-shucks grin.

"I enjoy the game," Romo said. "For some reason, people like that."

Coach Bill Parcells tried keeping Romo humble by telling him about Greg Cook, who dazzled when he burst onto the scene for Cincinnati in 1969 only to become the NFL's ultimate one-year wonder. He also warned Romo against becoming a "celebrity quarterback."

Romo sure tempted fate. An avid golfer, he played in celebrity events and tried qualifying for the U.S. Open. He took new girlfriend Carrie Underwood to the Country Music Awards and judged the Miss Universe Pageant. Then he started dating Jessica Simpson; that's the blonde many blamed for derailing his career, much as the character played by Kim Basinger did to Robert Redford's Hobbs, except the ruinous shots fired against Romo came from a camera, not a gun.

Simpson joined Romo on a trip to Mexico during a bye week before a playoff game. Pictures led to all sorts of questions about priorities. Her name came up again the following season, with Terrell Owens making some comments that required an apology. Romo dumped her before the 2009 season, a season in which his on-field decision-making was widely praised.

Through it all, Romo has proven worthy of carrying on the Cowboys' proud legacy at quarterback. A sports-history buff, Romo appreciates it too, and he takes pride in his relationship with Troy Aikman and Roger Staubach.

"This is my job, this is what I've been preparing to do," Romo said. "And I really want to win badly."

Despite the off-field turmoil, Terrell Owens led the NFL with 13 receiving touchdowns in 2006, including 3 during a 34–6 romp of Houston in mid October. *Ronald Martinez/Getty Images*

Although he turned a 5-point deficit into a 14-point loss, Romo's infectious charisma lifted teammates and fans. Parcells liked what he saw so much that he let Romo start the next game.

"Romo-mania" quickly followed.

Romo won five of his first six starts. He was named NFC offensive player of the week twice in a span of three weeks; the week he didn't get it, all he did was outduel Peyton Manning and the 9–0 Colts in a 21–14 Cowboys victory.

In his first Thanksgiving start, Romo tied the club record with five touchdown passes—in just three quarters. Fans were so gaga they hung his name on a blank part of the Ring of Honor. Security made them take it down; Jerry Jones later joked about firing those stadium workers.

Romo was so smooth that he even hooked up with the Thanksgiving halftime performer, Carrie Underwood. He also impressed another starlet in the stands, Jessica Simpson. Despite Parcells' repeated warnings for Romo not to become "a celebrity quarterback," things were going just fine. He was even voted into the Pro Bowl despite just 10 starts.

A big part of Romo's success was throwing to Owens. Keeping him happy and productive kept the Cowboys rolling. Romo also learned that Jason Witten was the guy to throw to for first downs, and backup running back Marion Barber was the man for short touchdown runs.

Dallas peaked at 8–4, leading the division and challenging for the NFC's No. 1 seed. Then came the now-predictable December meltdown.

COWBOY LEGENDS
JASON WITTEN

Jason Witten's defining play was a 53-yard catch that didn't even produce a touchdown. What made it so special? The lack of a helmet.

On a Sunday night in Philadelphia in 2007, two Eagles smacked Witten just as he caught a pass across the middle. His helmet popped off, but he stayed on his feet while both defenders fell. Witten instinctively took off toward the end zone, wind in his hair, caution be damned.

"I'm a tight end, man," Witten said. "I can't go down."

Witten has made the Pro Bowl catching passes from Vinny Testaverde, Drew Bledsoe, and Tony Romo. Quarterbacks just know they can trust him to be in the right place at the right time and to make every catch.

Witten and Romo have a deeper bond. They arrived in 2003 as part of Bill Parcells' first rookie class. There's no telling how many thousands of passes they'd completed before getting to do it for real in 2006. So it only made sense that Witten became Romo's "security blanket," as Jay Novacek had been for Troy Aikman. Terrell Owens eventually made an issue of how often and in what situations Romo looked for Witten. If indeed the huddle wasn't big enough for both T. O. and Witten, well, look at which one the Cowboys kept.

Rob Tringali/SportsChrome/Getty Images

Facing a New Orleans squad that featured several former Dallas coaches, the Cowboys were thumped 42–17 as the Saints exploited Romo. Dallas lost two of its last three to finish 9–7 and settle for a wild card.

Romo's playoff debut came on a Saturday night in Seattle. He still wasn't back in his midseason groove, but he did well enough to put the Cowboys in position to win with a short field goal by Martin Gramatica.

Romo was still the holder, and he bobbled the snap. He couldn't get the ball down in time for Gramatica, so he took off for the end zone, hoping to at least get the yardage for a first down.

He didn't.

Romo lost the game, then tearfully apologized. Later there was talk of how slick the "K" ball was, which was set aside just for kicking, but Romo never used that as an excuse.

Showing what a good sport he was, he asked to be the holder at the Pro Bowl. He did it flawlessly.

With the season over, a new drama began: Would Parcells stay?

The coach dragged out his decision until many top candidates were off the market. Jones wanted him to stay, so he didn't rush a decision. Then Parcells decided to leave.

As Jones began interviews, he was smitten by Jason Garrett, Troy Aikman's longtime backup and confidante whose dad had been a Dallas scout for many years. Garrett had spent the previous two seasons as the quarterbacks coach in Miami, and the Dolphins gave Jones a deadline for hiring him. Jones

YOU MAKE THE CALL

WAS BILL PARCELLS' TENURE A SUCCESS?

At his first three stops in the NFL, Bill Parcells went a combined 11–6 in the playoffs, reaching at least the conference championship with each team.

In Dallas, he went a combined 0–2 in the playoffs.

At his first three NFL stops, Bill Parcells won eight division titles, at least one with each team, and always had a season with at least 11 wins.

In Dallas, he never won a division title or more than 10 games in a season.

But didn't Parcells inherit a worse mess in Dallas than he did anywhere else?

Quite the opposite. The Cowboys were coming off a five-win season; at his previous stops, the Giants were coming off a four-win season, the Patriots a two-win season, and the Jets a one-win season.

So maybe Parcells' performance in Dallas didn't live up to the standard he set for himself.

He made a huge difference, nevertheless, and left the organization much better off than he found it.

"This isn't going to be a simple, overnight, one-stop-does-all process," Parcells said during his tenure. "This isn't like driving into the Texaco station, where you tell the guy to change the plugs and adjust the brakes."

Parcells went 34–30 and made two playoff trips in four years with a club that had gone 23–41 with one playoff trip the previous four years.

He drastically raised the talent level, launching the career of Tony Romo and drafting DeMarcus Ware, Jason Witten, and more.

Most of all—and this is the part that often gets overlooked—he brought some stability and respect back to the Dallas front office. Nobody ever accused Bill Parcells of being anyone's "puppet." The energy and excitement he helped revive also went a long way toward getting Arlington voters to pass the stadium plan.

did but wasn't sure whether he wanted Garrett as head coach or offensive coordinator.

The finalists for the top job ended up being Norv Turner, the popular offensive coordinator from the 1990s heyday who had been a flop thus far as a head coach, and Wade Phillips, a highly respected defensive coordinator for three decades who had a winning record as a head coach but had never won a playoff game.

Jones figured the offense was in good shape with Romo, Owens, et al., and he trusted Garrett to make the most out of them. So he hired Phillips to crank up the defense.

A LOT OF FUN . . . 'TIL THE END

Just like Bill Parcells' stern style was once what this club needed, the soft touch of Wade Phillips was the perfect follow-up.

Training camp wasn't as punishing, physically or mentally. Maybe easing up early would keep the Cowboys fresher at season's end and prevent another disastrous December.

As Tony Romo went into his first full season in charge, he had to prove that 2006 was no fluke and that there was no emotional damage for the playoff flub. Jerry Jones was confident enough not to take highly touted Notre Dame quarterback Brady Quinn when he fell to the Cowboys in the draft, but the owner still took a wait-and-see approach toward a contract extension for Romo. Jones decided to risk having the quarterback put up a big year and drive up the price. It was a problem he'd love to have.

That's exactly what happened. Romo led the Cowboys to 12 wins in their first 13 games, with the only loss coming on the road to a New England team on its way to a perfect season.

Romo passed for four touchdowns and ran for a fifth in a 45–35 shootout against the Giants in September 2007. *Greg Nelson/Sports Illustrated/ Getty Images*

In cementing himself as the heir to Troy Aikman and his predecessors, Romo had many highlights:

- Four touchdowns in the opener against the Giants.
- A snap over his head against the Rams that he recovered 33 yards behind the line of scrimmage and turned into a 4-yard gain on a third-and-3, the kind of move not seen by a Cowboys quarterback since Roger Staubach.
- Overcoming five interceptions to beat Buffalo on a Monday night.
- The Wisconsin native outplaying Green Bay's Brett Favre in a late-season showdown for the best record in the conference.

During the bye week, Jones gave Romo a $67.5 million contract, $30 million guaranteed and $11.5 as a bonus. (Jones keeps the canceled check mounted under glass in his home, alongside one of his whopper payments to Aikman.)

When the calendar flipped to December, trouble followed.

Romo needed a touchdown pass with 18 seconds left to beat lowly Detroit, 28–27, and a week later the Cowboys lost 10–6 at home to Philadelphia. Romo's new girlfriend, Jessica Simpson, was televised wearing a pink No. 9 jersey, and fans decided to blame her for everything.

Dallas lost two of its last three games, "settling" for a 13–3 record that matched the best in club history. Team records fell left and right, especially on offense, and the Cowboys made NFL history by sending 13 players to the Pro Bowl, including backup running back Marion Barber. (He led the club in yards rushing and touchdowns but never started.) Another first-time honoree was linebacker Greg Ellis, who returned from a torn Achilles' tendon to have a career-best 12 1/2 sacks and earn the NFL's comeback player of the year award.

What could possibly go wrong?

Phillips trusted his guys so much that he let them do whatever they wanted during the bye week before the playoff opener. Romo and several teammates jetted down to Cabo San Lucas, Mexico, with their playbooks and significant others.

Paparazzi found them, turning this siesta into a big story about Romo's priorities. While controversy

raged, Phillips was more interested in spinning the notion that by making it to the second weekend of the playoffs, he'd broken the playoff losing streak that loomed over his career record and the Cowboys' recent history. His message: Dallas was the bye-week champion!

The Giants arrived at Texas Stadium a week later plenty focused.

New York—which already had lost twice to Dallas this season—barely had the ball in the first half but scored just before halftime to tie it at 14. The Cowboys went ahead with a third-quarter field

Pro Bowl running back Marion Barber led the Cowboys with 975 yards rushing in 2007. He gained a season-high 110 yards against Carolina in December. *Rex Brown/ Getty Images*

goal, but the Giants got a fourth-quarter touchdown from Brandon Jacobs for a 21–17 victory. A wide-open pass dropped by Patrick Crayton and a bunch of penalties were among the many regrets as the Cowboys lost what turned out to be the final playoff game at Texas Stadium.

"I'm dying," Jones said a half-hour after the game. "I'm absolutely dying."

Dallas became the first No. 1 seed in the NFC to bow out right away since this playoff format began in 1990. Phillips' career oh-fer continued, as did the team's drought that stretched to 1996. High school seniors at that time had been in first grade the last time the Cowboys won a playoff game.

Romo was 0-for-2 in the playoffs, and his south-of-the-border getaway remained a big deal. Sure, other players had traveled too, but he was the guy who set the tone.

Terrell Owens refused to blame Romo. "That's my quarterback," he said, his voice cracking as tears slid below his sunglasses.

The next day, Phillips said that he'd seen the tape and was convinced the better team lost.

That argument lost steam when the Giants ended New England's perfect season in the Super Bowl. Still, getting knocked out by the eventual champions was no solace. It just meant the division was going to be even tougher next season.

"We have a special team," cornerback Terence Newman said, "but someone else has a more special team."

T.O.RN APART

The Cowboys had won the Super Bowl their first season in Texas Stadium, and they had reason to believe they could do it again in their last season.

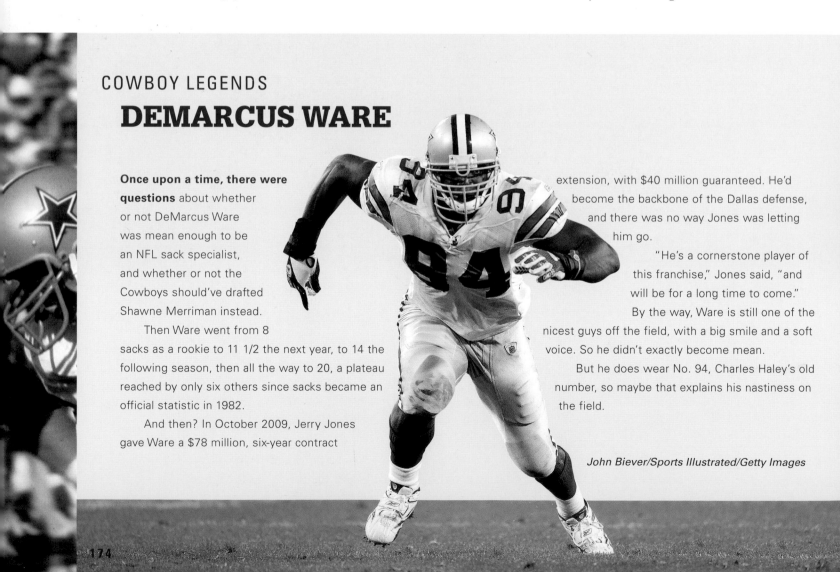

COWBOY LEGENDS
DEMARCUS WARE

Once upon a time, there were questions about whether or not DeMarcus Ware was mean enough to be an NFL sack specialist, and whether or not the Cowboys should've drafted Shawne Merriman instead.

Then Ware went from 8 sacks as a rookie to 11 1/2 the next year, to 14 the following season, then all the way to 20, a plateau reached by only six others since sacks became an official statistic in 1982.

And then? In October 2009, Jerry Jones gave Ware a $78 million, six-year contract extension, with $40 million guaranteed. He'd become the backbone of the Dallas defense, and there was no way Jones was letting him go.

"He's a cornerstone player of this franchise," Jones said, "and will be for a long time to come."

By the way, Ware is still one of the nicest guys off the field, with a big smile and a soft voice. So he didn't exactly become mean.

But he does wear No. 94, Charles Haley's old number, so maybe that explains his nastiness on the field.

John Biever/Sports Illustrated/Getty Images

The core of the 13–3 team remained intact, with some upgrades like electrifying running back/returner Felix Jones, cornerback Mike Jenkins, and cornerback Adam "Pacman" Jones. Jones had been a star for Tennessee in 2005 and 2006 but missed the 2007 season due to a league suspension for extensive trouble with the law. Jerry Jones gave up little to get him, wasn't paying him much, and hired a bodyguard to keep him out of trouble.

The biggest changes were behind the scenes.

Bill Parcells was now in charge of the Dolphins and had hired away personnel director Jeff Ireland to be general manager and Tony Sparano as his coach. Sparano had called plays in Romo's first season and had worked closely with offensive coordinator Jason Garrett. Garrett turned down head coaching offers from Atlanta and Baltimore, a clear indication he was waiting for the head coaching job in Dallas.

Things were chugging along OK through five games, as the Cowboys won four and lost the other by just two points. They were far from dominant, though, and questions about the so-called ugly wins annoyed the players.

Then they really had something to be angry about—an overtime loss in Arizona during which Romo broke the pinkie on his throwing hand and punter Mat McBriar broke his kicking foot. Days later, Jones tried sparking the offense by trading for receiver Roy Williams, giving up a stash of draft picks and a $45 million, five-year contract extension.

Backup quarterback Brad Johnson found a way to lose to St. Louis, which was 1–4 and would lose its next 17 games. He barely beat Tampa Bay, then got clobbered by the Giants.

It was only November 2 and Dallas already had more losses than the previous season.

"Talent's never won nobody nothing. Nothing," special teams captain Keith Davis said. "It's got to be a complete team."

They were 5–4 when Romo returned, and he led them to three straight wins. Williams still wasn't producing, and Owens' numbers were way down too. Still, Dallas was in great position to win the division when December came along.

After leading Dallas to a division title in 2007, Wade Phillips could barely stand to watch as his team failed to make the playoffs a year later. *Bob Rosato/Sports Illustrated/Getty Images*

The Cowboys kept themselves out of the playoffs by losing three of their last four. The losses exposed what a fragile bunch this was.

First they blew a fourth-quarter lead in Pittsburgh. Then, two weeks later, in the final home game at Texas Stadium, they blew a fourth-quarter lead by giving up a record-tying 77-yard touchdown run, went back ahead, then lost by giving up a record-setting 82-yard touchdown run.

At 9–6, the Cowboys went into the finale against the Eagles knowing that a win would put them in the playoffs. Instead, they gave one of the most pathetic performances in team history, losing 44–6 in Philadelphia.

"If this is the worst thing that ever happens to me, then I'll have lived a pretty good life," Romo said, opening himself up to an offseason filled with criticism.

This difficult season included Pacman getting into a fight with his bodyguard, accusations of name-calling and shoving between T. O. and Jason Witten, receivers complaining to Garrett, and Phillips taking the defensive play-calling duties away from coordinator Brian Stewart. The rare bright spot was DeMarcus Ware's 20 sacks, challenging the league record of 22½.

Phillips' day-after speech this time was a declaration that the Cowboys weren't changing coaches, so the old coach was going to change.

Interpretation: No more Mr. Nice Guy.

Reaction: Defensive captain Bradie James just laughed.

SHOWCASE STADIUM; SHOWCASE TEAM

Jerry Jones had some cleaning up to do to get ready for the 50th season in Cowboys history. There was no way this club was worthy of the $1.2 billion stadium they were about to move into.

He started by getting rid of guys who might have been to blame for various problems. Out went Terrell Owens, Adam "Pacman" Jones, Tank Johnson (another character-reclamation project that didn't

POLISHING THE STAR

GOODBYE, TEXAS STADIUM

Few stadiums have been as iconic as Texas Stadium, with its signature "hole in the roof" and all those Super Bowl banners hanging inside the lip of the semi-dome.

In its final years, however, the home to so many memorable games and great Cowboys teams was . . . well, not quite a dump, but certainly past its prime.

Jerry Jones never bothered fixing it up much because he knew he was leaving. By the time the Super Bowl comes to North Texas in February 2011, Texas Stadium won't even exist. It will have been imploded, all that concrete and steel turned to dust.

The memories, of course, will never fade.

The Cowboys played their final game at Texas Stadium on December 20, 2008. The loss locked their all-time

Harry How/Getty Images

record there at 213 wins and 100 losses, including the playoffs.

After the finale, there was a ceremony featuring most members of the Ring of Honor (one of the many innovations launched in the building) and a countdown of the team's 10 greatest moments in that stadium. The top pick: Emmitt Smith's run that made him the NFL's all-time rushing leader.

"This stadium is the only one home to five world championships and seven conference championships," Jones told the crowd. "These players and coaches know it was nothing without the fans."

Those were the people Roger Staubach saluted too.

"We won a lot of games because we were a good team," he said, "but also because you were our fans. Thank you."

The billion-dollar Cowboys Stadium opened to much fanfare on September 20, 2009, for the team's regular-season opener against the New York Giants. *Ronald Martinez/ Getty Images*

pan out), Brad Johnson, Greg Ellis, defensive coordinator Brian Stewart, and special-teams coach Bruce Read. There were no splashy hires to take their places. It was addition by subtraction.

Tragedy struck in May.

A freak storm hit the team's indoor practice facility while a rookie minicamp was going on, with about 70 players, coaches, other team employees, and media inside. Scouting assistant Rich Behm was paralyzed, and new special-teams coach Joe DeCamillis needed surgery to repair a broken neck.

A few weeks later, DeCamillis showed up for the first full-squad workout wearing a neck brace and barking into a bullhorn last used by Tom Landry. DeCamillis set an example for the toughness, selflessness, and passion needed to get this club out of its funk.

The team's new home was pretty inspiring too.

Jones scrapped plans to build a "regular" stadium and decided to go for a quantum leap beyond anything ever built. He put on a retractable lid in the shape of the "hole in the roof" from Texas Stadium,

and retractable glass doors on each end of the field. He left room for more than 100,000 fans, many destined for areas designed specifically for folks to stand and watch. The signature pieces are the world's largest high-definition televisions—two of them, one facing each sideline.

The video boards cost a total of $35 million, the same price it cost to build all of Texas Stadium. They are about 20 yards tall and 60 yards wide, looming right over the center of the field—low enough to get hit by a punt during a preseason game.

Before the first game, Cowboys Stadium already had booked a Super Bowl, a Final Four, the NBA All-Star Game, the Cotton Bowl, the Big 12 football championship, and a Notre Dame "home" football game. It cost Jones more than $800 million of his own money, and it was worth every penny.

The home opener drew 105,121, the biggest crowd ever for an NFL regular-season game, but the Cowboys lost on a last-minute field goal to the New York Giants.

Receiver Miles Austin leaps high to make a grab during the Cowboys' victory over New Orleans in 2009. It was Austin's fifth 100-plus-yard receiving game of the season. *Al Messerschmidt/Getty Images*

The first month of the 2009 season was rocky, but then Tony Romo—who had endured an offseason filled with questions about his commitment, conditioning, decision-making, and leadership—found a new favorite receiver to replace Terrell Owens.

Miles Austin, a former undrafted kid who had spent three years waiting for his chance, just like Romo had once done, pulled in a team-record 250 yards receiving in his first career start, including the game-winning touchdown in overtime at Kansas City. He had 171 yards the next week, giving him the best two-start total for a receiver in NFL history. He would finish the year in the Pro Bowl.

As the season progressed, more youngsters stepped up. Anthony Spencer became a solid outside linebacker opposite DeMarcus Ware. Mike Jenkins blossomed into a shutdown cornerback. Felix Jones got healthy and made big, breathtaking plays. Even rookie kickoff specialist David Buehler became a reliable weapon, booming touchback after touchback.

The season's turning point came the third weekend of December.

Dallas was coming off back-to-back losses, the first time that had happened all season. The timing

RIVALRY IN REVIEW
NEW YORK GIANTS

Because Tom Landry played for the New York Giants and subsequently launched his coaching career there, it's hard to hold too much of a grudge against that team.

When the Cowboys fell on hard times in the early 2000s, it was another guy with strong ties to the Giants, Bill Parcells, who brought Dallas back to respectability.

Although the Giants have been a frequent foe since the start, there's not as much enmity toward them as other longtime rivals.

Beyond the coaching connections, New York provided Dallas its first non-loss (a tie on December 4, 1960) and was the

foil in Emmitt Smith's incredible, one-armed performance in the 1993 season finale.

The teams didn't meet in the playoffs until January 2008, and that encounter did not work out so well for the Cowboys, as they became the first No. 1 seed in the NFC to lose its playoffs opener under the current format.

Of course, that Giants squad went on to knock off the unbeaten Patriots to become Super Bowl champions, which made the loss a tiny bit less embarrassing.

DALLAS COWBOYS RECORD BOOK

THROUGH THE 2009 SEASON

DALLAS COWBOYS YEAR-BY-YEAR

Year	W–L–T	Postseason	Points Scored	Points Allowed	Head Coach
1960	0–11–1		177	369	Tom Landry
1961	4–9–1		236	380	Tom Landry
1962	5–8–1		398	402	Tom Landry
1963	4–10		305	378	Tom Landry
1964	5–8–1		250	289	Tom Landry
1965	7–7		325	280	Tom Landry
1966	10–3–1*	0–1; lost conference championship	445	239	Tom Landry
1967	9–5*	1–1; lost conference championship	342	268	Tom Landry
1968	12–2*	0–1; lost divisional round	431	186	Tom Landry
1969	11–2–1*	0–1; lost divisional round	369	223	Tom Landry
1970	10–4*	2–1; lost Super Bowl	299	221	Tom Landry
1971	11–3*	3–0; won Super Bowl	406	222	Tom Landry
1972	10–4	1–1; lost conference championship	319	240	Tom Landry
1973	10–4*	1–1; lost conference championship	382	203	Tom Landry
1974	8–6		297	235	Tom Landry
1975	10–4	2–1; lost Super Bowl	350	268	Tom Landry
1976	11–3*	0–1; lost divisional round	296	194	Tom Landry
1977	12–2*	3–0; won Super Bowl	345	212	Tom Landry
1978	12–4*	2–1; lost Super Bowl	384	208	Tom Landry
1979	11–5*	0–1; lost divisional round	371	313	Tom Landry
1980	12–4^	2–1; lost conference championship	454	311	Tom Landry
1981	12–4*	1–1; lost conference championship	367	277	Tom Landry
1982	6–3	2–1; lost conference championship	226	145	Tom Landry
1983	12–4	0–1; lost wild card game	479	360	Tom Landry
1984	9–7		308	308	Tom Landry
1985	10–6*	0–1; lost divisional round	357	333	Tom Landry
1986	7–9		346	337	Tom Landry
1987	7–8		340	348	Tom Landry
1988	3–13		265	381	Tom Landry

Year	W–L–T	Postseason	Points Scored	Points Allowed	Head Coach
1989	1–15		204	393	Jimmy Johnson
1990	7–9		244	308	Jimmy Johnson
1991	11–5	1–1; lost divisional round	342	310	Jimmy Johnson
1992	13–3*	3–0; won Super Bowl	409	243	Jimmy Johnson
1993	12–4*	3–0; won Super Bowl	376	229	Jimmy Johnson
1994	12–4*	1–1; lost conference championship	414	248	Barry Switzer
1995	12–4*	3–0; won Super Bowl	435	291	Barry Switzer
1996	10–6*	1–1; lost divisional round	286	250	Barry Switzer
1997	6–10		304	314	Barry Switzer
1998	10–6*	0–1; lost wild card game	381	275	Chan Gailey
1999	8–8	0–1; lost wild card game	352	276	Chan Gailey
2000	5–11		294	361	Dave Campo
2001	5–11		246	338	Dave Campo
2002	5–11		217	329	Dave Campo
2003	10–6	0–1; lost wild card game	289	260	Bill Parcells
2004	6–10		293	405	Bill Parcells
2005	9–7		325	308	Bill Parcells
2006	9–7	0–1; lost wild card game	425	350	Bill Parcells
2007	13–3*	0–1; lost divisional round	455	325	Wade Phillips
2008	9–7		362	365	Wade Phillips
2009	11–5*	1–1; lost divisional round	361	250	Wade Phillips

* = won division title
^ = tied for best record in division, but lost tiebreaker

INDIVIDUAL HONORS

DALLAS COWBOYS RING OF HONOR

Name (uniform no.)	Position	Years with Cowboys	Induction Year
Bob Lilly (74)	DT	1961–1974	1975
Don Meredith (17)	QB	1960–1968	1976
Don Perkins (43)	RB	1961–1968	1976
Chuck Howley (54)	LB	1961–1973	1977
Mel Renfro (20)	DB	1964–1977	1981
Roger Staubach (12)	QB	1969–1979	1983
Lee Roy Jordan (55)	LB	1963–1976	1989
Tom Landry	head coach	1960–1988	1993
Tony Dorsett (33)	RB	1977–1987	1994
Randy White (54)	DT	1975–1988	1994
Bob Hayes (22)	WR	1965–1974	2001
Tex Schramm	team executive	1959–1988	2003
Cliff Harris (43)	S	1970–1979	2004
Rayfield Wright (70)	OT	1967–1979	2004
Troy Aikman (8)	QB	1989–2000	2005
Michael Irvin (88)	WR	1988–1999	2005
Emmitt Smith (22)	RB	1990–2002	2005

DALLAS COWBOYS IN THE PRO FOOTBALL HALL OF FAME

Name	Position	Years with Cowboys	Induction Year
Herb Adderley	DB	1970–1972	1980
Troy Aikman	QB	1989–2000	2006
Lance Alworth	WR	1971–1972	1978
Mike Ditka	TE	1969–1972	1988
Tony Dorsett	RB	1977–1987	1994
Forrest Gregg	OT	1971	1977
Bob Hayes	WR	1965–1975	2009
Michael Irvin	WR	1988–1999	2007
Tom Landry	head coach	1960–1988	1990
Bob Lilly	DT	1961–1974	1980
Tommy McDonald	WR	1964	1998
Mel Renfro	DB	1964–1977	1996
Tex Schramm	team executive	1960–1989	1991
Emmitt Smith	RB	1990–2002	2010
Jackie Smith	TE	1978	1994
Roger Staubach	QB	1969–1979	1985
Randy White	DT	1975–1988	1994
Rayfield Wright	OT	1967–1979	2006

DALLAS COWBOYS FIRST-TEAM ALL-PROS

Bob Lilly	DT/DE	1964, 1965, 1966, 1967, 1968, 1969, 1971
Randy White	DT/LB/DE	1978, 1979, 1981, 1982, 1983, 1984, 1985
Larry Allen	G/T	1996, 1997, 1998, 1999, 2000, 2001
Chuck Howley	LB	1966, 1967, 1968, 1969, 1970
Emmitt Smith	RB	1992, 1993, 1994, 1995
Cornell Green	DB	1966, 1967, 1969
Ralph Neely	T/G	1967, 1968, 1969
Rayfield Wright	T/TE	1971, 1972, 1973
Drew Pearson	WR	1974, 1976, 1977
Cliff Harris	DB	1976, 1977, 1978
Darren Woodson	DB	1994, 1995, 1996
Deion Sanders	DB/WR	1996, 1997, 1998
DeMarcus Ware	LB	2007, 2008, 2009
Bob Hayes	WR	1966, 1968
John Niland	G	1971, 1972
Herb Scott	G/T	1980, 1981
Erik Williams	T	1993, 1996
Nate Newton	G/T	1994, 1995
Don Perkins	RB	1962
Frank Clarke	E	1964
George Andrie	DE	1969
Calvin Hill	RB	1969
Lee Roy Jordan	LB	1969
Mel Renfro	DB/RB	1969
Ron Widby	P	1969
Efren Herrera	K	1977
Harvey Martin	DE/DT	1977
Tony Dorsett	RB	1981
Rafael Septien	K	1981
Ed "Too Tall" Jones	DE	1982
Everson Walls	DB	1983
Michael Irvin	WR	1991
Jay Novacek	TE	1992
Charles Haley	DE/LB	1994
Richie Cunningham	K	1997
Roy Williams	DB	2003
Terrell Owens	WR	2007
Jason Witten	TE	2007
Jay Ratliff	DE	2009

DALLAS COWBOYS PRO BOWLERS

* includes only players with five or more Pro Bowl selections.

Bob Lilly	DT/DE	11 (1962, 1964–1973)
Mel Renfro	DB/RB	10 (1964–1973)
Larry Allen	G/T	10 (1995–2001, 2003–2005)
Randy White	DT/LB/DE	9 (1977–1985)
Emmitt Smith	RB	8 (1990–1995, 1998, 1999)
Don Perkins	RB	6 (1961–1963, 1966–1968)
Chuck Howley	LB	6 (1965–1969, 1971)
John Niland	G	6 (1968–1973)
Roger Staubach	QB	6 (1971, 1975–1979)
Rayfield Wright	T/TE	6 (1971–1976)
Cliff Harris	DB	6 (1974–1979)
Troy Aikman	QB	6 (1991–1996)
Nate Newton	G-T	6 (1992–1996, 1998)
Jason Witten	TE	6 (2004–2009)
George Andrie	DE	5 (1965–1969)
Cornell Green	DB	5 (1965–1967, 1971, 1972)
Lee Roy Jordan	LB	5 (1967–1969, 1973, 1974)
Michael Irvin	WR	5 (1991–1995)
Jay Novacek	TE	5 (1991–1995)
Darren Woodson	DB	5 (1994–1998)
Flozell Adams	T/G/TE	5 (2003, 2004, 2006–2008)
Roy Williams	DB	5 (2003–2007)

PLAYER RECORDS

SERVICE

Most Seasons

15	Ed "Too Tall" Jones, 1974–1978, 1980–1989
15	Bill Bates, 1983–1997
15	Mark Tuinei, 1983–1997
14	Lee Roy Jordan, 1963–1976
14	Bob Lilly, 1961–1974
14	Mel Renfro, 1964–1977
14	Jethro Pugh, 1965–1978
14	Randy White, 1975–1988
14	Tom Rafferty, 1976–1989

Most Games

217	Bill Bates, 1983–1997
201	Emmitt Smith, 1990–2002
188	Jim Jeffcoat, 1983–1994
180	Ed "Too Tall" Jones, 1975–1989
178	Darren Woodson, 1992–2003

OFFENSE

SCORING RECORDS

Most Points Scored

Career

986	Emmitt Smith, RB, 1990–2002
874	Rafael Septien, K, 1978–1986
516	Tony Dorsett, RB, 1977–1987
456	Bob Hayes, WR, 1965–1974
392	Michael Irvin, WR, 1988–1999

Season

150	Emmitt Smith, RB, 1995
132	Emmitt Smith, RB, 1994
131	Nick Folk, K, 2007
127	Chris Boniol, K, 1995
127	Richie Cunningham, K, 1998

Game

24	Bob Hayes, WR, 12/20/1970
24	Calvin Hill, RB, 9/19/1971
24	Emmitt Smith, RB, 12/16/1990
24	Emmitt Smith, RB, 9/4/1995
24	Terrell Owens, WR, 11/18/2007

Touchdowns Scored

Career

164	Emmitt Smith, RB, 1990–2002
86	Tony Dorsett, RB, 1977–1987
76	Bob Hayes, WR, 1965–1974
65	Michael Irvin, WR, 1988–1999
51	Frank Clarke, End, 1960–1967
51	Tony Hill, WR, 1978–1986

Season

25	Emmitt Smith, RB, 1995 (25 rush.)
22	Emmitt Smith, RB, 1994 (21 rush., 1 rec.)
19	Emmitt Smith, RB, 1992 (18 rush., 1 rec.)
16	Dan Reeves, HB, 1966 (8 rush., 8 rec.)
16	Marion Barber, RB, 2006 (14 rush, 2 rec.)

Game

4	Bob Hayes, WR, 12/20/1970
4	Calvin Hill, RB, 9/19/1971
4	Emmitt Smith, RB, 12/16/1990
4	Emmitt Smith, RB, 9/4/1995
4	Terrell Owens, WR, 11/18/2007

PASSING RECORDS

Quarterback Chart (min. 100 attempts)

	Years	Games	Completions	Attempts	Comp. %	Yards	Yards per Att.	Yards per Comp.	Yards per G	Long Pass	Touchdown Passes	TD %	Interceptions	Int. %	QB W–L Record	QB Rating
Troy Aikman		165	2,898	4,715	61.5	32,942	7.0	11.4	199.6	90	165	3.5	141	3.0	94–71–0	81.6
Roger Staubach		131	1,685	2,958	57.0	22,700	7.7	13.5	173.3	91	153	5.2	109	3.7	85–29–0	83.4
Danny White		166	1,761	2,950	59.7	21,050	7.4	12.5	132.3	80	155	5.3	132	4.5	62–30–0	81.7
Don Meredith		104	1,170	2,308	50.7	17,199	7.5	14.7	165.4	95	135	5.8	111	4.8	48–33–4	74.8
Tony Romo		61	1,178	1,857	63.4	15,045	8.1	12.8	246.6	80	107	5.8	55	3.0	38–12–0	95.6
Craig Morton		97	685	1,308	52.4	10,279	7.9	15.0	106.0	89	80	6.1	73	5.6	32–14–1	75.6
Steve Pelluer		46	520	922	56.4	6,555	7.1	12.6	142.5	84	28	3.0	38	4.1	8–19–0	71.7
Quincy Carter		31	507	902	56.2	5,839	6.5	11.5	188.4	80	29	3.2	36	4.0	16–15–0	70.0
Eddie LeBaron		52	359	692	51.9	5,331	7.7	14.8	102.5	85	45	6.5	53	7.7	4–21–1	67.2
Drew Bledsoe		22	390	668	58.4	4,803	7.2	12.3	218.3	71	30	4.5	25	3.7	12–10–0	80.1
Gary Hogeboom		42	279	518	53.9	3,550	6.9	12.7	84.5	68	13	2.5	23	4.4	6–6–0	65.4
Vinny Testaverde	2004	16	297	495	60.0	3,532	7.1	11.9	220.8	53	17	3.4	20	4.0	5–10–0	76.4
Jason Garrett		23	165	294	56.1	2,042	6.9	12.4	88.8	80	11	3.7	5	1.7	6–3–0	83.2
Chad Hutchinson		10	128	252	50.8	1,563	6.2	12.2	156.3	58	7	2.8	8	3.2	2–7–0	66.3
Steve Walsh		9	114	228	50.0	1,411	6.2	12.4	156.8	46	5	2.2	9	3.9	1–4–0	60.4
Steve Beuerlein		24	80	155	51.6	1,061	6.8	13.3	44.2	66	5	3.2	3	1.9	4–0–0	76.3
Anthony Wright		8	70	151	46.4	766	5.1	10.9	95.8	80	5	3.3	8	5.3	1–4–0	50.8
Randall Cunningham	2000	6	74	125	59.2	849	6.8	11.5	141.5	76	6	4.8	4	3.2	1–2–0	82.4
Kevin Sweeney		6	47	106	44.3	605	5.7	12.9	100.8	77	7	6.6	6	5.7	2–2–0	61.2

Quarterback Wins

Career

94	Troy Aikman, 1989–2000
85	Roger Staubach, 1969–1979
62	Danny White, 1976–1988
48	Don Meredith, 1960–1968
38	Tony Romo, 2006–2009

Season

13	Troy Aikman, 1992
13	Tony Romo, 2007
12	Roger Staubach, 1977
12	Danny White, 1980
12	Danny White, 1983
12	Troy Aikman, 1995

Pass Attempts

Career

4,715	Troy Aikman, 1989–2000
2,958	Roger Staubach, 1969–1979
2,950	Danny White, 1976–1988
2,308	Don Meredith, 1960–1968
1,857	Tony Romo, 2006–2009

Season

550	Tony Romo, 2009
533	Danny White, 1983
520	Tony Romo, 2007
518	Troy Aikman, 1997
505	Quincy Carter, 2003

Game

57	Troy Aikman 11/26/1998

Pass Completions

Career

2,898	Troy Aikman, 1989–2000
1,761	Danny White, 1976–1988
1,685	Roger Staubach, 1969–1979
1,178	Tony Romo, 2006–2009
1,170	Don Meredith, 1960–1968

Season

347	Tony Romo, 2009
335	Tony Romo, 2007
334	Danny White, 1983

302	Troy Aikman, 1992
300	Drew Bledsoe, 2005

Game

41	Tony Romo, 12/6/2009

Completion Percentage

Career (min. 100 attempts)

63.4%	Tony Romo, 2006–2009 (1,178–1,857)
61.5%	Troy Aikman, 1989–2000 (2,898–4,715)
60.0%	Vinny Testaverde, 2004 (297–495)
59.7%	Danny White, 1976–1988 (1,761–2,950)
59.2%	Randall Cunningham, 2000 (74–125)

Season (min. 50 attempts)

69.1%	Troy Aikman, 1993 (271–392)
66.7%	Wade Wilson, 1995 (38–57)
65.3%	Tony Romo, 2006 (220–337)
65.3%	Troy Aikman, 1991 (237–363)
64.8%	Troy Aikman, 1995 (280–432)

Game (min. 10 attempts)

87.5%	Danny White, 11/6/1983

Passing Yards

Career

32,942	Troy Aikman, 1989–2000
22,700	Roger Staubach, 1969–1979
21,959	Danny White, 1976–1988
17,199	Don Meredith, 1960–1968
15,045	Tony Romo, 2006–2009

Season

4,483	Tony Romo, 2009
4,211	Tony Romo, 2007
3,980	Danny White, 1983
3,639	Drew Bledsoe, 2005
3,596	Roger Staubach, 1979

Game

460	Don Meredith, 11/10/1963

Longest Pass Play from Scrimmage

95 yards   Don Meredith to Bob Hayes, vs. Washington, 11/13/1966

Most Yards per Game

Career

246.6	Tony Romo, 2006–2009 (15,045–61)
220.8	Vinny Testaverde, 2004 (3,502–16)
218.3	Drew Bledsoe, 2005–2006 (4,803–22)
199.6	Troy Aikman, 1989–2000 (32,942–165)
188.4	Quincy Carter, 2001–2003 (5,839–31)

Season

280.2	Tony Romo, 2009 (4,483–16)
265.2	Tony Romo, 2008 (3,448–13)
263.2	Tony Romo, 2007 (4,211–16)
248.8	Danny White, 1983 (3,980–16)
237.9	Danny White, 1987 (2,617–11)

Most Yards per Attempt

Career (min. 100 attempts)

8.10	Tony Romo, 2006–2009 (15,045–1,857)
7.86	Craig Morton, 1965–1974 (10,279–1,308)
7.70	Eddie LeBaron, 1960–1963 (5,331–692)
7.67	Roger Staubach, 1969–1979 (22,700–2,958)
7.45	Don Meredith, 1960–1968 (17,199–2,308)

Season (min. 50 attempts)

8.92	Roger Staubach, 1971 (1,882–211)
8.85	Craig Morton, 1968 (752–85)
8.79	Craig Morton, 1970 (1,819–207)
8.67	Craig Morton, 1969 (2,619–302)
8.65	Eddie LeBaron, 1962 (1,436–166)

Touchdown Passes

Career

165	Troy Aikman, 1989–2000
155	Danny White, 1976–1988
153	Roger Staubach, 1969–1979
135	Don Meredith, 1960–1968
107	Tony Romo, 2006–2009

Season

36	Tony Romo, 2007
29	Danny White, 1983
28	Danny White, 1980
27	Roger Staubach, 1979
26	Tony Romo, 2008
26	Tony Romo, 2009

Game

5	Accomplished 9 times

Consecutive Games with a Touchdown Pass

17	Tony Romo, 12/10/2006–12/9/2007

Most Interceptions Thrown

Career

141	Troy Aikman, 1989–2000
132	Danny White, 1976–1988
111	Don Meredith, 1960–1968
109	Roger Staubach, 1969–1979
73	Craig Morton, 1965–1974

Season

25	Eddie LeBaron, 1960
25	Danny White, 1980
23	Danny White, 1983
21	Craig Morton, 1972
21	Quincy Carter, 2003

Game

5	Accomplished 6 times

Fewest Interceptions per Attempt

Career Percentage (min. 100 attempts)

1.70%	Jason Garrett, 1993–1999 (5–294)
1.94%	Steve Beuerlein, 1991–1992 (3–155)
2.96%	Tony Romo, 2006–2009 (55–1,857)
2.99%	Troy Aikman, 1989–2000 (141–4,715)
3.17%	Chad Hutchinson, 2002–2003 (8–252)

Season Percentage (min. 50 attempts)

0.00%	Bernie Kosar, 1993 (0–63)
1.46%	Steve Beuerlein, 1991 (2–137)
1.53%	Troy Aikman, 1993 (6–392)
1.56%	Jason Garrett, 1999 (1–64)
1.59%	Troy Aikman, 1998 (5–315)

Most Completions Without an Interception, Game

41	Tony Romo, 12/6/2009

Quarterback Rating

Career (min. 100 attempts)

95.6	Tony Romo, 2006–2009
83.4	Roger Staubach, 1969–1979
83.2	Jason Garrett, 1993–1999
82.4	Randall Cunningham, 2000
81.7	Danny White, 1976–1988

Season (min. 50 attempts)

104.8	Roger Staubach, 1971
102.5	Rodney Peete, 1994
99.0	Troy Aikman, 1993
97.9	Danny White, 1986
97.6	Tony Romo, 2009

RUSHING RECORDS

Attempts

Career

4,052	Emmitt Smith, 1990–2002
2,755	Tony Dorsett, 1977–1987
1,500	Don Perkins, 1961–1968
1,166	Calvin Hill, 1969–1974
1,160	Robert Newhouse, 1972–1983

Season

377	Emmitt Smith, 1995
373	Emmitt Smith, 1992
368	Emmitt Smith, 1994
365	Emmitt Smith, 1991
361	Herschel Walker, 1988

Game

35	Emmitt Smith, 11/7/1994

Yards

Career

17,162	Emmitt Smith, 1990–2002
12,036	Tony Dorsett, 1977–1987
6,217	Don Perkins, 1961–1968
5,009	Calvin Hill, 1969–1974
4,784	Robert Newhouse, 1972–1983

Season

1,773	Emmitt Smith, 1995
1,713	Emmitt Smith, 1992
1,646	Tony Dorsett, 1981
1,563	Emmitt Smith, 1991
1,514	Herschel Walker, 1988

Game

237	Emmitt Smith, 10/31/1993

Rushing Yards per Carry

Career (min. 100 carries)

6.5	Felix Jones, 2008–2009 (146–951)
5.9	Steve Pelluer, 1985–1988 (120–709)

5.5   Roger Staubach, 1969–1979 (410–2,264)
5.3   Tashard Choice, 2008–2009 (156–821)
5.0   Don Meredith, 1960–1968 (242–1,216)

Season (min. 75 carries)
5.9   Felix Jones, 2009 (116–685)
5.6   Amos Marsh, 1962 (144–802)
5.3   Duane Thomas, 1970 (151–803)
5.3   Emmitt Smith, 1993 (283–1,486)
5.1   Troy Hambrick, 2001 (113–579)

Game (min. 8 rushes)
12.1   Walt Garrison, 12/9/1972 (10–121)

Rushing Touchdowns

Career
153   Emmitt Smith, 1990–2002
72   Tony Dorsett, 1977–1987
43   Marion Barber, 2005–2009
42   Don Perkins, 1961–1968
39   Calvin Hill, 1969–1974

Season
25   Emmitt Smith, 1995
21   Emmitt Smith, 1994
18   Emmitt Smith, 1992
14   Marion Barber, 2006
13   Emmitt Smith, 1998

Game
4   Calvin Hill, 9/19/1971
4   Emmitt Smith, 12/16/1990
4   Emmitt Smith, 9/4/1995

Consecutive Games with a Rushing Touchdown
11   Emmitt Smith, 11/7/1994–9/24/1995
11   Emmitt Smith, 10/8/1995–12/25/1995

Longest Scoring Run from Scrimmage
99 yards Tony Dorsett, 1/3/1983

RECEIVING

Receptions

Career
750   Michael Irvin, 1988–1999
523   Jason Witten, 2003–2009
489   Drew Pearson, 1973–1983
486   Emmitt Smith, 1990–2002
479   Tony Hill, 1977–1986

Season
111   Michael Irvin, 1995
96   Jason Witten, 2007
94   Jason Witten, 2009
93   Michael Irvin, 1991
88   Michael Irvin, 1993

Game
15   Jason Witten, 12/9/2007

Receiving Yards

Career
11,904   Michael Irvin, 1988–1999

7,988   Tony Hill, 1977–1986
7,822   Drew Pearson, 1973–1983
7,295   Bob Hayes, 1965–1974
5,965   Jason Witten, 2003–2009

Season
1,603   Michael Irvin, 1995
1,523   Michael Irvin, 1991
1,396   Michael Irvin, 1992
1,355   Terrell Owens, 2007
1,330   Michael Irvin, 1993

Game
250   Miles Austin, 10/11/2009

Yards per Reception

Career (min. 50 receptions)
20.0   Alvin Harper, 1991–1994 (2,486–124)
20.0   Bob Hayes, 1965–1974 (7,295–365)
19.2   Lance Rentzel, 1967–1970 (3,521–183)
18.6   Frank Clarke, 1960–1967 (5,214–281)
18.3   Golden Richards, 1973–1978 (1,650–90)

Season (min. 20 receptions)
26.1   Bob Hayes, 1970 (889–34)
24.9   Alvin Harper, 1994 (821–33)
24.0   Bob Hayes, 1971 (840–35)
22.4   Frank Clarke, 1961 (919–41)
22.3   Lance Rentzel, 1969 (960–43)

Game (min. 4 receptions)
42.0   Frank Clarke, 9/30/1960 (168–4)

Touchdown Receptions

Career
71   Bob Hayes, 1965–1974
65   Michael Irvin, 1988–1999
51   Tony Hill, 1977–1986
50   Frank Clarke, 1960–1967
48   Drew Pearson, 1973–1983

Season
15   Terrell Owens, 2007
14   Frank Clarke, 1962
13   Bob Hayes, 1966
13   Terrell Owens, 2006
12   Bob Hayes, 1965
12   Lance Rentzel, 1969

Game
4   Bob Hayes, 12/20/1970
4   Terrell Owens, 11/18/2007

SPECIAL TEAMS

KICKOFF RETURNS

Most Kickoff Returns

Career
144   Kevin Williams, 1993–1996
101   James Dixon, 1989–1991
98   Tyson Thompson, 2005–2007
89   Miles Austin, 2006–2009
87   Reggie Swinton, 2001–2003

Season
57   Tyson Thompson, 2005
56   Reggie Swinton, 2001
51   Jason Tucker, 2000
50   Herschel Walker, 1997
49   Kevin Williams, 1995

Game
8   Mel Renfro, 11/29/1964

Kickoff Return Yardage

Career
3,416   Kevin Williams, 1993–1996
2,416   Tyson Thompson, 2005–2007
2,315   James Dixon, 1989–1991
2,246   Mel Renfro, 1964–1974
2,146   Miles Austin, 2006–2009

Season
1,399   Tyson Thompson, 2005
1,327   Reggie Swinton, 2001
1,181   James Dixon, 1989
1,167   Herschel Walker, 1997
1,148   Kevin Williams, 1995

Game
247   Felix Jones, 9/20/2009

Longest Return
102 yards Alexander Wright, vs. Atlanta, 12/22/1991

Yards per Kickoff Return

Career (min. 30 returns)
26.4   Mel Renfro, 1964–1974 (85–2,246)
25.7   Cliff Harris, 1970–1977 (63–1,622)
25.3   Herschel Walker, 1996–1997 (77–1,946)
25.2   Craig Baynham, 1967–1969 (41–1,035)
24.7   Tyson Thompson, 2005–2007 (98–2,416)

Season (min. 15 returns)
30.0   Mel Renfro, 1965 (21–630)
28.9   Herschel Walker, 1996 (27–779)
28.4   Cliff Harris, 1971 (29–823)
27.9   Jason Tucker, 1999 (22–613)
27.1   Felix Jones, 2008 (16–434)

Kickoffs Returned for Touchdown

Career
2   Mel Renfro, 1964–1974
2   Ike Thomas, 1971
2   Alexander Wright, 1990–1992
1   Held by 9 players

Season
2   Ike Thomas, 1971

Game
1   15 times (last: Felix Jones, 9/15/2008)

PUNT RETURNS

Most Punt Returns

Career
179   Kelvin Martin, 1987–1996
146   Butch Johnson, 1976–1978

111	Patrick Crayton, 2004–2009
109	Mel Renfro, 1964–1974
104	Bob Hayes, 1965–1974

Season

54	James Jones, 1980
54	Gary Allen, 1984
51	Butch Johnson, 1978
50	Butch Johnson, 1977
45	Butch Johnson, 1976

Game

8	Butch Johnson, 11/15/1976

Punt Return Yardage

Career

1,803	Kelvin Martin, 1987–1996
1,313	Butch Johnson, 1976–1978
1,184	Deion Sanders, 1995–1999
1,158	Bob Hayes, 1965–1974
1,066	Patrick Crayton, 2004–2009

Season

548	James Jones, 1980
532	Kelvin Martin, 1992
489	Butch Johnson, 1976
446	Gary Allen, 1984
437	Patrick Crayton, 2009

Game

124	Kelvin Martin, 12/15/1991

Yards per Punt Return

Career (min. 20 returns)

13.3	Deion Sanders, 1995–1999 (89–1,184)
11.1	Bob Hayes, 1965–1974 (104–1,158)
10.9	Reggie Swinton, 2001–2003 (51–555)
10.4	Wane McGarity, 1999–2001 (39–407)
10.1	Kelvin Martin, 1987–1996 (179–1,803)

Season (min. 10 returns)

20.8	Bob Hayes, 1968 (15–312)
15.6	Deion Sanders, 1998 (24–375)
15.1	Dennis Morgan, 1974 (19–287)
13.4	Reggie Swinton, 2001 (31–414)
13.1	Mel Renfro, 1964 (32–418)

Punts Returned for Touchdown

Career

4	Deion Sanders, 1995–1999
3	Bob Hayes, 1965–1974
3	Kelvin Martin, 1987–1996
3	Kevin Williams, 1993–1996
2	Patrick Crayton, 2004–2009
2	Wane McGarity, 1999–2001

Season

2	Bob Hayes, 1968
2	Kelvin Martin, 1992
2	Kevin Williams, 1993
2	Deion Sanders, 1998
2	Wane McGarity, 2000
2	Patrick Crayton, 2009

Game

1	Held by many players

KICKING

PAT Attempts

Career

398	Rafael Septien, 1978–1986
182	Mike Clark, 1968–1973
131	Nick Folk, 2007–2009
128	Danny Villanueva, 1965–1967
121	Toni Fritsch, 1971–1975
121	Chris Boniol, 1994–1996

Season

60	Rafael Septien, 1980
59	Rafael Septien, 1983
56	Danny Villanueva, 1966
54	Mike Clark, 1968
53	Nick Folk, 2007

Game

8	Danny Villanueva, 10/9/1966
8	Mike Clark, 9/15/1968
8	Rafael Septien, 10/12/1980

PATs Made

Career

388	Rafael Septien, 1978–1986
180	Mike Clark, 1968–1973
131	Nick Folk, 2007–2009
125	Danny Villanueva, 1965–1967
119	Toni Fritsch, 1971–1975

Season

59	Rafael Septien, 1980
57	Rafael Septien, 1983
56	Danny Villanueva, 1966
54	Mike Clark, 1968
53	Nick Folk, 2007

Game

8	Danny Villanueva, 10/9/1966
8	Mike Clark, 9/15/1968
8	Rafael Septien, 10/12/1980

PAT Percentage

Career (min. 30 attempts)

100%	Nick Folk, 2007–2009 (131–131)
100%	Richie Cunningham, 1997–1999 (95–95)
100%	Ken Willis, 1990–1991 (63–63)
100%	Eddie Murray, 1993–1999 (48–48)
100%	Tim Seder, 2000–2001 (39–39)
100%	Mike Vanderjagt, 2006 (33–33)

Most PATs Without a Miss

Season

56	Danny Villaneuva, 1966
54	Mike Clark, 1968
53	Nick Folk, 2007
48	Chris Boniol, 1994
47	Mike Clark, 1971

Field Goal Attempts

Career

226	Rafael Septien, 1978–1986
119	Mike Clark, 1968–1973
107	Toni Fritsch, 1971–1975
94	Richie Cunningham, 1997–1999
93	Chris Boniol, 1994–1996

Season

39	Ken Willis, 1991
37	Richie Cunningham, 1997
36	Mike Clark, 1969
36	Toni Fritsch, 1972
36	Chris Boniol, 1996

Game

8	Billy Cundiff, 9/15/2003

Field Goals Made

Career

162	Rafael Septien, 1978–1986
81	Chris Boniol, 1994–1996
75	Richie Cunningham, 1997–1999
69	Mike Clark, 1968–1973
66	Toni Fritsch, 1971–1975

Season

34	Richie Cunningham, 1997
32	Chris Boniol, 1996
29	Richie Cunningham, 1998
28	Eddie Murray, 1993
27	Rafael Septien, 1981
27	Ken Willis, 1991
27	Chris Boniol, 1995

Game

8	Chris Boniol, 11/18/1996
8	Billy Cundiff, 9/15/2003

Most Field Goals of 50+ Yards, Career

8	Rafael Septien, 1978–1986

Longest Field Goal Made

56 yards   Billy Cundiff, 11/20/2005

Field Goal Percentage

Career (min. 20 attempts)

87.1%	Chris Boniol, 1994–1996 (81–93)
83.3%	Eddie Murray, 1993–1999 (35–42)
79.8%	Richie Cunningham, 1997–1999 (75–94)
79.0%	Nick Folk, 2007–2009 (64–81)
73.2%	Billy Cundiff, 2002–2005 (60–82)

Season (min. 10 attempts)

96.4%	Chris Boniol, 1995 (27–28)
91.9%	Richie Cunningham, 1997 (34–37)
90.9%	Nick Folk, 2008 (20–22)
88.9%	Chris Boniol, 1996 (32–36)
88.0%	Roger Ruzek, 1987 (22–25)

PUNTING

Most Punts

Career

610	Danny White, 1976–1985
591	Mike Saxon, 1985–1992

371	Mat McBriar, 2004–2009	
338	Toby Gowin, 1997–2003	
253	John Jett, 1993–1996	

Season
94	Toby Gowin, 2003
86	Mike Saxon, 1986
86	Toby Gowin, 1997
82	Danny White, 1984
81	Mike Saxon, 1985
81	Toby Gowin, 1999
81	Mat McBriar, 2005

Total Yardage

Career
24,542	Mike Saxon, 1985–1992
24,509	Danny White, 1976–1985
16,712	Mat McBriar, 2004–2009
14,099	Toby Gowin, 1997–2003
10,593	John Jett, 1993–1996

Season
3,665	Toby Gowin, 2003
3,592	Toby Gowin, 1997
3,500	Toby Gowin, 1999
3,498	Mike Saxon, 1986
3,493	Mat McBriar, 2005

Yards per Punt

Career (min. 100 punts)
45.0	Mat McBriar, 2004–2009
44.7	Sam Baker, 1962–1963
41.9	John Jett, 1993–1996
41.8	Ron Widby, 1968–1971
41.7	Toby Gowin, 1997–2003

Season (min. 50 punts)
48.2	Mat McBriar, 2006
47.1	Mat McBriar, 2007
45.4	Sam Baker, 1962
45.1	Mat McBriar, 2009
44.2	Sam Baker, 1963

Longest Punt
84 yards   Ron Widby, vs. New Orleans, 11/3/1968

DEFENSE

INTERCEPTIONS

Most Interceptions

Career
52	Mel Renfro, 1964–1977
44	Everson Walls, 1981–1988
41	Charlie Waters, 1970–1981
36	Donnie Thurman, 1978–1985
34	Cornell Green, 1963–1974
34	Michael Downs, 1981–1988

Season
11	Everson Walls, 1981
10	Mel Renfro, 1969
9	Dennis Thurman, 1981
9	Everson Walls, 1985
8	Don Bishop, 1961

Game
3	Herb Adderley, 9/26/1971
3	Lee Roy Jordan, 11/4/1973
3	Dennis Thurman, 12/13/1981
3	Terence Newman, 12/14/2003

Interception Return Yardage

Career
626	Mel Renfro, 1964–1977
584	Charlie Waters, 1970–1981
562	Dennis Thurman, 1978–1985
552	Cornell Green, 1963–1974
472	Lee Roy Jordan, 1981–1988

Season
211	Cornell Green, 1962 (7 int.)
187	Dennis Thurman, 1981 (9 int.)
182	Herb Adderley, 1971 (6 int.)
172	Don Bishop, 1961 (8 int.)
153	Deion Sanders, 1998 (5 int.)

Game
121 yards Mike Gaechter, 11/13/1963 (2 int.)

Most Interceptions Returned for Touchdown

Career
4	Dennis Thurman, 1978–1985
4	Dexter Coakley, 1997–2004
3	Lee Roy Jordan, 1963–1976
3	Mel Renfro, 1964–1977
3	Larry Cole, 1968–1980
3	Roy Williams, 2002–2008

Season
2	Dexter Coakley, 2001
2	Roy Williams, 2002

Longest Interception Return for Touchdown
100 yards Mike Gaechter, 10/14/1962

SACKS

Note: Sacks first became an official statistic tracked by the NFL in 1982.

Most Sacks

Career
94.5	Jim Jeffcoat, 1983–1994
77.0	Greg Ellis, 1998–2008
64.5	DeMarcus Ware, 2005–2009
59.0	Tony Tolbert, 1989–1997
57.5	Ed "Too Tall" Jones, 1975–1989

Season
20	DeMarcus Ware, 2008
14	Jim Jeffcoat, 1986
14	DeMarcus Ware, 2007
13	Ed "Too Tall" Jones, 1985
12.5	Randy White, 1983
12.5	Randy White, 1984
12.5	Charles Haley, 1994
12.5	Greg Ellis, 2007

Game
5	Jim Jeffcoat, 11/10/1985

FUMBLE RETURNS

Most Fumble Return for Touchdown

Career
3	Bob Lilly, 1961–1974
2	Cornell Green, 1963–1974
2	Drew Pearson, 1973–1977
2	Benny Barnes, 1973–1982
2	Mike Hegman, 1976–1987
2	Michael Downs, 1981–1988
2	Jim Jeffcoat, 1983–1994

TEAM RECORDS

Super Bowl Wins
    5 (1971, 1977, 1992, 1993, 1995)
Conference Championships
    8 (1970, 1971, 1975, 1977, 1978, 1992, 1993, 1995)
Division Titles (outright)
    21 (1966–1971, 1973, 1976–1979, 1981, 1985, 1992–1996, 1998, 2007, 2009)
Playoff Berths
    30 (1966–1973, 1975–1983, 1985, 1991–1996, 1998, 1999, 2003, 2006, 2007, 2009)
Winning Seasons   33
Most Wins, Regular Season   13 (1992, 2007)
Most Consecutive Wins, Regular Season
    8 (1977)
Most Consecutive Wins, All Games
    12 (11/7/1971–9/24/1972)
Most Losses, Season   15 (1989)
Most Consecutive Games Without a Win
    11 (1960)

SCORING AND TOTAL OFFENSE

Most Points, Season   479 (1983)
Most Points, Game
    59 (vs. Detroit, 9/15/1968; vs. San Francisco, 10/12/1980)
Largest Point Differential, Season
    245 (1968; 431–186)
Largest Margin of Victory, Game
    49 (56–7, vs. Philadelphia, 10/9/1966)
Fewest Points Scored per Game, Season
    12.75 (1989; 204 points/16 games)
Fewest Points Scored, Game   0 (11 times)
Largest Margin of Defeat
    44 (44–0, vs. Chicago, 11/17/1985)
Most Touchdowns, Season   60 (1980)
Most Touchdowns, Game
    8 (vs. Philadelphia, 9/9/1966; vs. Detroit, 9/15/1968; vs. San Francisco, 10/12/1980)
Most Yards Total Offense, Season
    6,390 (2009)
Most Yards Total Offense, Game
    652 (vs. Philadelphia, 9/9/1966)
Most Total Offensive Plays, Season
    1,122 (1979)

Fewest Yards Total Offense per Game, Season
    255.1 (1990; 4,081 yards/16 games)
Most First Downs, Season   364 (1995)
Most First Downs, Game
    33 (@ Detroit, 9/15/1985)

PASSING

Most Pass Attempts, Season   604 (1984)
Most Pass Completions, Season   347 (2009)
Highest Completion Percentage, Season
    66.7% (1993; 317–475)
Most Yards Passing, Season   4,287 (2009)
Most Yards per Pass Attempt, Season
    8.0 (1969; 2,846 yards/355 attempts)
Most Yards per Pass Completion, Season
    15.1 (1969; 2,846 yards/189 completions)

Fewest Pass Attempts per Game, Season
    21.2 (1970; 297 attempts/14 games)
Fewest Pass Completions, Season
    149 (1970, 14 games); 210 (2001, 16 games)
Fewest Yards Passing per Game, Season
    138.6 (2001; 2,218 yards/16 games)
Fewest Yards Passing, Game
    -1 (@ Green Bay, 10/24/1965)
Most Touchdown Passes, Season   36 (2007)
Most Interceptions Thrown, Season   33 (1960)
Fewest Interceptions per Attempt, Season
    1.3% (1993; 6 interceptions/475 attempts)

RUSHING

Most Rushing Attempts, Season   630 (1981)
Most Rushing Yards, Season   2,783 (1978)
Most Yards per Rush, Season
    4.8 (2009; 2,103–436)
Most Rushing Touchdowns, Season   29 (1995)
Fewest Rushing Attempts per Game, Season
    22.2 (1989; 355 attempts/16 games)
Fewest Rushing Yards per Game, Season
    87.4 (1960; 1,049 yards/12 games)
Most Rushing Yards, Game
    354 (@ Baltimore Colts, 12/6/1981)
Fewest Rushing Yards, Game
    1 (@ Washington, 12/30/2007)

SPECIAL TEAMS

Most Punts, Season 112 (2002)
Fewest Punts, Season
    51 (1972); 37 (1982, 9 games)
Most Yards per Punt, Season   48.2 (2006)
Fewest Yards per Punt, Season   36.7 (1961)
Most Punt Returns, Season   63 (1978)
Most Punt Return Yards, Season   573 (1974)
Most Yards per Punt Return, Season   12.6 (1998)
Most Punt Return Touchdowns, Season
    2 (1968, 1992, 1993, 1998, 2000, 2009)
Most Kickoff Returns, Season   78 (2004)
Most Kickoff Return Yards, Season
    1,709 (1989)
Most Yards per Kickoff Return, Season   27.5 (1971)
Most Kickoff Return Touchdowns, Season
    2 (1971, 2002)

DEFENSE

Fewest Points Allowed per Game, Season
    13.3 (1968; 186 points/14 games)
Fewest Points Allowed, Game
    0 (accomplished 17 times)
Fewest Touchdowns Allowed per Game, Season
    1.25 (1996; 20 TDs/16 games)
Fewest Total Yards Allowed per Game, Season
    229.5 (1977; 3,213 yards/14 games)
Fewest Total Yards Allowed, Game
    62 (vs. Seattle, 10/11/1992)
Lowest Average Yards Per Play, Season
    3.7 (1977; 3,213 yards/880 plays)
Fewest Passing Yards Allowed per Game, Season
    111.6 (1977; 1,562 yards/14 games)
Fewest Passing Yards Allowed, Game
    -10 (@ Green Bay, 10/24/1965)

Fewest Rushing Yards Allowed per Game, Season
    75.0 (1969; 1,050 yards/14 games)
Fewest Rushing Yards Allowed, Game
    7 (vs. Pittsburgh, 10/30/1966)
Fewest Opponent First Downs per Game, Season
    14.2 (1974; 199 first downs/14 games)
Fewest Opponent First Downs, Game
    5 (@ Philadelphia, 9/23/1974; @ Philadelphia, 11/6/1966)
Most Interceptions Made, Season   37 (1981)
Most Interceptions Made, Game
    7 (@ Philadelphia, 9/26/1971)
Highest Interception Percentage, Season
    7.7% (1961; 25 interceptions/326 attempts)
Most Yards on Interception Returns, Season
    549 (1963)
Most Interceptions Returned for Touchdown, Season   4 (1985, 1995, 1999)
Most Sacks, Season (since 1976)   62.0 (1985)
Most Sacks, Game (since 1976)
    12.0 (@ Houston, 9/29/1985)
Most Opponent Punts, Season   108 (1978)
Lowest Opponent Punting Average, Season
    37.1 (1977)

TURNOVERS AND PENALTIES

Most Fumbles Lost, Season   21 (1961)
Most Fumbles Lost, Game
    5 (@ New Orleans, 11/3/1968; vs. NY Giants, 10/11/1971; vs. Kansas City, 11/10/1975)
Fewest Fumbles Lost, Season   5 (2007)
Most Takeaways, Season   53 (1981)
Most Takeaways, Game
    10 (vs. San Francisco, 10/12/1980)
Most Turnovers, Season   50 (1960)
Most Turnovers, Game   7 (accomplished 6 times)
Fewest Turnovers, Season   15 (1998)
Best Turnover Differential, Season
    +18 (1981; 53–35)
Best Turnover Differential, Game
    +10 (vs. San Francisco, 10/12/1980)
Worst Turnover Differential, Season
    -25 (1989; 17–42)
Worst Turnover Differential, Game
    -6 (vs. Minnesota, 11/13/1988)
Most Yards Penalized, Season   1,196 (1999)
Fewest Yards Penalized, Season   427 (1961)
Most Opponent Penalty Yards, Season
    1,015 (2005)
Fewest Opponent Penalty Yards, Season
    362 (1964)

INDEX